A WINDOW TO HEAVEN

A
WINDOW
to
HEAVEN

The Daring First Ascent of Denali,
AMERICA'S WILDEST PEAK

Patrick Dean

PEGASUS BOOKS
NEW YORK LONDON

A WINDOW TO HEAVEN

Pegasus Books, Ltd.
148 West 37th Street, 13th Floor
New York, NY 10018

First Pegasus Books cloth edition March 2021

Interior design by Maria Fernandez

Library of Congress Cataloging-in-Publication Data is available.

ISBN: 978-1-64313-642-4

10 9 8 7 6 5 4 3 2 1

Printed in the United States of America
Distributed by Simon & Schuster
www.pegasusbooks.com

To
Susan

And to
Honey & Dino

CONTENTS

A NOTE FROM THE AUTHOR

T hroughout this book, the letters, diaries, and other correspondence from Hudson Stuck and other main players are quoted verbatim. All spelling errors and grammar inconsistencies are consistent with the original source. The title of this book, *A Window to Heaven,* is a play on the quote from Robert Tatum, uttered upon reaching the summit of Denali, which he described as "a window of heaven."

PROLOGUE

Hudson Stuck could barely breathe. A tough and experienced outdoorsman who had spent the last decade dogsledding and tramping across Alaska and the Yukon, Stuck nevertheless gasped in the high, thin air 20,000 feet above sea level.

He and his three companions stood just below the summit ridge of Denali, the highest peak in North America, on a clear, windy, 4°-below day. Stuck wore six pairs of socks inside his leather moccasins, with iron "ice-creepers" or crampons attached to the bottom. Immense lynx-fur-lined mitts covered inner Scotch-wool gloves, and his torso was layered beneath a fur-hooded Alaskan parka. "Yet," Stuck wrote, "until high noon feet were like lumps of iron."[1]

Behind them stretched what Stuck called the "dim blue lowlands" of the future Denali National Park, "with threads of stream and patches of lake that still carry ice along their banks."[2] A few smaller peaks squatted off to the northeast. In every other direction, the immensity of the mountain they perched on blocked their views of Mount Foraker and the other peaks in the Alaska Range. Above them, just a few hundred more yards of climbing and the prize—to be the first humans to set foot atop Denali—would be theirs.

It was June 7th, 1913. They were Stuck, Episcopal Archdeacon of Alaska and the Yukon, the oldest of the group at nearly fifty years old, short and wiry, his neatly-trimmed beard the only one among the four; Walter Harper, the youngest at age twenty, half Alaskan Native, fit and confident; Harry Karstens, thirty-four, calmly competent from his years in the Alaskan backcountry; and Robert Tatum, twenty-one, the greenest member of the team. They had launched this expedition eight weeks earlier, enduring bitter cold, severe altitude, and the loss of key supplies to a camp fire.

The team had arrived at their last camp, just below 18,000 feet, the night before. Awakening to a brilliant, bitterly cold morning, the party had reached the summit slope after eight grueling hours, with Harper in the lead. Surrounded by nothing but snow and ice, their toes and fingers numb, they approached the final ridge to the summit.

Though all the men were unable to fully take in air—"it was curious to see every man's mouth open for breathing," Stuck would later write—it was hardest for him. Everything kept turning black for Stuck as he choked and gasped, almost unable to get any breath at all. The missionary's load had already been reduced; the other members had divided up the contents of his pack, leaving him only the bulky mercurial barometer he had stubbornly carried up the mountain to make scientific observations on the summit. Now he struggled even under the barometer's weight. Finally, Harper, the youngest and strongest member of the expedition on this day, doubled back to where Stuck knelt in the snow, took the barometer and hoisted it onto his back.

Harper's presence on the mountain was important to Stuck for more than just his youthful vigor and physical strength. Since coming to Alaska in 1904 to become Archdeacon of Alaska and the Yukon, Stuck had become a fervent champion of the rights of the Native people. In the Alaska of this era, a raucous and deeply unsettled meeting point between traditional Native ways and the modern white culture—"a center of feverish trade and feverish vice," in Stuck's words—Stuck spent most of his time ministering to the Athabascan peoples in his region. He bore no illusions that their lives would be improved by the onslaught of Western ways.[3]

Harper, who was half Athabascan and half Irish, represented Stuck's aspirations for the Natives of the Far North. Walter's father, Arthur Harper, a distant figure in his life, was a pioneer in the history of white Alaska, the first to imagine gold in the Yukon, where he met Walter's mother. Walter was raised by his mother in an Athabascan village and at sixteen met Stuck at the mission school in Tenana.[4] They forged a lifelong connection. On Denali, in Stuck's words, Harper "ran Karstens close in strength, pluck, and endurance."[5]

Robert Tatum was a Tennessean who had come to Alaska to study for Holy Orders in the Episcopal Church. He had proved himself the previous winter by joining a heroic relief effort, helping deliver by dogsled desperately-needed supplies to two women missionaries down the dangerous ice of the frozen Tanana River. His experience with surveying tools and other scientific instruments and his willingness to serve as the cook for the expedition, along with what Stuck termed "his consistent courtesy and considerateness," made Tatum "a very pleasant comrade."[6]

Harry Karstens had been in Alaska for almost two decades, and learned its often-harsh lessons first-hand. He had earned the right to be considered a "Sourdough"—a term derived from prospectors' habit of carrying a starter of sourdough bread in a pouch around their neck, later expanded to describe those who'd been in the Far North long enough to prove themselves. He had made his reputation in the backcountry since the Klondike Gold Rush of 1897, making his reputation on the mail routes, prospectors' streams, and hunting expeditions of early-1900s Alaska. Stuck explicitly relied on Karstens for his outdoor skills and experience, as well as his toughness.

Karstens, on the other hand, had less sympathy than Harper for Stuck's difficulties. To Karstens, a hardened miner and backwoodsman, Stuck's insistence on spending time with the books and writing materials he brought to Denali—not to mention the burden that carrying such extra weight imposed on everyone—amounted to little more than "lying in the tent." Karstens's antagonism toward Stuck, which increased with each step up the mountain, was fated to flare into far worse.

For his part, Stuck had always admired Karstens, describing him as "strong, competent, and resourceful, the true leader of the expedition in the face of difficulty and danger."[7] He would never understand his former partner's antagonism in the wake of the expedition's success and fame. But for now, Stuck and the others had to put all animosities aside, and focus on putting one foot in front of the other, slowly and deliberately gasping, and grasping, for the summit.

&

How did an Episcopal Archdeacon, well into middle age by the standards of the time, come to find himself in the freezing final summit push on the highest, coldest peak on the continent? The answer lay in two equally potent forces, woven into his being. Just as strong as Hudson Stuck's belief in doing good—"I am sorry for a life in which there is no usefulness to others," he once wrote—was his love of wild places. He had grown up reading the exploits of the polar explorers, thanks to the library of a relative lost at sea. As a youth Hudson Stuck had explored the mountains of his native England, including the Lake District peaks Scafell Pike (the highest mountain in England, at 3200 feet), Skiddaw, and Helvellyn. Although they weren't much more than scrambles, much less technical climbs, they gave the youthful Stuck a glimpse of what could be found in the world's high, wild places.[8]

The twenty-two-year-old Englishman's pursuit of change and adventure led him and a friend to leave England in 1885 and make their way by steamship to New Orleans, then to San Antonio. Stuck loved the stark beauty of the West Texas rolling prairie. Working as a cowboy and ranch hand, on horseback with his Remington rifle, he witnessed a vanishing world.[9]

After three years of alternating teaching and ranch work, Stuck's future path became clear. Always devout and with a keen sense of duty to serve others, his involvement with the Episcopal Church as a layman earned him a scholarship to the University of the South in Sewanee, Tennessee, to study for the ministry. The university, founded in 1868 by the Episcopal Church, was created to offer a liberal-arts education and as training for the priesthood.

Stuck's time in Sewanee began a lifelong love of the school and the place. With its stone Gothic buildings situated amid the rocky streams, waterfalls, and dramatic views of the Cumberland Plateau, Sewanee gave full flower to Stuck's intelligence and desire for engagement with the wider intellectual world. By the end of his life, Stuck would be one of Sewanee's favorite sons.

Feeling expansive after his time in Sewanee, Stuck returned to Texas and a small parish church in Cuero. Before long, however, he was inevitably lured to the largest and most powerful church in the state: St. Matthew's, the Episcopal Cathedral of Dallas. There, among his wealthy and influential parishioners, Stuck would first make a reputation—though not, in some quarters, a favorable one.

As dean of St. Matthew's Cathedral, Stuck founded St. Matthew's School for boys, a night school for mill workers, and a home for indigent young mothers. But when Stuck took up the reform of child-labor laws, he found himself at odds with the powers that be and in a public-relations battle with Dallas's leading newspaper, the *Dallas Morning News*. In 1903, after a campaign by Stuck and his allies, the Texas legislature passed the first factory law of any kind in the state, requiring a minimum age of twelve and restricted hours of employment.

Even while fighting these battles as dean, Stuck continued his quest to challenge himself in the strenuous pursuit of natural, rugged beauty. He spent annual holidays in wild and mountainous places, from the Colorado Rockies and "the Grand Cañon of the Yellowstone" to the summit of Washington's Mount Rainier.[10]

Chafing under the direction of his more-conservative bishop in Dallas, Stuck jumped at the chance to work in Alaska. At last, he felt he had found a place and a job with scope for his ambitions, as well as the landscape of his wildest dreams. First in Fairbanks, and later in Fort Yukon, Stuck continued the work he had begun in Texas: building hospitals and schools as well as churches; founding libraries as alternatives to saloons; condemning the lax morals of the whites and their corrosive effects on the Natives of the North.

After accepting his new position in Alaska, he routed his trip north through the Canadian Rockies, climbing Mount Victoria, "my first snow mountain,"[11] as well as reaching Glacier House on present-day Revelstoke. Stuck then sailed north from Seattle with stops along the Alaskan coastal range. Almost from the moment of his arrival in Fairbanks, Stuck began visiting his mission churches by dogsled in winter and by boat after the spring thaw, awed by the wild rivers and mountains, the Northern Lights, and the rugged grandeur of the high latitudes. His book about his winter trips, *Ten Thousand Miles with a Dogsled*, earned him acclaim in the Lower Forty-Eight and respect as an outdoorsman who was willing to visit his far-flung mission churches in the dead of the Alaskan winter.

Yet even as he criss-crossed his region by dogsled and boat, Hudson Stuck would catch a glimpse from time to time of Denali. The mountain, "the Big One" in the Athabascan language, was as yet unclimbed; with the arrival of prospectors in the 1890s it also acquired a new name, Mount McKinley. Thoughts of the glory and acclaim to be won from its first ascent never really left Stuck's mind. When the persistent clouds cleared and he grabbed a glimpse of the mountain, the "splendid vision" made him ever more eager to "scale its lofty peaks."[12] For Stuck, Alaska was a place where his physical and spiritual aspirations, his goals for himself and for his mission, could be united into a single purpose. "I would rather climb Mount McKinley than own the richest gold mine in Alaska," he claimed.[13] He was not alone in his desire.

Given its status as the grandest peak in the Northern Hemisphere, Denali became one of the primary prizes of the age. This immense young mountain, geologically speaking—the Alaska Range at 5 to 6 million years old is far younger than the Appalachians or Rockies—sheds massive glaciers, largely on its southern flanks due to the accumulated moisture swept up from the North Pacific. Its height from base to peak, rising 18,000 feet from the plain, is several thousand feet more than that of Everest. In addition, due to its position as the northernmost 6,000-meter mountain in the world, Denali's weather is extremely hazardous, to say the least. In 2003, a North American-record windchill of -118° F was recorded near the mountain's summit; the next day, the same weather station recorded a temperature of -75.5° F. This ferocious, frigid massif was destined to become the next great prize in that era of exploration and discovery. The only question was who would be the first to claim its undisputed ascent.

Attempts to summit Denali had begun not long after whites first came into the country. The year before Stuck's arrival in Alaska, the first notable expedition had been organized by Judge James Wickersham, who with a party of five men attempted to ascend by way of the northern face of the mountain in 1903. There they were stymied by the enormous ice-encrusted cliffs of the Peters Glacier.

Then came Dr. Frederick Cook from New York, who had parlayed experience in the Antarctic into a shot at Denali. On his second attempt, in 1906, he claimed the summit, and produced photo evidence. The claim isn't acknowledged today, over a century later; most don't believe Cook. Stuck, for one, flatly dismissed Cook's claim.

So did a group of four Alaskans who would become known as the Sourdough Expedition of 1910. With no mountaineering experience but plenty of pioneer confidence, the Sourdoughs attempted to dash up Denali's slopes to plant a flagstaff that would be visible in Fairbanks. Amazingly, they made it to the lower North Summit, though as with Cook, not everyone believed their account. And just the year before, Belmore Browne and Herschel Parker had been driven off the summit approach by bad weather, only 200 feet from the top.

Stuck and Karstens left Tenana two months behind schedule, on St. Patrick's Day, March 17, 1913. They aimed their dogsleds toward the mission at Nenana, stopping there to pick up

Harper, Tatum, and two Indian boys who would help with the dogsleds. By April 11, they had reached the base of Denali and had their first glimpse of the Muldrow Glacier, the river of ice they planned to follow to the summit. Stuck named it "the highway of desire."

Overcoming one setback after another—some natural, some man-made—the team made the first foray onto the Northeast Ridge toward the summit. Much to their dismay, the path up the ridge, which Belmore Browne had described as "a steep but practical snow slope," was instead fractured and jumbled thanks to a 1912 earthquake. Slowly, laboriously, exhaustingly, Karstens led the effort to hack a safe three-mile path through the house-sized boulders and enormous ice sheets. What should have been a three-day climb up the ridge consumed three weeks. "Anyone who thinks that the climbing of Denali is a picnic," wrote Stuck, "is badly mistaken."

❧

Now, on the clear morning of June 7, dressed in "more gear than had sufficed at 50° below zero on the Yukon Trail," Stuck and the others turned toward the final slopes. The group made steady progress, with Harper in the lead and Stuck stumbling in the rear. As the four men stood, one behind the other, desperate for air, Denali's South Peak lay within reach. The weather gods had blessed them with brilliantly clear, though numbingly cold, weather this day. Now it was up to them to take advantage of their luck.

Each man lifted a frozen, heavy foot, and, one after the other, took another step upward toward their goal.

1

TALL MOUNTAIN

The Alaska Range echoes the southern coast of the forty-ninth state, sprawling in a massive eyebrow-shaped arc from the Canadian boundary in the east all the way to the root of the Alaska Peninsula six hundred miles to the west. On the map, its mountains loom over and seem to shelter Anchorage and the Cook Inlet. This effect is far more than visual or cartographic, as the range defines the climate of the state: within the concave curve of the range, to the south, the Gulf of Alaska produces warmer, wetter maritime weather, while to the north the drier, more extreme heat and cold scrapes raw the landscape of Alaska's interior. In between, ten major peaks push themselves up into the airstream, combining to brew up some of the harshest weather in the world.

The tallest of those peaks, Denali, lies one-third of the way around the arc from the west, ringed by lesser mountains including Mount Foraker, known to some Alaska Natives as Menlale, "Denali's Wife." The Alaska Range, three hundred miles from the Gulf of Alaska, is the highest in the world outside of the Himalaya and the Andes; Denali itself, measured from base to peak, is a mile taller than Everest, rising three-and-a-half miles from base to its summit of 20,310 feet.[1] The topography, and the range's position so far north (Everest, by contrast, is on the same latitude as Miami), produce some of the rawest, coldest, windiest conditions on Earth.

Statistics, though, don't account for the place that Denali holds in the imagination of its people. For in addition to its height and the weather that it both produces and endures, Denali and the rest of its range seize the skyline near the middle of the Alaskan landmass, visible from much of the surrounding land, as well as from the Alaskan Sea. As long as people have lived in the Far North, the mountains have loomed large in their lives.

∞

One summer day over eleven thousand years ago, in a river valley 150 miles northeast of Denali, the bodies of two infant girls were carefully laid to rest in a pit in the floor of a hut built of poles and skins. The children—one born prematurely, the other three to five weeks old—were placed into the space along with spear-rods made of antler, and lanceolate (elongated oval) stone projectile points. Everything, including the bodies, was dusted with a coat of red ocher, a common burial practice in Neolithic times.[2] According to Craig Childs in *Atlas of a Lost World: Travels in Ice Age America*, "This spectral, blood-red mineral . . . is the ceremonial stone of our species," and its use on this continent is "considered to be a sign of a direct relationship with Old World Upper Paleolithic complexes."[3]

Four millennia before, humans had begun to cross the land bridge connecting two continents, traveling east from Asia to America. Not far from where the children were found, other archaeological discoveries have yielded tools and other remnants that are 14,500 years old. Ten thousand years ago, melting glaciers and rising waters caused the inundation of that land bridge, creating fifty-mile-wide seas, later to be named the Bering Strait, between Russia and Alaska.[4]

The girls' burial site is in what is now known as the Tanana River Valley, at Upward Sun River, or Xaasaa Na' in the present-day Middle Tanana Athabascan tongue. The Tanana, a major tributary of the Yukon, flows northwest from the Canadian border and curves around the foothills of the Alaska Range before emptying into the Yukon at the town of Tanana. When non-natives arrived in the Tanana Valley in the 1880s, Upward Sun River was in the territory of the Salchaket band of Athabascan Alaska Natives, though none are left in the area now; two of the last speakers of Middle Tanana, a mother and daughter, gave oral histories in the 1960s, when the Alaska Native name for Upward Sun River was recorded. After the burial site was found, the local indigenous community gave the girls names in that same language: Xach'itee'aanenh T'eede Gaay, "Sunrise Girl-Child," and Yełkaanenh T'eede Gaay, "Dawn Twilight Girl-Child."[5]

The discovery of the infants in 2013, by Dr. Ben Potter of the University of Alaska at Fairbanks, provided the oldest-yet evidence of humans on the continent, and changed what we know about the prehistory of North America. The people of Upward Sun River lived during the Terminal Pleistocene epoch in geology, the term for the end of the last Ice Age, and also at the end of the Paleolithic ("Old Stone") Age of archaeology. Culturally, they are considered part of what scientists call the Denali Complex, occurring between 12,000 and 6,000 years ago.[6]

As Potter's team excavated the pit in close consultation with Native tribal organizations and state agencies, they made further contributions to our knowledge of the Denali Complex people. Their discovery that the burial site also contained a cooking pit, with several hearths and a semi-underground shelter nearby, meant that in addition to the highly mobile, nomadic foraging for which they had long been known, humans in this era also had settled camps—and rituals for dealing with life's eternal mysteries. "There was intentionality in the burial ceremony," Potter told a journalist. "These were certainly children who were well-loved."[7]

Late-Pleistocene people "would have worn skins and leggings and carried a pouch of small stone blades of Asian design . . . and eyed sewing needles made from mammoth ivory," according to Childs. "[They] would have used the small blades to cut skins, and the needles to sew tailored, tight-fitting clothes . . . These were people with preferences and sensibilities." They came from the Eurasian landmass "with languages and customs, body adornments, styles of weaponry, tailored clothing, pole-and-hide structures, and burial rites involving red ochre. They were not a blank slate."[8]

From their camp, the Upward Sun Valley people would have ranged widely as a matter of routine, in search of game. The same Alaska Range weather patterns that prevail today kept the interior from being covered with ice during the glaciations of the Pleistocene era. While the last Ice Age glaciation covered the Brooks Range to the north and southern Alaska from Denali to the sea, the interior between remained grassland and shrub—ideal habitat for Denali-period fauna.[9] From the summer camp where they would later bury the little girls, the Upward Sun Valley people hunted bison, elk, and sheep. They also pursued small game like ground squirrels, hare, and ptarmigan or grouse, and fished for salmon in the nearby Tanana River.[10] What they harvested they brought back to the site to become food, clothing, and tools.[11]

Roaming southwest from the Tanana River Valley in search of these ever-moving animals and fish, the Upward Sun River clan could have looked up and glimpsed Denali and the rest of the Alaska Range.[12] Like the eternal questions of life and death, the mountains would have loomed over them, overshadowing their lives, filling them with awe and wonder. What did they think about the white ice-clad pyramids? Did they worship the peaks as gods, and give them supernatural powers? Were the roars of avalanches and screams of winds considered the speech of a higher power? Did they give a name to the highest point that they could see?

Some time after Sunrise Girl-Child and Dawn Twilight Girl-Child were carefully interred with the antler spears and rust-colored dust, perhaps the next summer, their people placed in the pit and cremated another child (Xaasaa Cheege Ts'eniin, "Upward Sun River Mouth Child").[13] The fire, made of poplar wood, burned untouched for one to three hours; neither the skeleton nor the embers were ever touched while the fire lasted.[14] Then, they abandoned the camp permanently. With them, the archeological record of the Alaskan interior slams shut, not to be opened again for almost five thousand years.

⚬

In 1778 Captain James Cook sailed into the inlet which would be named for him, and Russians appeared there in 1785 in search of furs. But George Vancouver is credited with being the first non-Native to document a glimpse of Denali. While surveying Cook Inlet from aboard HMS *Discovery* May 6, 1794, Vancouver spotted what he described in his journal as 'distant stupendous mountains,' which would have included Denali, the most stupendous of all. Hudson Stuck would note in the margin of his copy of Vancouver's *A Voyage of Discovery to the North Pacific Ocean*, printed in 1801, that Cook's was "the first reference to Denali and Denali's Wife (Mt McKinley and Mt Foraker) that has been discovered in any literature."[15]

Thus the history of Alaska, in the modern, Western sense, began. From that date, over the following century, outsiders, non-natives, have flocked to the Far North. Russian fur traders crossed the Bering Strait and aimed south and east; English explorers pushed north up the Pacific coast from the mouth of the Columbia River; miners, missionaries, adventurers, and wanderers from the south followed. All of them, upon arrival, encountered Aleut and Athabascan cultures which had been in the region for thousands of years, and who thought of the physical features of their world as being imbued with spirits. For these Native cultures, all of the natural world, including Denali, contained spiritual force as well as physical presence. Seven different indigenous languages name the mountain—and all of them refer to either 'the tall one' or 'big mountain.'

Had these cultures developed in place from the Pleistocene people who had hunted mammoth six millennia before? Had humans lived along the rivers and coasts of Alaska in unbroken succession ever since the time of the Upward Sun River settlement? That remains an open question; no human remains have been found in the Alaskan interior dating from the interval between 6000 and 3000 years ago.[16] The story of Alaska between the late Pleistocene and the earliest accounts of the Alaska Natives is, for now, a closed book.

∽

The first Westerners to come to Alaska were the Russians. In 1741, Vitus Bering, sailing for Czar Peter the Great at the command of the *Sv. Piotr*, and Alexei Chirikov, a Russian commanding the *Sv. Pavel*, both reached the southeast coast of Alaska. Chirikov landed on what is thought to be Prince Edward Island on July 14, and Bering sighted Mount St. Elias on or about July 15. Within two years, small groups of fur traders were voyaging east across the 51-mile-wide Bering Strait to the Aleutian Islands. There the Russian trade in otter furs began in earnest.

According to two modern scholars, "The end of the nineteenth century gave Alaska a gold rush, but earlier, in the eighteenth century a fur rush had emerged in this land."[17] We know from indigenous stories passed down orally and recorded in the 1970s that contact between Russians and Alaska Natives was sometimes bloody.[18] One oral account of a Russian-Native encounter, perhaps in 1794–5, was translated and transcribed in the late 20th century as "When Russians Were Killed at 'Roasted Salmon Place.'" The Russians named the territory "Russian America," exploiting and enslaving indigenous people in their desire for sea-otter and other furs, the most sought-after commodity of the time.[19] Although "in Russian Alaska colonizers consciously acknowedged the skills and ways of knowing possessed by native peoples," this was acompanied by Russian "coercion of these local labor forces."[20] As one recent historian, Bathsheba Demuth, says, "'small peoples' [the Russian term for the indigenous tribes] struggled to hunt what they needed while paying tribute and enduring the smallpox and syphilis and abuse that came with its extraction."[21]

By the time of Russia's sale of Alaska to the United States in 1867, competition with England and the US for the fur trade, combined with overhunting, had shriveled the Russian involvement in Alaska. Captain Cook had sailed from Alaska for the Sandwich Islands, only to be murdered in Hawaii; his men continued their voyage of discovery, arriving in China in December 1799. There they learned that "the spectacularly lustrous sea otter furs purchased for one dollar's worth of trinkets from Northwest Coastal Indians" on the American coast "sold for the equivalent of a hundred dollars cash in Macao and Canton."[22] The ensuing encroachment of the British North West Company and the American Pacific Fur Company into the North left little room for the Russians. The number of Russians living in Alaska had never been more than 700 (compared to 40,000 Alaska Natives); now, they abandoned North American altogether. The fur rush was over. The gold rush was two decades ahead.

The cruel and harsh treatment of Alaska Natives by the Russian fur traders, however, established a pattern which would typify encounters between indigenous peoples and the Western colonial powers, and reverberate through the centuries. In a lasting counterpoint, the missionaries of the Russian Orthodox Church, who had followed in the wake of Russian colonialism, fought against their countrymen's mistreatment of Alaska Natives. Hudson Stuck would later write of the "frightful ravages" of the Alaska Natives routinely committed by fur traders before "the most noted and vigorous" of the Russian missionaries, John Veniaminoff, arrived in Russian Alaska in 1824. Veniaminoff's career of "devoted labours" among the Natives, including translations of the Bible and other writings into Aleut, "justify [in Stuck's eyes] the very honourable place that is given him in Alaskan history."[23]

The Russian missionaries' policies stressing sympathy for, and taking care to retain, Native customs, languages, and culture would be taken up by others in the decades to come—most notably by the Episcopal Church for which Hudson Stuck would labor in the Far North as Archdeacon of Alaska and the Yukon.[24] The introduction of Christianity by Russian, Anglican, Episcopal, and other missionaries in the period before 1869 undermined and devalued the former belief systems of the Alaska Natives; however, in the words of one Alaska scholar, "this early contact did far less to destabilize Athabascan languages and lifeways than the waves of gold-seeking migrants and later official English-only language policies."[25]

Those policies, and the overall policy of assimilation, were the work of other Protestant denominations, especially the Presbyterians led by Sheldon Jackson, who were put in charge of Alaska Native education beginning in 1885. They sincerely believed that the best thing to do for the indigenous people of Alaska, as for those in the rest of the United States, was to "civilize" them, forcing them to abandon their language and culture for that of white nineteenth-century Americans.[26] Presbyterian missionary S. Hall Young, who had established the denomination's first church in Alaska at Wrangell in 1879, wanted to let the "old tongues with their superstition and sin die—the sooner the better—and replace these languages with that of Christian civilization."[27] The era's burgeoning of pseudo-scientific theories on race supported these actions. As one modern historian has noted, "The assertion of power by people of European descent . . . called out for justification. Racial theorists of all stripes were eager to provide it."[28]

Then with the onset of the gold rush in August 1896, white greed, amorality, and environmental destruction were brought into the lives of a vastly greater number of Alaska Natives.[29] Although some of the seekers after gold may have been searching for "the end of the great American rainbow [that] was located somewhere near the junction of the Klondike and Yukon rivers,"[30] their overcrowded shanty towns, unthinking destruction of riverine habitats, and shameless exploitation of Native women were the most destructive influences yet inflicted upon Alaska Natives.

Not only were Alaska Natives forced to deal with these effects of the Gold Rush; they were also systematically denied participation in what benefits there were to be gained from it. They were shoved aside, not allowed to work the mining claims which by right of eons of inhabitation should have been theirs. Ancient patterns of subsistence were lost, to be replaced, the whites claimed, by gardens, farms, and manufactured food. Native ways of dwelling, traveling, eating, learning, surviving would become replaced by the patterns of the outside, twentieth-century Western civilization.[31] These—the sanctimonious culture war of the white assimilators, and the depredations of whites attempting to profit from the resources of the North—were the forces that Hudson Stuck would encounter on his arrival in 1904.

All of these invaders, though, whatever their attitudes toward Alaska Natives—whether trappers, miners, merchants, or missionaries—could see the soaring and daunting mountain ranges which crowded the landscape. They would have shared the common human emotions, that mixture of attraction and fear, toward the massive upthrusts and avalanche-laden slopes of Alaska's mountains. Many no doubt dreamed of climbing those mountains, especially the prize: Denali.

2

FROM LONDON TO THE AMERICAN FRONTIER

When Hudson Stuck was born in the London suburb of Paddington on November 11, 1863, Queen Victoria had ruled over the United Kingdom of Great Britain and Ireland for three decades. With its recent victory over Imperial Russia in the Crimean Wars, Great Britain gloried in the height of its Empire. The forty-four-year-old queen, however, remained in semi-seclusion as winter neared, mourning, as she had for almost two years, the death of her husband and soulmate, Prince Albert. The royal household was bathed in gloom, dressed in black, forbidden by Victoria from any show of frivolity or laughter.[1]

For four decades London had been the largest city in the world,[2] and it continued to display everything that was new and advanced, with all the swagger of an imperial capital. Not far from the Stucks' house on Irongate Wharf Road, the first section of the London Underground had opened earlier that year, between Paddington and Farringdon Road.[3] A short distance to the southeast, just two weeks before Hudson Stuck joined the world, the Football Association had been founded at the Freemasons' Tavern on Great Church Road; on December 19 the first-ever match would be played under the rules of the Football Association (shortened by Rugby School slang to "soccer," as it became known in the US and Canada).[4]

But all wasn't bright and shiny in 1860s London, either literally or figuratively. Charles Dickens began serializing his last novel, *Our Mutual Friend*, in the spring after Stuck's birth in May 1864. He described London as "a black shrill city . . . a gritty city . . . a hopeless city, with no vent in the leaden canopy of its sky."[5] Nor did the wealth derived from India, "The Jewel in the Crown," make any real difference in the lives of most Londoners. The stifling social and moral strictures which would give the adjective "Victorian" its negative connotations remained in force, as did as the rigid class system, to say nothing of the environmental and social evils of the ongoing Industrial Revolution. These conditions drove some Londoners to find escape in the British countryside beyond the city; others chose to join the hundreds of thousands of emigrants who left during the first two decades of Stuck's life, when he was a resident of the British Isles.

Hudson Stuck, for his part, did both.

∽

He had been born to James and Jane (nee Hudson) Stuck; his father was a "moderately successful foreman and part owner of a lumber yard" whose strict Presbyterianism failed to take hold in his son, to put it mildly.[6] Stuck would much later write of the "forgotten religious books to which . . . it was sought to confine my reading with notable unsuccess."[7] Clara Burke, who knew him well in Alaska, claimed that "When he decided to join the Episcopal Church and study for the ministry, his father was so incensed by his son's disloyalty to the family church that he refused to finance his education. So young Stuck had come to the United States."[8] Presumably she was told this by Stuck himself, although there is no indication in any of his early letters from Texas that he had decided to be a priest before 1889. Perhaps Stuck was tidying up his timeline, for others as well as for himself.

Young Hudson Stuck's preference for the Church of England (known as the Episcopal Church in the United States) had cultural as well as theological implications. The Anglican Church, as it was also known, with its elaborate rituals and centuries-old Prayer Book, was the church of the well-born, the social elite, in England as well as in America. The Presbyterianism of Stuck's father, on the other hand, would have been a dissenter's church, populated mainly by working-class believers.

Hudson Stuck, with his love of the English language, doubtless was drawn to the beauty of the Anglican service, and its liturgy written during Shakespeare's time. But he also was disavowing his family's social status, and choosing a more elevated church home. Esthetically, socially, and theologically, this choice was key to his subsequent life as a clergyman in America.

Hudson and his younger sister Caroline moved with his parents to Westbourne, a London district just west of Paddington, where he attended Westbourne Park Public School and the King's College School, a secondary school attached to the college.[9] Westbourne around this time contained "one of the capital's leading shopping centres," Westbourne Grove, but also the area by the Lock bridge, "one of six poor patches amid the general affluence of north-west London."[10] Stuck would describe in *A Winter Circuit of Our Arctic Coast* the prints by the artist and satirist George Cruikshank, "full of action and character," that hung upon the walls of his childhood home, perhaps because of Cruikshank's strong patriotism (he invented "John Bull" as a symbol of England) or his fierce support of the temperance and anti-smoking movements.[11]

Two anecdotes from Stuck's early life in England seem to point him in the direction of escape, of lighting out for the territory, of pursuing adventure. The first concerns his father's cousin, a sailor in the merchant marine until he sailed from Australia and, as Stuck recounted, "he and his ship were never seen or heard of again." The cousin left with Stuck's family a pet green parrot, as well as books on exploration in the Arctic: beautiful leather-bound editions describing the exploits of Vancouver, Parry, and Richardson. In Stuck's words, those fine old quartos, with their delicate and spirited engravings of ships beset by fantastic icebergs, their coloured plates of auroras and parhelia, of Eskimos and their igloos and dog-teams, are amongst the most vivid recollections of my childhood.[12]

"New country," Stuck would say, remained "of special interest to me all my life," perhaps because of his uncle's books of exploration and adventure, which "were my companions and delights as a boy."[13]

The second indicator, less detailed but no less intriguing, consists of a single sentence in Stuck's book *The Ascent of Denali*: "Scawfell [sic] and Skiddaw and Helvellyn had given [me my] first boyish interest in climbing."[14] This seems to indicate that the young Stuck traveled to these peaks in the famous Lake District of northwest England at a historic place and time in mountaineering history. A 1913 profile of Stuck in a Scottish newspaper, which claimed that he "learnt his mountaineering in Cumberland, his mother's county" (where Scafell is located), offers another tantalizing clue.[15]

Scafell Pike, the highest mountain in England at an elevation of 978 meters (3,209 feet) above sea level, and its twin Scafell, the second-highest at 964 meters (3,162 feet), had long drawn the imagination of outdoor lovers. The Romantic poet Samuel Taylor Coleridge had survived his own mini-epic adventure there in 1802. In the middle of a nine-day hike around the district, Coleridge made it to the top of Scafell. However, while trying to scramble down a steeper, more direct route from the top, a route that today is classified as 'moderate'—the easiest rating—Coleridge struggled to keep his footing and his composure. He said in a letter to his love interest at the time that his "whole Limbs" were "in a Tremble," until finally he safely reached the bottom.[16]

By the 1860s, the exploits of pioneering mountaineers, such as Edward Whymper's first ascent of the Matterhorn in 1859, had given rise to the first wave of British mountaineering in the Lake District. During this time, according to an article written in a Lake District climbing journal a half-century later, "Alpine Clubmen, Norwegian Explorers, and Pyrenean Mountaineers" came to the area for "the rock work available in the District. Many who now bear honoured names in the mountaineering world vied with each other in their search for new courses."[17] These progenitors of English mountain ascents "wore rough old tweed suits, thick socks and stout country boots, usually hobnailed." Their route information came "not from detailed guide books but from what they could gather from predecessors of accounts in the newspapers."[18]

The mystery persists: When—if ever—did Hudson Stuck go to these accessible, non-technical peaks in the Lake District? Six hours from Westbourne by modern transportation, they must have been harder to reach in the late nineteenth century. Stuck emigrated in 1885, at the age of twenty-two, but "boyish" would imply sometime in the previous decade. Did he venture to the fells with his family?

Stuck, if he went, would have gone to the "awesome rock architecture and writhing ethereal mists"[19] of Scafell and the Lake District not only to bag the peaks, but also for "the stretching of muscles and mind in God's fresh air, the escape from all the pressures and . . . occupations of everyday life in the city."[20] He certainly fit one historian's description of climbers of the day as coming from "comfortable middle-class homes in the industrial cities." They were seeking, as present-day climber and author Doug Scott wrote, "to escape the restrictions society was imposing upon them."[21] Stuck's desire to leave the constraints of Victorian London would eventually take him much farther than the Lake District.

⁓

Finally, it all came down to the flip of a coin. Tiring of his first job, clerical work in the city of Bristol, Stuck dreamed of going to Texas, but his friend and boss's son, Jim Hall, leaned toward Australia. One of them flipped a coin to decide the matter. Texas it was.

At least, that is the better-known and more widespread explanation for Stuck's decision to emigrate to Texas at the age of twenty-three. According to Frank Juhan, however, who knew Stuck later in Dallas and who eventually became Bishop of Florida, there was another reason: Stuck, he wrote, had tuberculosis, and West Texas along with Colorado was considered to have the most healthful climate for sufferers of the disease. According to Juhan, by 1889, when Stuck left Texas, there were no traces of the illness.[22] (Coming as it did from a retired Episcopal bishop, the story of Stuck's illness may have been a more genteel explanation for his choice of destination, in place of the more cavalier story of the coin-flip.)

Whatever the reason, on March 1, 1885, Stuck, Hall, and a third friend, Jim Kerr, left Antwerp and traveled by steamship to New Orleans, final destination San Antonio. Six years before, a journalist for London's *Pall Mall Gazette* had taken passage in steerage class aboard a Cunard liner. "Words are incapable of conveying anything like a correct notion" of conditions below decks for those who can't afford luxury or saloon passage, the reporter wrote; "a glance around filled me with dismay and disgust."[23] So Stuck found his time in the steerage compartment of *La Gaul*, a converted cattle boat. The voyage, he wrote a friend back in England, was horrible from the beginning: the 140 passengers were often trapped by heavy seas below decks, with little light or air, and had to contend with "vile smells, vile atmosphere, and sleeping wet" as the leaky portholes dropped water on the bunks.[24]

On April 1, the three arrived in New Orleans, purchased pistols and tickets, and boarded a train the same day for San Antonio. Three days later, they were there.

≈

Texas in the nineteenth century, as today, was an idea and a crucible, as much as a place. In the wake of a civil war which had shattered the Southern economy and landscape, and left psychological, familial, and economic damage behind it, Texas seemed to be the answer to the hopes of many Americans.

Hudson Stuck and his friends therefore joined thousands of others who, in that era, were "GTT—Gone to Texas." The phrase was popularized in the early 19th century, when Texas was known for both producing and harboring outlaws. Frederick Law Olmsted, who would later design New York's Central Park, mentioned in his book *A Journey Through Texas* (1857) that the initials were used to describe any "rascal who skipped out." By Stuck's time, "GTT" was used more broadly to refer to anyone heading to the one-time republic and 28th state in search of a new life.[25]

The three young immigrants were part of a huge influx into the state after the Civil War. In the two decades from 1870 to 1890, Texas's population almost tripled, from 818,579 to 2,235,527. Most of the immigrants were fleeing the demoralized and destroyed farms, towns, and cities of the defeated South. Although Texas had been part of the Confederacy, it was spared any major military action, and offered land and opportunity largely undamaged by the war. Germans, following a trail blazed by their countrymen since the 1830s, and African-Americans fleeing the ruined Deep South also greatly increased their numbers in Texas during that time.[26] Historical forces were propelling the state into a more powerful twentieth-century role in the newly re-formed United States.

∽

The three arrived "in high spirits" in San Antonio, but were quickly discouraged. There was no work. In fact, they encountered men who had been trying for three weeks to a month to find work; some of them were "on the eve of taking a resolution to return to England." Stuck and his companions stayed for a week before deciding to catch a freight wagon bound for Junction City in search of work. "Our journey occupied eight days and we enjoyed it very much," wrote Stuck:

We generally camped beside a river or creek—for several nights we camped beside the Guadaloupe—and before breakfast, we used to get a swim. Tis a grand life and a life that I enjoyed immensely, the only drawback . . . being the uncertainty as to whether we should get a job at the end of our journey.[27]

"A regular frontier town of about a score of wooden shanties called 'stores,'" was Hudson Stuck's description of Junction City, Texas upon his arrival in 1885. The town, named for its location 120 rolling prairie miles west of Austin at the confluence of the North and South Llano Rivers, had around 300 residents at the time, as well as a drugstore, a livery stable, a sawmill, and more than one general store.

Stuck immediately found work when a Mr. Bundy chose him from among his group—"a proof of his bad judgment as [Stuck's friend] Fred remarked"—to perform general work on his ranch (not including sheep herding, as Stuck took care to point out; this must have been an important distinction at the time). The ranch was twenty-five miles from Junction City, and Stuck found it to be "wild and picturesque." He liked the place and the people, game was plentiful, and the food "far better than I expected to find in so remote a region." On the other hand, Stuck yearned for news of the outside world. "I am exceedingly anxious to hear about the war between England and Russia," he wrote. "When you get hold of a 'Punch' or 'Society' or anything of that sort you might save it to send."[28]

When Stuck arrived in search of adventure and wide-open spaces, Junction City and much of Texas was still a not-quite-settled frontier. The US Army had fought Kiowa, Cheyenne, and Comanche warriors near Amarillo in the Red River War only a decade before. After a major engagement in Palo Duro Canyon in the summer of 1874, the tribes' warriors never again posed a military threat to the Texas frontier,[29] though skirmishes continued for several years. In 1878, just two years after Junction City's founding, a news item noted that "a large force of Indians" had been "raiding near Johnson Fork and Junction City, Texas, and mounted men have gone in pursuit."[30] Like a Wild West cliche, an 1883 newspaper account spoke of "an impromptu shooting affray" near Junction City, in which "one of the parties was mortally wounded and the other had a thigh and hand shattered."[31]

The frontier, however, was fast disappearing. The extension of railroads throughout Texas and the West, as well as the invention of refrigerated railcars, put an end to the epic cattle drives along the Chisholm Trail, while the invention of mass-produced barbed-wire fencing spelled the demise of the open range. Junction City had its own post office and a newspaper, the *West Texan*. In 1890, five years after Stuck reached the west Texas plains, the US Census Bureau would state that all the land within the United States was claimed, and that there was no longer a frontier. But the West, and what it represented, still attracted the romantics, the dreamers—the seekers after adventure, a challenge, or a new start. Just a year before Stuck, another young man in search of the strenuous life had headed westward. Theodore Roosevelt, who at twenty-six was only four years older than Stuck, had told an interviewer en route to the Dakota Bad Lands, "For good healthy exercise I would strongly recommend some of our gilded youth to go West and try a short course of riding bucking ponies, and assist at the branding of a lot of Texas steers."[32]

∞

Stuck quickly learned how hard the "good healthy exercise" of a cowboy's life could be. Most men only stayed with the work a couple of years before moving on, and the economics of ranch work quickly became apparent to the young Englishman. "I don't know whether I am going to do here or not," he wrote:

> I should not mind the hard work if I saw some prospect of doing better in the immediate future but it is very hard indeed for a man without capital to get a start and save enough money from the ten dollar a month after paying for clothes and washing and tobacco. To start in any way is next to impossible.

Stuck needed to find a way forward, a path out of cowboying that suited his ambitions. Finally, he conceived of a plan "that may possibly save me for two or three years out here—it is to become a school teacher." He planned to continue ranch work, as school was held for only six months out of the year.[33]

His search for a teaching position took Stuck to San Angelo, 100 miles northwest of Junction City. The town was founded in 1867 with the establishment of Fort Concho, home of the African-American cavalry regiments nicknamed Buffalo Soldiers by Native Americans. Stuck found himself in a bustling trade center for farmers and settlers in the area, as well as "a fairly lawless cowtown filled with brothels, saloons, and gambling houses."[34]

For a time, it seemed that his gamble had been a failure. "I have suddenly been so supremely miserable and low spirited ever since I came to San Angelo that I haven't had the heart to write to anyone," Stuck wrote, as prospects of a teaching position refused to come true. To support himself he 'rode the line' for the telegraph company, "nearly 400 miles and climbing up poles like a monkey when anything was wrong." Once he discovered that cowboys had shot off fifteen glass insulators in a row, and "I only had ten." He fell from the ninth pole and when he got up, he "swore a terrible oath that come what might I would climb no more posts." Stuck also took work building fences and dipping sheep (the latter involving "days from five in the morning till seven at night" for $1 a day plus board).[35]

Finally, he obtained a teaching job at $40 a month for five months. Over the next two years he taught in one-room schools at Copperas Creek, San Angelo, and San Marcos, and by 1888 he was able to report that he was doing fairly well: "I like my work better than I have liked it before, also the principal is a gentleman and a good fellow." He also had saved enough to embark on Spanish lessons ("when I have mastered it, I shall be qualified for my Mexican trip").

The trip to Mexico never happened, however. Before it could take place, Stuck's fortunes changed forever.

After the Civil War, one institution above all others drove Texas's transformation from a frontier to a settled, industrializing state. In historian T.R. Fehrenbach's words, "[churches] were the single most important cultural and social force behind the Texas frontier." Stuck's denomination, the Episcopal Church, was "among the first to build edifices" in Texas, along with the Presbyterians, Lutherans, and Roman Catholics, though they were mainly to be found in the towns.[36]

In the same letter in which Stuck detailed his low spirits, he mentioned his involvement in a local Episcopal church. "Today being Good Friday we have a holiday, a thing of my doing and hitherto unknown in this town." He had attended services all Holy Week, as he felt it incumbent upon himself to be there whenever the small congregation met. "I cannot help in any other way, so I can help by lighting the church and sweeping the floor."[37] While there he and Dr. Stanley, the Episcopal priest of that town became great friends and the latter asked him why he did not enter the university. Stuck replied that "'that was his great wish,' but that he had not the funds to finish his course and get his degree."[38]

This was to be a turning point in Hudson Stuck's life. The opportunity to advance that Stuck had been seeking appeared, in the form of Bishop James Steptoe Johnston, who had in that same year of 1888 been elected to be the second Bishop of the Missionary District of Western Texas. Stuck's bearing and intellect caught the attention of the bishop, someone with means and connections. From their meeting would come Stuck's path to his future self.

The bishop was liberal for his diocese, responsible for the integration of the district and admitting an African-American congregation previously affiliated with the Methodist Church. He would found the West Texas Military Academy (now TMI, The Episcopal School of Texas) in 1893 to give young men in the area a classical and Christian education, and five years later create St. Philip's Female College (now St. Philip's College). His activism and open-mindedness would be echoed throughout Hudson Stuck's career in Texas and Alaska.[39]

Bishop Johnston was in charge of a funded bequest by an American churchwoman for the college education and seminary training of candidates for Holy Orders, and Stuck fit the bill perfectly. The fund would guarantee Stuck $30 a month for as long as necessary. With this, he would depart Texas in 1889 for the University of the South in Sewanee, Tennessee.[40]

Hudson Stuck had left England full of romanticism, eager for adventure, seeking his own mountain to climb, pole to reach, or desert to traverse. On the edge of the frontier, he had found that, and more besides. Texas taught the youth from London to ride a horse, shoot a Winchester rifle, and navigate a rough and alien world by his wits. Four years had brought Stuck far; his ambition and resourcefulness had led him across the plains and up telegraph poles, and driven him to poverty in search of experience. Though no photos of Stuck from his early years in Texas exist, we know from later descriptions that he looked much younger than his twenty-eight years. Unafraid of new experiences and challenges, he must have surprised the Americans he encountered in those small Texas towns as he pursued his destiny with focus and determination.

In the process, he had also discovered a career path which would challenge his mind as well as his body. In Tennessee, he would hit his intellectual stride, and begin to make his mark in a larger sphere. His days as cowboy and schoolteacher behind him for good, Stuck would embark on the career which would occupy the rest of his life, and make him a bestselling author, a renowned missionary, and an important figure in the history of Alaska and of mountaineering.

3

"THE MOUNTAIN,"
EXPLORING THE WEST,
AND FIGHTING FOR JUSTICE

The Gothic sandstone buildings of the University of the South stand among the hemlocks and magnolias of Sewanee, Tennessee, on the southwestern end of the Cumberland Plateau. The most famous description of the place, in William Alexander Percy's 1940 memoir *Lanterns on the Levee: Recollections of a Planter's Son*, described Sewanee as "a long way away, even from Chattanooga, in the middle of woods, on top of a bastion of mountains crenellated with blue coves."[1] The architectural style of those stone buildings has been described as "Oxbridge tempered with Tennessee mountain orneriness."[2] Taken as a whole, they embody the South's long-running infatuation with all things British. A sense of transatlantic kinship ran in both directions, as can be seen in the British aristocracy's support of the South during the Civil War and their donations to help build the University after the war. Confederate General Robert E. Lee's surrender at Appomattox was barely a quarter-century gone when Hudson Stuck arrived in Sewanee in 1889.

The smells and noises of a rapidly-growing rural town greeted Hudson Stuck on his arrival on "The Mountain," as it has long been known locally. Wooden fences surrounded all the buildings, keeping away the cattle and hogs which roamed freely in the dirt streets. The grandest of the buildings was the just-completed Convocation Hall and Breslin Tower, designed to mimic the halls of the great British universities. Below those aspirational edifices, wagons pulled by mules hauled trash, while the more-refined rode in carriages pulled by horses; equine droppings were ubiquitous on the town's streets. Horses and townspeople alike might have started at the cannon firing blanks as the students, mustered as the Sewanee Light Artillery, marched on the parade ground in front of St. Luke's Hall.

Downhill, south on Tennessee Avenue (present-day University Avenue), sat the Sewanee village, with its three dozen businesses, including general store, confectionary, blacksmith, and a shop making ecclesiastical furniture. The Black people of Sewanee lived mostly in or near the ravines and their log houses were generally in very poor condition. For all of Sewanee's residents, the sounds of the railroad that ran regularly through the village would have competed with the half-dozen sawmills operating nearby and the constant banging of construction.[3]

At twenty-six, Stuck was a mere five years older than the university he had arrived to attend. Founded by ten dioceses of the Episcopal Church in the Southeast and deliberately patterned on the universities of Oxford and Cambridge, the University of the South in the town of Sewanee was designed to furnish a liberal-arts education to the sons of the white Southern planters, as well as to provide well-trained Episcopal clergymen for the region. One of its founders, Leonidas Polk, resigned as an Episcopal bishop to serve as a Confederate major-general and fight for the preservation of his plantations on which he held four hundred slaves; the school's ties to the Old South and the Lost Cause would complicate its path forward for the next century and beyond. One modern critic has described the Sewanee of Stuck's time as "an isolated retreat for a defiant intellectual elite when the South was licking the wounds of its civil war."[4] Stuck himself described some of the faculty as "reactionaries and status quo ante-bellum advocates."[5]

On October 10, 1860, a crowd of hundreds had gathered at University Place in Sewanee to hear speeches and benedictions from congressmen, bishops, and university presidents, enjoy a band which had traveled the hundred miles from Nashville to perform, and witness the laying of the six-ton marble cornerstone.[6] A month later, Abraham Lincoln was elected president of the United States; less than a month after that, South Carolina seceded. War was only four months away.

The five years of fighting "deprived the university of virtually all of its tangible assets except for the land on which it was to be built."[7] In the war's aftermath, on March 22, 1866, the Episcopal Bishop of Tennessee Charles Todd Quintard and several others visited Sewanee. All the buildings except an old log cabin had been burned or dismantled by the Union army that had camped there, or by Union sympathizers in the neighborhood. In an echo of the ceremony of six tragic years before, they selected a site for the chapel and erected a wooden cross. By May 1868 the "Sewanee Training and Divinity School" had nine students.[8] These students, wrote Thomas Frank Gailor, vice-chancellor during Stuck's time in Sewanee and later Bishop of Tennessee, "set a standard of scholarship and life at Sewanee which influenced the whole South . . . Sewanee . . . made the first stand for higher education and held the banner high when State Governments were paralyzed with the desolation of war and when private benefactions had not reached the prostrate South."[9] In 1874, three Bachelor of Arts degrees and one Bachelor of Letters were awarded—the first earned degrees granted by the university.[10]

The Theological Department, as it later became known, offered courses in five areas: New and Old Testament, Dogmatic Theology, Ecclesiastical History and Polity, and Homiletics and Pastoral Theology.[11] Like all theology students, Stuck was expected to wear "the scholastic cap and gown" in yet another bow to the traditions of the oldest universities in England.[12] The school's calendar was designed to take advantage of Sewanee's elevation; a thousand feet above the surrounding countryside, the area had become a haven for planters fleeing the heat and malaria of the Deep South. Students would attend classes through the summer, with a long winter vacation around Christmas. Stuck signed the University's enrollment book on August 11, 1889, listing his hometown as San Marcos, Texas.[13] He would be one of just nineteen students enrolled in the Theological Department in each of the years from 1889 to 1892.[14]

Four years before Stuck's arrival, one of his professors, William A. Guerry, had introduced to the university a course called "Practical Christianity." Later, Guerry would write that "the problems of this age are social problems and therefore the Gospel for this age must be a social Gospel." He also claimed that "the early church believed that she had a mission to fulfill to society as well as to the individual, and that the individual was to be saved only as he is part of the visible society and Kingdom of God."[15] Stuck would live out this Social Gospel for the rest of his life, focusing his work at least as much on improving social conditions as on serving the spiritual needs of individuals.

∽

Hudson Stuck thrived in the intellectual and social atmosphere of Sewanee, acting more like a giddy undergraduate than a seminarian. (Later, as a Sewanee trustee, he would write, "I want to see theologues mixing with the other fellows and taking part in everything.")[16] He joined the Delta Tau Delta fraternity, eventually becoming president, and founded a student literary journal, *The University of the South Magazine*, the forerunner of *The Sewanee Review*. Launched in 1892, today the *Review* is the oldest surviving critical and literary quarterly in the United

States.[17] Stuck also won academic prizes for English and Composition. The newspaper in Stuck's old hometown of Junction ("City" had been dropped from the name in 1894) would later claim that Stuck "graduated with the highest honors up to that date in the Theological Department of the University of the South."[18]

Situated amid ten thousand acres owned by the university—"the Domain"—the rocky streams, waterfalls, and dramatic views which surrounded the school, gave Stuck as much pleasure as his intellectual pursuits. He became known for his energy, for a sometimes-brusque manner, and for strenuous enjoyment of the outdoors. He spent a great deal of time walking mountain trails, and exploring the local caves. A story credited to a Queenie Woods Washington recounted an outing with Stuck:

> We were returning home from Wet Cave. Mr. Stuck told me if we ran up the mountain we would feel the fatigue much less than if we took the climb leisurely. I was completely exhausted but we reached the top quite three-quarters of an hour before the wagon. Mr. Stuck who suggested this uphill running later climbed Mt. McKinley.[19]

Stuck's reputation for being prickly also began during his time in Sewanee. The school's yearbook *Cap & Gown* one year used the quotation, "At his stern command all hell grew silent—pandemonium was stilled." The next year's yearbook used a line from Shakespeare's *Coriolanus*, "Hear you this triton of the minnows," referring perhaps sarcastically to his status as a

Gulliver among Lilliputians.[20] Students made fun of his accent, and of his insistence on doing things right.

Using a word more common then than now for someone who acts in a smug and morally superior way, Hudson Stuck said, "I don't see why a man should feel called to be a prig as soon as he feels that he is called to be a clergyman. But lots do." He called this priggishness the "curse of St Luke's Hall,"[21] the general term for Sewanee's theology school. A quarter-century later, further betraying his bias for action, Stuck would write, "I doubt that a professional theologian, as a professional theologian . . . ever helped to make a Christian since Christianity began."[22]

On August 4, 1892, Stuck received the degree of Graduate in Divinity, newly created the year before.[23] Three days later, Bishop Johnson of Texas ordained him as a deacon of the Episcopal Church. Stuck's three years of seminary training had instilled in him a deep love for Sewanee, and for the steep trails and intricate caves of the university's ten thousand acres, which would last the rest of his life, along with friendships and alliances forged at the university. In turn, Stuck would become one of Sewanee's favorite sons, and be offered several faculty positions there, though none could lure him away from Alaska.

∽

After his time in Sewanee, Stuck, flush with academic and social success, returned to Texas and a small parish church in Cuero, ninety miles southeast of San Antonio. At Grace Church the newly-minted priest began learning his profession, and also learning to be the head of a household. "I have a boy as servant who cooks my simple meals, tends to my horse, cleans up the house, smokes my tobacco & robs me generally," Stuck wrote. "Someone asked me yesterday whether I 'still had Ally' (for my valet rejoiceth in the name of Nathan Allen Bunker). I replied that I thought it might be better expressed that Ally still 'had' me." He had realized that "keeping house as a bachelor is not the way to save money—and I'm not a marrying man. But I will not board. I hate boarding." In spite of his lack of domestic tranquility, Stuck could claim in the same letter that "I think I'm learning to preach."

The Episcopal community must have thought so as well, as only five months into his career in Cuero he was offered a position in Palestine, Texas, 240 miles to the northeast. Loyalty to his new parish led him to refuse that call, though no one would say that he was content to be where he was. For one thing, he found it impossible to create a boys choir in Cuero, because, he said bluntly, "the boys here can't sing." For another, he missed Sewanee terribly.

On October 4, 1892, just two months after graduating from Sewanee, Stuck had written the first letter in what would be a thirteen-year correspondence with the university's new vice-chancellor, Benjamin Lawton Wiggins. (In accordance with the Oxbridge model, the chancellor, a bishop of one of the controlling dioceses, was and is the ceremonial leader of the university, while the vice-chancellor is the school president.) Wiggins, the first Sewanee graduate to serve as vice-chancellor, would become noted among Southern college presidents of this day, attaining "the most prominent position ever enjoyed by a Sewanee vice chancellor."[24] In these letters Stuck reveals himself as he does nowhere else, speaking of his love for and despair at leaving Sewanee, and his feelings about his work in Texas and, later, Alaska.

"Leaving Sewanee has been I think, the greatest wrench of my life. It hit me harder than even my friends knew. For the first week here I was utterly miserable," Stuck wrote from Cuero. "[W]hen I got to my room and had locked the door, again & again I have rolled on the bed tearing my hair and wishing that I might . . . stay at Sewanee and see the boys sometimes." Although he realized that the Mountain was dear to others beside himself, "I don't think the place ever twined itself about the heart-strings of anyone as it has about mine." He was doing his best and working hard, "but anyone that says I'm happy lies in his throat."

He then relates a pointed exchange with his superior: "I had to write to my bishop that first week, and I wrote as I felt, as is my wont, [whether] to Bishop or butcher. And I felt at the bottom of the deep blue sea." To Stuck's chagrin, the bishop "felt called upon to administer some episcopal admonition." Stuck "should be like St. Paul. St Paul was never 'blue.' I should be above such petty infirmity, and so on, the worst stuff that ever right reverend prelate wrote to a 'green gosling of a deacon.'" Stuck replied that "I didn't care whether St Paul was ever blue or not; I was, and that St Paul was never at Sewanee anyhow, or he would have written an epistle to the Mountain when he left, more passionately lugubrious than anything I had penned."[25]

But Stuck also enjoyed himself while in Cuero. He recounted a week-long outing in Gonzalez, which included an evening of singing college songs with Sewanee friends. He displayed his sardonic side in his description of local church culture: "The indigenous Texas idea of a 'preacher' (how I hate that word) is a man with a long face and a sanctimonious snuffle."[26]

Before long, however, he was inevitably lured from Cuero to the largest and most powerful church in the state: the Cathedral of Dallas. The Fort Worth *Gazette*'s correspondent in Cuero reported, "Rev. Hudson Stuck, the Episcopal preacher here, has received a call to the cathedral of Dallas, which he will accept." Stuck was described as "one of the ablest and most eloquent young divines in Texas and while his parishioners here regret exceedingly to have him leave they rejoice in his well merited promotion."[27]

Just who was this rising man? A photo taken in 1894, the year Stuck left Cuero for Dallas, shows a young priest, cleanshaven and neat, boyish and seemingly undaunted. He has a cleft chin, rather oversized ears, dark hair, and dark piercing eyes. One who knew him then wrote, "He was lean and spare just under six feet tall, a great walker." Stuck would take that energy and intensity to Dallas, where he would find a growing city big enough for his ambitions.

4

GRIT, GOOD WORKS, & THE GRAND CANYON

No one has ever determined exactly how Dallas got its name. In 1841, John Neely Bryan had established a town where three branches of the Trinity River converged, and where surveyors were plotting the Preston Trail, a frontier highway which would connect Austin and the Red River.[1] Bryan decided to name it "for my friend Dallas," but died in 1877 in the Texas State Lunatic Asylum having never clarified who the friend was.[2]

Nor was the source of its name the only unusual thing about the early history of the city. In 1854, an exile from Napoleon III's France, Victor Prosper Considerant, founded La Réunion, a utopian settlement a few miles west of Dallas. The European emigres attracted to La Réunion included "highly educated professionals as well as scientists, artists, writers, musicians, artisans, and naturalists," and the settlement's cooperative store drew Dallas residents to its superior goods. After La Réunion was disbanded in 1857, most of its settlers remained; by 1860 it was incorporated into Dallas proper, adding an exotic and cosmopolitan tinge to the young and growing city.[3]

During the town's Wild West phase, "Doc" Holliday, Belle Starr, and Jesse James's brother Frank spent time in this growing north-Texas center for business and trade, which boasted three red-light districts. In 1873, the Texas & Pacific Railroad's first locomotive pulled into town; with the Houston & Texas Central Railway's existing line already in Dallas, the resulting crossroads began the city's boom era.[4] By the time of Hudson Stuck's arrival in 1894, Dallas was "a T-shaped city with a fairly even distribution of prosperous and working-class neighborhoods" as well as "separate shanty towns along flood plains inhabited by improverished Whites and Blacks."[5] The turn of the twentieth century saw increasing numbers of Mexican immigrants into Dallas; by 1920 "Little Mexico" would be an established neighborhoood. In an overwhelmingly rural state—in 1890 only 16 percent of residents lived in towns and cities[6]—Dallas was one of five Texas towns, along with Fort Worth, San Antonio, Galveston, and Houston, with more than 20,000 people. The growing city's "mix of southerners, migrants from border states,

European immigrants, and original . . . settlers cooperated to lure capital and businesses to Dallas in much the same way that they attracted the railroads."[7]

Historian Randolph B. Campbell has written, "While Texans living west of the 98th meridian (in modern terms, west of Interstate Highway 35) closed the Indian frontier and expanded the cattle kingdom," both participating in and helping to create the legend of the Old West, "those east of that line—the great majority of the total population—remained clearly a part of the South." But the Old South of the prewar, preindustrial era was giving way to what was being called the "New South." The creed of those who preached the New South "emphasized economic growth—railroad building, urbanization, and industrialization."[8] As it happened, in Hudson Stuck's move from Junction City east to Dallas he had crossed that geographic and social boundary. His social-justice initiatives in Dallas would bring him into direct conflict with the forces of the industrializing New South.

∽

On December 20, 1899, an august gathering of eight Episcopal bishops from across the South celebrated the consecration of St. Matthew's Cathedral on the corner of Canton and Ervay Streets, near present-day Dallas City Hall. The *Houston Daily Post* proclaimed it "a notable event in church history." The "very solemn and impressive" ceremonies also marked the twenty-fifth anniversary of the patrician, Irish-born Rev. Alexander Charles Garrett's ordination as bishop. "There is no better known or better loved churchman in the State than Bishop Garrett," the

Post asserted, "and the success of today's ceremonies has been particularly gratifying to his friends."[9]

St. Matthew's had been made a cathedral in 1874 when Garrett was ordained the first missionary bishop of Northern Texas. This first cathedral, which according to the *Dallas Morning News* was at the time "the finest church in Dallas,"[10] had been located downtown on Commerce and Kendall Streets; however, "the rapid growth of the congregation and the noise from the nearby Santa Fe railroad yards made worship services nearly impossible." The new cathedral, built of blue-gray Comanche sandstone in the Norman Gothic style, had been built in 1894 and '95.[11]

Five years before the consecration ceremonies, Hudson Stuck had arrived to take his new position at St. Matthew's, first as rector and then eighteen months later as Dean of the Cathedral. (In the Episcopal church, although the cathedral is the official headquarters of the bishop, the dean is the clergy member in charge. Other assisting clergy at the cathedral are given the title of Canon.)[12] In Cuero he had lacked a canvas large enough to effect meaningful change; it was in Dallas that Stuck's lifelong work came into focus, and here that his guiding philosophy, and his attitude toward life and work, coalesced.

∞

Hudson Stuck's career and achievements can best be seen in light of the movement known as Muscular Christianity. This mid-nineteenth-century trend, which had its roots in Great Britain and spread to the United States, stressed a type of religion which valued physical strength, social action, and above all, grit. Writing in the *Saturday Review* in 1857 about British clergyman/author Charles Kingsley's *Two Years Ago*, T. C. Sandars described Kingsley's ideal as "a man who fears God and can walk a thousand miles in a thousand hours," and who "at the same time can hit a woodcock, doctor a horse, and twist a poker around his fingers."[13]

The movement's adherents felt compelled to do something for the world in which they found themselves. Not for them the passive-martyr model of some saints or ascetic figures; instead, they were convinced that duty required them to strive mightily in service to their fellow humans. In this way the idea of the Social Gospel overlapped to some degree with Muscular Christianity. Whether helping to modernize child-labor laws in the historic British Reform Acts of 1832 and 1867, or heading to the farthest reaches of the British Empire as missionaries, muscular Christians saw it as their responsibility to improve the lot of others.

Muscular Christianity, though, was not immune to larger, less-benevolent forces at work in the late 19th and early 20th centuries. At its worst, its adherents substituted thoughtless action for sensitivity, saw violence as essential in warding off physical and moral softness, and were suspicious of intellectual engagement with the world. Hudson Stuck, who read Shakespeare by campfire-light and founded Sewanee's literary magazine, could hardly have been less of a Muscular Christian in this regard.

Nor did the more imperialist and racist aspects of Muscular Christianity seem to adhere to this British emigre.

While service to others could, and often did, devolve into paternalism—with frequent side helpings of condescension and superiority—Hudson Stuck would always treat the communities with which he worked, whether the mill-workers of Dallas or the indigenous peoples of Alaska, as human beings worthy of respect as equals before God.

Stuck had prominently opposed what he regarded as an unhealthy emphasis on sports, especially football, at Sewanee. He wrote Vice-Chancellor Wiggins in 1897 that academics were being "sacrificed on the altar of Varsity athletics." At the time Sewanee was a football powerhouse; its 1899 team was 12–0 and even today is famous for having defeated five teams, including Texas and LSU, in five cities in six days. (Perhaps inevitably, you can find today posters in Sewanee commemorating the team with the headline: "On the Seventh Day, They Rested.") A trip by the football team to Dallas in 1898 to play the University of Texas drew a sarcastic rebuke from Stuck: "Are there no teams in Porto Rico or Manilla [sic] that your enterprising manager could arrange games with?"[14]

However, Stuck's grievance wasn't with the sport per se, but rather with the extent to which its demands, especially the extensive travel, interfered with players' educations. In fact, Stuck formed a football team at St. Matthew's Grammar School almost immediately after its founding, and defended the sport when Texas's Southern Methodists in 1900 voted to ban the game from church schools in the state. In an essay for the *Dallas Morning News* in response, Stuck argued that "zealots" had caused "uneasiness in the minds of many Dallas parents whose sons are addicted" to football. "For the healthy boy who plays the game under expert direction there is surely no finer sport," Stuck argued.

A modern commentator has written, "[Stuck] might not have been the Father of North Texas football, but he certainly was an early shepherd." On Jan. 29, 1898, two years before the first documented game was played between Texas public schools, St. Matthew's defeated Forney's Lewis Academy, 4–0, at the Dallas Fair Grounds. Several St. Matthew's players followed Stuck's pipeline and played for Sewanee, including Ormond Simkins, who played on the 1899 team. In another letter to Vice-Chancellor Wiggins, Stuck wrote, "I am today engaged in forming the 3rd St. Matthew's football team, having already two in the field . . . I am dropping everything this afternoon to go out in the drizzle and witness a game of my first team. I am most emphatically not prejudiced against athletics."[15]

In the end, Stuck's love for Sewanee overrode his concerns about the team's academic progress. Once the decision to send Sewanee's 1898 team to Texas was made, he cast aside his reservations, and often thereafter played host to the team in Dallas, including when it lost to Texas, 11–0, on Oct. 10, 1902.[16]

Stuck may have also introduced another sport to Texas. A precursor to cross-country running had been invented in England in the 1830s, when schoolboys invented a game they called Hares and Hounds, or "paper chasing." The boys who were "hares" would leave first, and drop a trail of paper for the "hounds" to follow.[17] According to a September 1902 *Dallas Morning News* story, the "newly organized Hare and Hounds Club at St. Matthew's School . . . held its first paper chase of the season yesterday afternoon." The hares were listed as Edward

Belsterling and Grafton Burke, and "eighteen or twenty boys of the school of all ages were hounds." Although the outgoing chase was a success, "a second chase on the way home was ruined by an irate agriculturalist, who . . . would by no means permit passage through his fields." The *News* reported that "amusement and enjoyment were afforded by the run to all who took part," and also that great interest had been aroused in the sport, which was "new to this section."[18]

In 1862, five years after Sandars described Kingsley's ideal Muscular Christian, Edward Whymper became the first to climb the iconic Matterhorn in the Swiss Alps. The two events are not unconnected; the nineteenth-century mountaineering boom, along with its close relation, polar exploration, as evident in the famed expeditions led by Robert Falcon Scott and Ernest Shackleton, had quite a lot in common with the Muscular Christianity movement. Both were given their impetus by, and both in the beginning predominantly sprang from, nineteenth-century British ideals. And like the reforming and missionary impulses of the Muscular Christians, exploration required qualities which were highly valued by the Victorians. As Robert Macfarlane wrote in 2003's *Mountains of the Mind*, "pluck and potency . . . resourcefulness, self-assurance, and manhood" were required for both, qualities which are often summed up in the term "grit":

Grit was ingrained in the imperial generations of Britain from an early age—the boarding-school system churned out generation after generation of boys allegedly full of the stuff—and it was considered to be the moral substance which underpinned Britain's success, its zeal for exploration and its Empire-building.[19]

And, it might be added, its social activism and missionary work. "Football," Stuck had written in his 1900 *Dallas Morning News* editorial, "is incomparably the one game that requires not only skill, not only strength, but courage—that quality which in the bright lexicon of youth is known as 'grit.'"[20] Stuck, who considered himself an Englishman by birth and breeding, would take that grit to his social work, both in Dallas and beyond. He would also take it into the wilds of the American West and, finally, to Alaska and Denali.

Stuck's fascination with the literature of mountaineering and exploration, originating in his childhood reading of his sailor relative's books on the Arctic and his youthful scrambles in the Lake District, persisted his entire life. Even while overseeing all his projects in Dallas, the energetic dean found time to travel, exploring Yellowstone National Park and the Rocky Mountains, and summiting Washington's Mount Rainier. In a sermon delivered at St. Matthew's on July 20, 1902, Stuck described how, en route to San Francisco, he took a detour to visit "that wonder of the world, the Grand Canyon of the Colorado River." After hiking down into "the stupendous chasm" and becoming "familiar with its mysteries, and incomparable grandeur," he had spent a day on the canyon's rim. Stuck used the view to good rhetorical advantage:

I had no notion that it was within the range of man's eyesight to see so far. In that pure air, at that altitude, nothing bounded one's view but the rotundity of the earth. A hundred and fifty miles away the Navajo Mountain in Utah stood out clearly against the sky . . . while in the other direction the San Francisco Mountains lifted their graceful cones 12,000 feet into the sky, seventy miles from where I stood.

Then Stuck pivoted to his moral lesson: "So those who have walked only on the commonplace level ground," he concluded, "their atmosphere dense with the mist of sordid pleasures, dense with the mist of the marketplace, know not what vision is possible in the clear air of spiritual exaltation."[21]

In his writings Stuck would often refer to the feats and travails of famous mountaineers and polar explorers with the ease of deep familiarity. "We are disposed to be a little scornful of man-drawn sleds [for polar travel] these days," he wrote, pausing in mid-account of his summer voyages up the Yukon for one of the digressions that were so typical in his writings. Then he went on to argue that for efficiency of travel, "I do not think McClintock's record of journeys made in this way in 1853 on the Franklin search has ever been surpassed by dogs or other means of traction."[22] He would leave to the University of the South a library of over two hundred volumes, ranging from the sixteenth-century chronicles of Richard Hakluyt to a 1915 edition of John Muir's *Travels in Alaska*, published the year after Muir's death.

Stuck brought these precepts of Muscular Christianity—grit, devotion to doing good, love of the rugged and the mountainous—with him to the fast-rising town of Dallas.

⁖

In October 1894, two months after his arrival, Stuck wrote Vice-Chancellor Wiggins, "There is an immense work here, one that a man may well be content to devote his life to." As for the people, they "cannot be kinder [and] cooperation cannot [be] more ready and willing." He described himself as "very ambitious for my parish," with "great plans of extensive new work," and claimed, "We shall soon possess the finest church in Texas, and one of the finest anywhere in the South."[23]

Stuck's "immense work" began almost immediately, with his establishment of St. Andrew's Mission in a storefront near the factories of Dallas, to serve the working class of the city. By 1896 Bishop Garrett was holding the service of confirmation for "the first-fruits of the work" done at the mission, which had been "recently started in the cotton mill district of the city."[24]

That same year Stuck began a night school for mill workers at the mission, telling the *Morning News* in 1899 that "the school is doing most satisfactory work, having more than forty scholars enrolled from all ages and both sexes, the only condition being imposed being inability to attend day school."[25] In 1901, another Sewanee graduate, George Clifton Edwards, became director of the night school. The twenty-three-year-old lawyer had grown up in Dallas, and was a socialist and Progressive political activist. Under Edward's direction, the school was so successful that Dallas school superintendent J. L. Long, "after listening to a fiery appeal by Edwards, had little difficulty convincing the school board" that the school was worthy of being publicly funded beginning in 1902. "Under the auspices of the school board, night school remained the only educational option of many young mill workers for several decades."[26] A modern historian described the night school as "Perhaps the most far-reaching institution established by Dallas socialists."

In 1898, Dean Stuck launched his next initiative, a shelter for abused children. St. Matthew's Home for Children, in his words, was "not an orphan asylum. Most of the children are not orphans . . . but they are all children who but for this home would be without care and without good influence." As of 1899 Stuck was able to say that the home "shelters and feeds and clothes and teaches thirty children between the ages of 4 and 10 or 11 years. There are no more inmates because there is no more room."[27] In November 1902 construction began on a new building for the shelter, and "by Christmas 1903, the new home, called by Garrett 'a monument to Stuck's untiring zeal and tenacity of purpose,' housed seventy-five children." Hudson Stuck came back to Dallas in 1907 from Alaska to attend the formal dedication.[28]

Yet another of Stuck's cathedral programs began in 1899: Saint Matthew's Home for Aged Women. He described the home as a "most attractive cottage" located four miles away and "at the other extreme of the city" from the mission, near the city hospital. He had procured "the kind gift of a lady of the cathedral" for the residence, which at his insistence was open to women of all creeds—as were all the charitable works he involved himself in.[29] Stuck believed that "next to the care of children . . . the care of the aged poor must appeal most to the Christian heart."[30]

Of all the initiatives begun in Dallas by Stuck, it was St. Matthew's School for Boys which came first in his heart. Stuck announced the opening of the school in the spring of 1899, describing it as "a school to prepare boys for college," but above all, "a feeder to Sewanee." All instructors had Sewanee connections, and Stuck, now teaching English literature at St. Matthew's, wrote, "Of course it will prepare for any college, but it will not be the fault of the school if the boys that it graduates do not go to Sewanee." Its headmaster was Frank Shoup, Stuck's college classmate and the son of the Confederate general and Sewanee professor, "thoroughly well educated and highly cultivated" as well as "a close personal friend of mine."[31]

Stuck based the school on the pattern of the English grammar school, with the classic curriculum of Greek, Latin, mathematics, history, literature, English, French, and German. It would not teach "little dabs of everything"; furthermore, "what it teaches, it will teach thoroughly."[32] By 1902, the school housed seventy pupils. Stuck's first recruit for Sewanee, Ormond Simkins, would star in baseball and football and be a part of the school's fabled 1899 football team.

Personally as well as professionally, Stuck created a full and enjoyable life in Dallas. In June 1896, the *Morning News* noted that Stuck and the cathedral choir boys "departed yesterday for Huddle's Point, on the Colorado River, where they will go into the camp for two weeks." The thirty men and boys "anticipate great sport" during the outing. Stuck repeated this choir trip almost every summer, "entering into their sports with the same whole-souled heartiness with which he pursued more serious tasks." For this and other reasons, "his boys loved him; and no wonder," according to a 1904 profile in *The Churchman*. "In their troubles as in their happiness, wrong or right, they had learned to come to him, and those who once learned never seemed to lose the habit, as his annual visits to Sewanee have proved year by year."[33]

When Stuck took his nearly-daily afternoon rides on Blacksmith, a stallion he had purchased from a bankrupt racehorse owner, he invariably had behind him a "small cavalcade" of schoolboys following on their ponies. "Stuck always had his favorites, but any youth who had a problem or sought a champion need look no farther than the dean's door."[34]

∽

During his time at St. Matthew's, Stuck was described by Bishop Juhan as "irascible around women. He had little use for them, but they, strangely enough, seemed to like him. He was very highly thought of by women's organizations at the Cathedral in Dallas. At times he was curt with them, almost sarcastic." No one who reads Stuck's letters will doubt this assertion.[35] He himself knew his tendency to fire off scathing words, either in person or on paper. He wrote Wiggins in November 1900, after one such blast, "I think that perhaps I owe you an apology . . . I wrote as I felt . . . But it was not my intention to insult you, and I ask your pardon if my phraseology was beyond the permitted limit of even the most caustic criticism."[36]

"Irascible around women;" "not the marrying kind;" devoted to young men and boys. In our time, the third decade of the twenty-first century, some will look suspiciously upon behavior like Stuck's. Others, of a more generous frame of mind, will wonder more generally about Hudson Stuck's sexuality. Later, in Alaska, Stuck would write in his diary of the night his protegé Grafton Burke told Stuck of his intention to marry, "Tonight Burke crawled into my cot." During an epic dogsled tour of the Arctic coast in 1917–18, he wrote, "Although I rose at 4 A.M. and started a fire I was very glad to creep into bed again and snuggle up against Walter."

One modern writer has examined how "in the nineteenth century, it was common for men to forge romantic friendships—fervid, life-defining connections—with other men," quite apart from marriage and erotic relationships with women. While these nonsexual romantic male friendships existed all over America—the writer points out that Abraham Lincoln shared a bed with his best friend for four years—"the particular Southern strand of romantic friendship tended to last much longer, throughout the entire lives of men."[37] As a son of the Victorian age, Stuck might best be seen in this light. And in terms of behavior, no evidence exists that Stuck ever acted in a sexual way with anyone, of any gender or age.

∽

Among all the boys Stuck took in at St. Matthew's and sent on to Sewanee, the one who would be most prominent in Stuck's future was Grafton "Hap" Burke. Burke had come to St. Matthew's in 1899 as a seventeen-year-old, and resided at the rectory with Stuck. His father, according to Bishop Juhan, was "an inimitable Irish doctor with a wonderful personality but a wild nature. He neglected his family and Stuck felt the promising . . . Burke should be separated from him."[38] In March 1903 Stuck wrote to Wiggins "to ask you for a scholarship on my own account," for Hap Burke. Stuck described the boy's father as "a physician of sorts," and his mother as dead. "I think he is the best and solidest boy I have ever known . . . thoroughly conscientious and steady." Stuck had kept him at St. Matthew's against his father's will, "who would have put him to work at anything he could get long ago, and resents my keeping him at school." In case it was not clear, Stuck made it so: "The father amounts to very little." Basically, Stuck said, "I keep my temper with 'the doctor' for the boy's sake."

"Now 'Hap,' as we call him . . . is short for 'Happy,' his well-earned nickname," Stuck continued. "I know that whatever his calling he will be a clean, upright, God-fearing man." Burke, said Stuck, is "a robust, broad shouldered, vigorous fellow . . . [with] amiability and sweetness of disposition, [but also] stability and strength of character." In sum, "I think that 'Hap' is about the best all round boy I have had to do with . . . Can you give me a scholarship for him?" At Sewanee, Burke would begin the medical career that would take him to Alaska, and then to Stuck's side for the rest of Stuck's life.

Stuck was determined to play a role in the future of his university. In the letter discussing Burke, Stuck asked Wiggins very specific questions, and delivered quite piquant opinions, about Sewanee's academic and social life. "How does the new degree business affect the Greek department? . . . Am I to come up next year prepared to fight for the chair of metaphysics . . . ? I shall be in the Board next year sure."[39] Of Sewanee's medical school, which trained doctors from 1891 to 1909, Stuck wrote Wiggins, "Bother the medical department. You know my sentiments about that grisly excrescence." He described some of the faculty as "reactionaries and status quo ante-bellum advocates" and admitted, "After all I know awfully little about the best things to do, though I am most anxious that they should be done."[40]

One Sewanee-bound student in Stuck's care offers a fascinating bit of Texas historical trivia. Writing to Wiggins in the fall of 1897, Stuck said, "Before you get this letter a little chap named Harry Houston of whom you have been written to will be at the S. S. [summer school]. I have had him with me for two days and I like the kid." He described Harry as "the only grandson of Sam Houston of Texas fame, but he has had little show of any kind, and is a sort of young heathen. I don't think he even knows the creed." With the promotion of both his state and his university in mind, Stuck wrote, "I would like to see that name borne by a thoroughly cultivated man for the honor of history and of Texas, and as an enthusiastic alumnus such a man would be a power for Sewanee here." Stuck ended with, "He will spend his vacation on the mountain—poor chap."[41] Sam Houston's grandson attended Sewanee's grammar school from 1897 to 1899.[42]

∽

On Sunday, October 28, 1900, Dean Stuck climbed the short steps to the Gospel podium in St. Matthew's Cathedral. The rainy, muggy weather dulled the light passing through the tall, narrow windows, across the two rows of arched inner columns, and landing weakly on the four ranks of pews in the nave, with seating for 1,000 congregants. Stuck's subject that day was illiteracy. But he had a specific type, and cause, of illiteracy on his mind.

St. Matthew's Children's Home and free public kindergarten, he said, "are in the midst of the center of illiteracy in Dallas, the cottonmill district." Many—including, one can assume, the members of the city's business elite in the pews before him—thought that mills were of the utmost importance: "You are told almost every day of the week, if you read the newspapers, that the great need of Dallas is factories." However, Stuck told his congregation, "For my part, there is one thing that I think we need more than . . . factories, and that is a factory law . . . At present there are no restrictions whatever upon child labor in the State of Texas."

Stuck continued, "At 10 years the children of the factory operatives go to work in the mill." He called it "a reproach upon our civilization that this is so. We are fifty years behind Europe and the East in that this is so." He asserted that "The reproach is on the State, and only the State can remove it." As for the church, "We look and long for the time when the conditions will be other than they are, but meanwhile we waste little strength in declaiming against the conditions." Stuck saw clearly what "total illiteracy," resulting from child labor in factories, meant for the future of Dallas: "It means low ideals. It means a low standard of material and intellectual life. It means immorality and vice. It means thriftlessness and penury. It means dirt and squalor and disease."[43]

It was Stuck's first shot in a historic two-year battle to pass the first child-labor laws in Texas.

∽

As Dean, most of Stuck's initiatives to improve conditions in Dallas weren't controversial, though he had always been unafraid to speak truth to power. In his Sunday sermons he castigated the plutocratic congregation of St. Matthew's for having "little time for anything but making money." Nevertheless, he was on cordial terms with his parishioners. The vestry, including such Dallas establishment names as Belo, Coke, and Scollard, would pass a resolution before his departure for Alaska praising Stuck's "indefatigable zeal, his courageous and vigorous personality," as well as his "untiring and unselfish efforts to build up the parish work . . . in which he was so eminently successful."[44] One man later quoted his boss as saying around this time, "Stuck is a great man. All business men of Dallas love him."[45] Following his often-repeated statement, "I am sorry for a life in which there is no usefulness to others," Stuck had created institutions and programs which enjoyed widespread support in his congregation and the larger community.

But when Stuck took on the cause of child-labor reform, he found himself at odds with the powers that be, and in a public-relations battle with Dallas's leading newspaper, the *Dallas Morning News*—which had been founded in 1885 and owned since by the Belo family,[46] one of whom, Alfred N. Belo, sat on the vestry of St. Matthew's Cathedral. Fortunately for Stuck, though, he had in his corner an ally as formidable as it was unlikely: women's clubs.

When the Civil War brought an end to slavery, finding an available source of labor became crucial to the plans of the New South boosters of industrialism. Cotton, especially, required large numbers of workers. Texas, like other southern states, needed children to help cultivate, harvest, and spin cotton into cloth. The resulting high rates of child labor and low school attendance inevitably drew the attention of social reformers. Children as young as age six picked cotton, with sacks sized for them; the mills hired youth as young as eight for twelve-hour shifts. One mill owner told the *Dallas Morning News* "with complete sincerity" that "one advantage a man has at a mill over the farm tenant is that he can get employment for the whole family every day in the year at the mill, and at the same time educate his children." The trick, the mill owner said, was to work half of the children at a time in the mill, sending the other half to school.[47] In 1900, 25,000 of the nearly 100,000 textile workers in the South were children under sixteen.[48]

The larger picture for children in the United States wasn't much brighter. The twentieth century dawned on an America where child mortality rates were high, school attendance was low, and two million children between the ages of ten and fifteen worked in factories, on farms, and on urban streets.[49] Nationwide, children's health reflected the nation's widespread poverty: about 1 in 4 children in 1900 died by age 5.

In Dallas, at least, the plight of children was not totally subordinated to the desires of business. In an indirect and old-fashioned but effective way, the Dallas Federation of Women's Clubs made their voices heard. These "female members of the elite" were able to exert "a powerful influence on civil affairs" even though they were not yet able to vote.[50] By use of thoroughly modern tactics, such as "effective organizing and manipulation of public opinion," the clubwomen "moderated their fathers', husbands', and sons' visions of largely unrestricted growth."[51] On January 12, 1902, the *Morning News* reported that the City Federation of Women's Clubs voted to condemn child labor. "The subject was brought up by Mrs. J. C. Roberts, who made a reference to what she called the growing tendency to employ little ones in factories. She said that she was unalterably opposed to it."[52]

The Dallas cohort was part of a statewide movement. The Texas Federation of Women's Clubs added the child labor problem to its agenda in 1902, at a time when, as Stuck pointed out, the state not only had no law restricting children from working, but also had no law requiring them to attend school. Then the clubs went into action: "since no one knew how many children worked in factories, mines, and street trades, the clubwomen assigned themselves the job of investigating child labor in their local communities." In 1902, the Dallas Federation attempted to find out how many children were at work in the city's cotton mills. When the owners refused to cooperate, "the clubwomen, all refined middle-class ladies, resorted to spying."[53]

The Texas clubwomen had examples to follow. In September 1901 the column "Clubdom" in the *Morning News* described

"An important step [that] was taken . . . by the owners of cotton mills in Georgia." The owners had agreed that no child under twelve would work in mills, unless they had attended school for four months in the year. No child under ten would be allowed to work in mills, "day or night." The columnist saw it as "the direct outcome of the fight against child labor in Georgia by the Women's Federated Clubs of that state."[54] The Dean of St. Matthew's was all too willing to join the women's clubs in this effort. A modern historian has asserted that "in 1902–3, Hudson Stuck . . . acted more or less as the women's 'front man.'"[55]

The *Dallas Morning News*, in an editorial on April 15, 1902, defended the use of child labor, referring to "sentimental reformers" who were "taking little notice of the progress that has been made" concerning conditions in modern factories. "There is no greater evil," the editorial proclaimed, "than that of allowing strapping boys and girls to grow up in idleness."[56] Two days later, Stuck struck back. In a letter to the *News*, Stuck said, "It is not a theory we are dealing with . . . It is one plain, notorious, indefensible abuse that we are seeking to abolish." Conditions in Dallas, he wrote, "are conditions that the British Parliament forbade exactly 100 years ago, in 1802," and in Massachusetts "sixty-six years ago, in 1836."[57]

The *News* responded three days later, in another unsigned editorial. "Women and children who work in factories are made up largely of those who have no opportunities," it argued. "Has any provision been made for them elsewhere? . . . Will it really help them to deprive them of a chance to work even in a mill?" There should be, "as the News sees it," a "general multiplication of manufacturing establishments in Grand Old Texas," and "nothing should be done" to "discourage the good work which we have so well begun in this line."[58] That same day H. W. Fairbanks, the owner of the South Dallas mill, had a letter published in the *News* arguing with Stuck's statistics. Unfortunately perhaps for him, Fairbanks referred to Stuck's "facile pen" and the "glittering generalities" Stuck had used with reference to the mill and its employment of children.[59]

"There were no glittering generalities . . . I was most precise and definite," Stuck began in his response, printed in the *News* on May 1. As to Fairbanks's numbers, Stuck wrote, "The day I had them counted there were actually sixty-seven. I think the lady who counted them for me can guess ages as well as Mr. Fairbanks, having been engaged in the care and instruction of children all her life." As to the payroll figures, "Mr. Fairbanks knows perfectly well that his payrolls do not tell the whole truth." Many children who work in the factories didn't appear on the payrolls, as they assisted their parents with piecework. More broadly, Stuck argued that wherever factories have been built, regulation by the state of child labor had been necessary. "If these are generalities I hope they glitter enough to attract the attention of those who are disposed to dispute such regulation . . . in Texas." And again: "Speaking generally—and there is no glitter about the statement; it is wrapped in melancholy gloom—the run of the mill operatives are almost totally illiterate." Stuck, who was willing to use any argument that would galvanize his audience, added archly: "The negro children at school, the white children in the mills—is that a situation that Texas should rest content with?"[60]

The next installment in the debate was a short letter from Stuck which ran on May 4. Striking a conciliatory note, he began, "When one feels strongly on any subject, one is apt to be led into overstatements." He described a conversation between himself and Fairbanks, who was "personally aggrieved at what he considers my attack upon his veracity." Disputing Stuck's count of sixty-seven, Fairbanks had suggested that "many of the children may have come into the mills with their mothers to get warm." For his part, Stuck was writing to say "that I regard Mr. Fairbanks as a man of honor," that "it is the system . . . that I am fighting," and that "I hope to have grace and strength to fight that until a legislative remedy is reached."[61]

For almost two months both Stuck and the *News* editorial page were quiet on the topic. Meanwhile, the Dallas Typographical Union, as well as Local No. 188 of the International Brotherhood of Electrical Workers, passed resolutions in support of Stuck's position on child labor. Stuck resurfaced in the *News* on July 16, with an open letter to the state Democratic convention then meeting in Dallas. "Gentlemen: An opportunity lies before you of striking a blow at a wrong . . . that will inevitably grow unless checked by legislative action," he began. He called the question of child labor "not a twentieth century question at all, but a nineteenth century question" which "belongs to the time of Lord Shaftesbury." He warned that although "the evil is in its infancy in Texas . . . it is growing and is bound to grow." He ended by appealing to the Democratic Party to decree "the prevention of this child labor which is child slavery."[62]

In the 1902–1903 legislative session, the House Labor Committee lowered the original bill's age limit of fourteen to twelve, with the condition that working children, twelve to fourteen years old, be able to read and write simple English. Children with a disabled parent or a widowed mother were, however, exempt from the literacy requirement—a major disappointment for Stuck. Children could only work between 6:00 A.M. and 6:00 P.M. A system of penalties for violators was included, although the law lacked enforcement procedures. This weak bill easily passed the legislature and was signed into law by the governor.[63]

"The 1903 legislation, marginal as it was, had been a start; it was the first factory law of any kind in Texas."[64] The debate typified and foreshadowed the fights that Hudson Stuck would take on for the rest of his life against injustice, on both the personal and social levels.

❧

Bishop Garrett had now been in charge of the Diocese of North Texas for almost three decades. In the natural way of things, the seventy-year-old bishop and his young, energetic dean clashed over both style and substance, including the future of St. Matthew's School. In the beginning, the two had worked together. Stuck developed a strategy for dealing with the bishop: "If differences arose over theology or a social problem, a five-mile gallop on horseback from his downtown rectory out Ross Avenue" would bring Stuck to Garrett's office. "There he would make peace."[65]

Stuck, though, came to feel that the bishop seldom "lifted a finger to help [any] enterprise," including especially the boys' school, which Garrett had described as "precariously tentative" and "somewhat hazardly venturesome."[66] There were other sources of friction. "The Bishop does not entertain at all," Stuck wrote Wiggins, "and everyone who comes to town puts up at the rectory. Which is one of the reasons that cause me to state that I have a three thousand dollar job at a fifteen hundred dollar salary."[67] It is not surprising that the energetic dean found himself looking for new challenges.

In contrast to the urbane Garrett, Bishop Peter Trimble Rowe of Alaska was outdoorsy and beloved, the son of a missionary. Stuck had met Rowe at the church's General Convention of 1901, where Rowe had lured Stuck with tales of adventure and mission in the Far North. Stuck jumped at the chance to work in Alaska. In a letter Stuck said, "I have determined to give up at least three years of my life to the work of the Church in the Arctic, to the hardest and most venturesome that I can find because I think the Church has a right to ask of every man that he do his share of roughing it and as yet I have none."[68] Stuck agreed to become Archdeacon of the Yukon and the Arctic, with responsibility for 250,000 square miles in the interior of Alaska "and all the camps and settlements northward to the Arctic Ocean." This was, in Stuck's own words, "a sufficiently wide scope for any man's wanderings and charge." At last, he felt as though he had found a place and a job vast enough for his energy and ambitions.

In an unsigned profile in *Spirit of Missions*, the journal of the Episcopal Church, the month Stuck left for Alaska, the author wrote,

> "Dean Stuck's work at Dallas was excellent. Not only
> the people of the parish, but the people of the city
> soon learned to look upon the young dean as a man

who could be depended upon for aggressive leadership in every good enterprise . . . In his direct and
virile fashion, he would tell the men and women who
sought his help how to break away from the sins and
shortcomings that bound them, and make progress
along the road of right living.

He also referred to "the new archdeacon's characteristic
loyalty," which one of Stuck's classmates had described as
"unqualified, unequivocal, fearless loyalty, to college, fraternity,
the movements and men that appeal to him, and a loyalty that
always seeks to base itself upon principle."[69]

Before he left, though, Stuck had unfinished business, especially
with regard to Grafton Burke. Stuck wrote to Vice-Chancellor
Wiggins on March 8, 1904, "Can you give me about half an hour?
I am troubled about many things, and one of them is Burke."
After reminding Wiggins "how much I care for the boy, and . . .
what a good fellow he is," Stuck added, "but he is not bright, and
all he learns he learns with difficulty." Adding to that Burke's
age—twenty-two—Stuck felt that Hap should abandon the college course for medical training, so that he might follow Stuck to
Alaska as a medical missionary. "Hap will never make a scholar . . .
But he might make an excellent medical man without scholarship."
Though Stuck had thought Burke might take holy orders, he had
decided that "a good doctor is better than a poor priest."

In the same letter, Stuck foresaw that his next visit to
Sewanee would be a sad one, "for it will be the last for a series
of years, no one can say how many." Still, he wrote, "I think of
the glorious emancipation that is before me, and take courage."[70]

5

GOING INSIDE BY DOGSLED AND YUKON RIVER BOAT

The glories of the Inside Passage, which connected the continental United States to the Alaska Territory, were "beyond pen to describe"—although Stuck then proceeded to try. For a thousand miles, from Seattle to Skagway, "the sea is like a river and the shores are close in on either hand," with "one unending panorama of mountains, wooded from top to bottom, glistening with cascades," and "dropping their almost perpendicular sides sheer into water so deep that in many places it has never been fathomed."[1]

To travel from Seattle to Alaska in 1904, the only real option was by boat along the route followed by the new archdeacon. The Inside Passage threads between the mainland shorelines of first British Columbia and then Alaska to the east, while to the west lie thousands of islands which temper the effects of the Pacific Ocean. Even today it is the route followed by the Alaska State Ferry; and even today, most of the towns and villages along it are accessible only by boat or plane. Although it is sometimes assumed to be a journey of calm seas, the passage contains some of the most dangerous water in the world, where "corridors can act as wind funnels, and the many islands jumble tides and stack up steep waves."[2] Stuck, who was never unmindful of history, especially the history of exploration, noted that he was "on the track of the great navigators of the eighteenth century," including "the two greatest of them all, Captain James Cook and Captain George Vancouver." Extend the voyage a little further west and "the track of still another will be crossed—Vitus Bering."[3]

He was also never unmindful of the original inhabitants of Alaska. From the boat he could see "the uncouth pageantry of the native monuments," the totem poles along the shore, with "the gules and vert and azure of primitive heraldry," the "grotesque animal carvings gaudily painted, but often rendered with an admirable vigor," more impressive "than much of the modern heraldry of note-paper and teaspoons." The totem poles were rotting away, and no longer were being made, Stuck wrote scathingly:

for the Thlinkets [Tlingit] have been educated out of regard for their ancestors by teachers who for the most part had no ancestors and therefore cannot see anything but heathenism in distinctions of family descent. There is no scorn more withering than the scorn of a man who does not know who his grandfathers were, for "the pomp of heraldry."[4]

"The steam-roller of our civilization," he feared, "is slowly passing over these people and flattening out any picturesque prominence of custom and costume into the dead level of modern uniformity." Anyone who hoped to see what what was left of "the dignity and parade of savage life, of massive-timbered communal houses flanked and surrounded by the bold blazonry of eagle and whale, of bear and wolf and beaver," as well as the Natives' "gorgeous and grotesque ceremonial dress and accoutrement," according to Stuck, "must not linger. It is nearly gone now."[5]

From the beginning, it seems, Hudson Stuck had a broad-minded view of Native art and culture. Whether due to his emigre's vantage point, as a result of his wide reading in literature and journals of exploration, or from some other cause, the new Archdeacon steamed north with an openness rare for his time.

∽

Stuck had left Dallas in July, stopping in Sewanee and St. Louis; the same issue of *The Churchman* which profiled the new Archdeacon of the Yukon also ran Stuck's impressions of the

St. Louis World's Fair[6] before landing in New York. There he spent ten days at the Church Missions House, run by the Episcopal Church, and met a man who would figure prominently in the rest of his life. John W. Wood was the Corresponding Secretary of the Board of Missions, and the editor of *Spirit of Missions*, the church's monthly journal. For the next sixteen years, Wood would be Stuck's editor and confidant. He would serve as Stuck's personal agent, forwarding book manuscripts, arranging bank drafts, and connecting Stuck with the world outside.

∽

On August 8, six days after boarding the S.S. *Spokane* from Seattle, Stuck arrived in Skagway, the last of "the little Alaska towns—Ketchikan, Juneau, Skagway—[which] are perched upon shoulders of mountains."[7] While in Skagway, on Alaska's panhandle, Stuck quickly jotted notes in his diary: "The David [Davidson] Glacier—landed from small boats—walked a mile through a forest that recalled tropical luxuriance, growing on the terminal moraine; climbed glacier by aid of ice-axe." He described the return hike to Skagway as "very jolly sport singing college songs all the way back."[8] The next day, the longtime student of Arctic exploration seemed overwhelmed by the beauty of Alaska's coast. "Muir Inlet—Glacier Bay—the splendid Fairweather Range—the floating ice" were the brief details he noted as he traveled from Skagway to Sitka to meet with Bishop Rowe. There he "fell in love with Sitka & with the Bishop over again." His entry for August 11 mentions "walks & talks with the Bishop."

From Skagway Stuck took the White Pass Railway to White-horse, a "bold mountain railway of an hundred and twenty miles." Stuck wrote that when the train makes the "exciting climb" over the White Pass, one of the two main mountain passes during the Yukon Gold Rush, the traveler is then "inside" according to the language of the country. All the rest of the world, he said, is "outside."[9]

En route he met a clergyman headed out, who told Stuck that a diptheria epidemic at Fort Yukon had ended, "which good news I at once wired the Bishop at Sitka." Stuck reached White-horse on the evening of August 11, and immediately boarded the steamer *White Horse* for Dawson, beginning his first journey on the great river whose course would shape the rest of his life.

∽

The Yukon River, the longest in Alaska or the Yukon Territory, begins in British Columbia slightly northeast of Juneau. It travels almost two thousand miles, half of that in Alaska, describing an arc on the map as it heads northwest to Fort Yukon, about two hundred miles from Fairbanks, before angling west and south toward the Bering Sea. The name "Yukon" comes from the Gwich'in people of Alaska, and is a contraction of a Gwich'in phrase meaning "white water river," referring not to rapids but to the glacial runoff which turns the water a pale color.[10] The Yukon, in Stuck's phrase, runs "right through the midst of this continental region of Alaska, almost bisecting it."

From Whitehorse to Dawson, Stuck's view along the river from the steamer *Susy* was "continually bounded by mountains," which dominated for another 300 miles downriver from Dawson. After that, the Yukon "[spread] out from fourteen to forty miles in width," creating "the 10,000 islands of the Yukon."[11] As it happened, Alfred Brooks, the head of the US Geological Survey for whom the Brooks Range was later named, was aboard Stuck's boat, and the new archdeacon took the opportunity to question him closely about the country into which they were headed.[12]

In a letter to editor John Wood published in *Spirit of Missions*, Stuck wrote upon seeing the Yukon Flats for the first time: "It is a great country and a noble river . . . the warm sunshine gilds the low willow and aspen banks just turning with the hints of autumn, and shines in a broad wake of glory behind the foaming paddle wheel." Occasionally "a great flock of wild geese rises with discordant cries to give life to the scene." He called the summer Yukon "a delightful river—in the afternoon. The sunshine is warm, and yet there is just enough tang in the air to make thick clothing pleasant to one who is not taking much exercise." Finally, "the long, long twilights, lasting till nearly ten o'clock . . . and leaving some sort of glow in the sky till eleven, make the nights beautiful."[13]

At Circle City, Stuck met Nurse Lizzie Woods, head of the mission there, who had traveled downriver to Fort Yukon and there almost single-handedly stopped the diptheria epidemic with "rigid sanitary measures" and a strict quarantine. There he also held his first church service with Alaska Natives; the Native lay-reader said evening prayer in Gwich'in, and Stuck preached through an interpreter. Miss Woods told him afterward that he had spoken too quickly for the interpreter; he later commented, "I am afraid they got very little, but I shall know better by and by."[14] On August 30 Stuck transferred from the *Susy* to the SS *Tanana* at Rampart; two days on the Tanana River brought him to Fairbanks.

⟡

When Hudson Stuck arrived in Alaska in September 1904, the territory was less than a decade removed from the discovery of gold in Canada's Klondike, and was in the full roar of its wild prospecting period. The discovery of gold in Nome in 1899 had brought the gold rush directly to Alaska; in Stuck's words,

> The 'rush' to Nome takes rank second only to the rush to the Klondike in the history of the North. The discovery of gold in the sands of the beach itself where anyone might sit down and rock it out, made a sensation throughout the United States . . . Never before or since was such a trail down the Yukon . . . Late in the spring men even made the whole journey on bicycles, so hard-beaten was the snow.[15]

Judge James Wickersham, the Judge for the Third Circuit in northern Alaska who arrived in Fairbanks a year before Stuck, wrote, "Prospectors are invariably optimists. Most of them then in Alaska, having gazed enviously upon five-gallon tin cans filled with placer gold [gold panned from gravel] in the Klondike, hoped to locate an equally rich camp on this border."[16]

Two years before Stuck's arrival, Captain E. T. Barnette had founded a trading post on the Tanana River to serve these hopeful prospectors. Judge Wickersham, meanwhile, had promised to put the courthouse at Barnette's trading post if Barnette agreed to name his post after Charles W. Fairbanks, then the senior US senator from Indiana, who had allowed Wickersham to be given his position by withdrawing his candidate's name.

In Wickersham's words, "When Barnette arrived . . . a few weeks later, on board his new boat, the *Isabelle* . . . he was amazed and delighted to find an active mining stampede." A few weeks before, in July 1902, an Italian named Felix Pedro had discovered gold at Golden City on Pedro Creek, just a few miles away. After Barnette "established his camp as its business center," the spot where he had stashed his trading goods became Fairbanks.[17]

The resulting rush created Fairbanks's boom; unlike other gold-strike towns, however, it had the government offices to keep it from permanent bust. Within the year hundreds of cabins had been built. At one point early on, there were six saloons and a brothel, but no churches; the first services were held by an Episcopal evangelist and a Presbyterian preacher in Marston's saloon.[18] Judge Wickersham once attended church services "held by Episcopal Bishop Peter T. Rowe in the room in which court had convened the previous week." The judge noted that "while the bishop was dressed in his beautiful church canonicals, he wore at the same time a pair of Indian-made moosehide moccasins." Apparently, "he had forgotten his shoes at some trail roadhouse where he had changed to moccasins as a rest for his sore feet." This episode made onlookers "[love] the good bishop just a little more for his disregard of the conventionalities of dress."[19]

Of Rowe, Stuck wrote, "Familiar all his life with canoe and snowshoes, with axe and rifle . . . he entered his fortieth year a few days before he entered his new office, and brought the vigor of his prime to the strenuous task that lay before him."[20] Describing the bishop's appeal to the sourdoughs of Alaska, Stuck pointed out that "here was a boatman preaching to boatmen, a 'musher' to 'mushers'; here was the equal in strength and skill and endurance of any of them to listen to." That this boatman and musher also happened to be a bishop "doubtless made appeal to some, but to others meant no more than if he had been a colonel."[21]

For Rowe and the Episcopal Church, having a presence in Fairbanks was of strategic importance. *Spirit of Missions* reported in May 1904, "Of the outlook at Fairbanks—the new town in central Alaska—Bishop Rowe speaks hopefully. It promises to be an important point." The bishop was "making plans and laying foundations" for a hospital, and a nurse to be sent to it that summer. Fairbanks would also be "the headquarters of the Rev. Hudson Stuck, who is to join the staff this summer as general missionary to all of Central Alaska." Fairbanks would require another missionary, though, "as Dean Stuck's long journeys will make sustained work at any one point impracticable."[22]

Whatever the Church thought about its possibilities in Fairbanks, Hudson Stuck had few illusions:

> Fairbanks was . . . the center of feverish trade and feverish vice in 1904–5, when the stores were open all day and half the night and the dance-halls and gambling dens all night and half the day; . . . when

the curious notion prevailed that in some mysterious way general profligacy was good for business, and the Commercial Club held an indignation meeting upon a threat of closing down the public gaming and refusing liquor licenses to the dance-halls, and voted unanimously in favor of an 'open town'; when a diamond star was presented to the 'chief of police' by the enforced contributions of the prostitutes; when the weekly gold-dust from the clean-ups on the creeks came picturesquely into town escorted by horsemen armed to the teeth.[23]

∞

The first months of Stuck's time in Alaska give a sense of his energy and determination. He arrived in Fairbanks on September 1, and "went at once to the hospital" according to his diary.[24] The hospital's building committee was so inept that Stuck fired them and took over construction himself. "The hospital was complete in only one story and whole interior was to finish, but the money gathered had all been spent." Less diplomatically, in his diary he called it "a cold cheerless barn of an unfinished structure." He borrowed money, purchased materials on credit, and within two weeks, St. Matthew's Hospital treated its first patient; "indeed before the carpenters left there were already two or three patients within it, so pressing was the need," he wrote.[25] By May 1905 Stuck could say that the hospital had taken care of more than a hundred cases of injury and sickness. "It is a much bigger thing already than anyone supposed it would be . . . but for Bishop Rowe's prompt support and remittances, it would not have been possible to keep [the doors] open."

Stuck noticed almost immediately that men in Fairbanks had no places to spend their evenings, other than saloons. His solution appeared in mid-October; when St. Matthew's Church opened its doors it boasted a library and reading-room. The small log church, a "picturesque structure amidst the wilderness of 'frame' houses and stores," was "the only building in Fairbanks worth making a picture of," Stuck quoted a visiting artist as saying. Bishop Rowe reported to Church authorities that he was "sending up a fine bell" from Troy, New York to Fairbanks "for the use of the congregation and the town."[26]

The archdeacon described St. Matthew's as "an exceedingly expensive little church" but "an exceedingly useful one" thanks to the reading room.[27] An article in *Spirit of Missions* described how after services ended, "a curtain is drawn across the chancel, tables are moved out upon the floor and are piled high with magazines." Along the walls were Stuck's contribution, one thousand "volumes of general literature" donated from his personal library. In the new reading room, "night after night, until eleven o'clock or later, forty or fifty rough-garbed men may be found deep in the fascination of good literature."[28] Stuck in his articles for outside readers would request that reading to be sent North, "books more especially . . . late good novels," sometimes with specific asks such as John Morley's life of British prime minister William Gladstone, which "I have been asked about . . . again and again."[29]

Charles Betticher, who arrived in 1905 to be the rector of St. Matthew's, wrote of the reading room, "The doors are never locked, and . . . it is not an uncommon thing to hear a man rejoice in the fact that it is not necessary to go to the saloons to be entertained and warmed." Magazines on offer included the *Outlook,* the *Literary Digest,* and the *Saturday Evening Post.*[30]

Stuck wrote a former Sewanee friend who had become vicar of St. Agnes's Chapel in New York, suggesting that his church raise funds for a gramophone, both for the miners in the reading-room and for the patients in the hospital. One was soon acquired and sent to Alaska, with a large number of records. Stuck wrote, "I cannot tell you how much pleasure it has already given to the ladies of the mission and to the patients in the hospital . . . I sometimes hear [tunes] borne on the breezes from the hospital to my cabin."[31]

Stuck also found time to start a weather station. The task of recording weather details which he began in 1904 was taken over seven years later by the University of Alaska Fairbanks; in 2018, having been in continuous service ever since, it was recognized as Alaska's longest-running weather station.[32]

Miners in Fairbanks may have appreciated the church's reading room, but Stuck found it difficult to get them to attend religious services during the summer. "In the winter it is different, but in the short Alaskan summers every effort is made to take advantage of every one of the twenty-four hours of daylight. People catch up on back sleep and catch up on back religion, it would seem . . . The hibernal Alaskan is by way of being devout; the equinoctial Alaskan still retains traces of piety, but the solstician Alaskan is a pagan."[33] Many others did find their way to St. Matthew's, and to the pulpits across Alaska which Stuck visited. *The Daily Alaskan* described him as "an eloquent divine" whose "church at Fairbanks, or wherever he may be, is always crowded to the doors."[34]

As in Dallas, the archdeacon's forcefulness and ambition, not to mention spendthriftiness, irritated his church superior. Stuck began a habit of spending money, whether on missions, hospitals, schools, or medicine, then sending his bishop the bill. Rowe supported (to an extent) his archdeacon, and the two always remained on good terms; but the bishop was also frustrated by his archdeacon's headstrong ways: "He is a terror. I am trying to hold him down."[35] According to an account sent to Sewanee historian Arthur Ben Chitty,

> When the great archdeacon died, an old sourdough said "I guess Bishop Rowe will succeed him, will be promoted." His listener explained, "You don't understand. A bishop is Number One. An archdeacon is Number Two." The old timer said "That can't be. I saw them together back in the bush one time and Archdeacon Stuck was giving the orders."[36]

In October 1904, not long after arriving in Fairbanks, Stuck wrote in his diary, "[I] hitched the dogs to Condon's sled and had them gee-ing and haw-ing." His initial work in Fairbanks done, the archdeacon decided it was time he learn to dogsled. After two months of almost daily practice, just after Christmas he began the first of what would become yearly circuits in winter to the mission churches scattered throughout his immense northern territory. Stuck's initial experience took him 101 days over the winter of 1904–1905, twenty of which averaged thirty degrees or more below zero; he covered 1,480 miles in sixty-two days of mushing. He later detailed his winter trips between 1904–1910 in his first book, *Ten Thousand Miles with a Dog Sled*, published in 1914.[37]

DNA analysis suggests that when humans began to cross the Bering land bridge from Asia to America 15,000 years ago, the domestic dog accompanied them. A modern study concludes, "Historical records of the use of sled dogs in the Siberian Sub Arctic appear in Arabian literature of the tenth century; in writings of Marco Polo in the thirteenth century; and of Francesco de Kollo in the sixteenth."[38] Martin Frobisher, Elizabethan explorer, privateer, and all-round shady character, led three trips to the New World between 1576 and 1578 in search of the Northwest Passage to Asia.[39] His crew were the first Westerners to contact the indigenous people of present-day Greenland. George Best, a gentleman-soldier who sailed with Frobisher, published an account of the 1578 voyage which included this passage describing the Inuit:

> They draw with dogges in sleds upon the Ise, and remove their tents therewithal, wherein they dwell in sommer, when they goe a hunting for their praye and provision against Winter.[40]

And in the 1920s, Fairbanks-area gold miners found frozen dog remains, which were donated to the American Museum of Natural History in New York City and then forgotten for more than seven decades. In 2002, scientists published the results of radiocarbon dating of the remains: they found the dogs had lived between 345 and 570 years ago—before the arrival of Europeans in Alaska.[41]

The eighteenth-century Russian explorers of the North American Arctic found a culture similar to the one Frobisher's crew had encountered. They brought with them several innovations in dog sledding, including arranging the dogs in pairs or single file as well as the concept of the lead dog.[42] The leader, "guided by the voice, 'geeing' and 'hawing,' stopping and advancing at the word of command," in Stuck's words, had eventually been universally adopted by Alaska Natives, along with the dog collar.[43] One scholar of Russian Alaska, Lydia T. Black, has argued that Russian innovations in several fields, including dogsledding, were taken up by the indigenous people into whose lands they had come. "Kamchadal [an ethnic tribe of Kamchatka] and Evenk [an ethnic tribe of northern Siberia] dog sleds and harness and joinery . . . were adopted from the Russians by several Native groups."[44]

The Klondike and Nome Gold Rushes caused increased demand for sled dogs, as everything delivered to or from gold camps and hunting camps in winter had to be done by sled. As a result, breeding of sled dogs also increased heavily.[45] The importance of dogs, and dogsleds, in Alaska in Stuck's day is reflected in metaphors from two men famous in the state's history. Judge Wickersham wrote, "The dog has been to this far northland what the horse has been to the great plains west of the Mississippi."[46] And the Geological Survey head Alfred Brooks asserted, "Countless generations of Alaskan natives have used the dog for transport, and he is to Alaska what the yak is to India or the llama to Peru."

Travel by sled in Stuck's day was arduous; only rarely were trails smooth and flat. More often, crusted river ice, laterally steep banks, and thick Alaskan bush made sledding an endurance event. When Bishop Rowe prepared for a season of mushing, his "preliminary work" was described in *Spirit of Missions*: "A run of five miles or more every day is good for the wind." The training included climbing hills, "though only child's play compared with climbing the mountains that must be crossed later." Also in the bishop's regimen was skipping rope, "a most unepiscopal occupation, it must be admitted, but . . . valuable in developing the muscles of the leg." Adding in prepping the sled, along with frequent runs with the dogs "to learn their several peculiarities," and it could take four to five weeks to make the Bishop "as hard and fit as a college athlete."[47] In all, according to a 1905 article in *Spirit of Missions*, "Two qualities are pre-eminently needed by the man who would travel the winter trail in Alaska, an instinct for finding one's way and bulldog grit."[48]

Stuck described his clothing for winter dogsledding trips: moose-hide breeches and mukluks "tied tight around my knees" below, and for the upper layers a "parkee [parka] without opening front or back, that pulls on over the head . . . [with a] fur-edged hood . . . pulled forward over cap and scarf." The hands were "enclosed in woolen gloves, and they in blanket-lined moose-hide mitts," and the feet "in caribou sock[s] with the hair on, strips of blanket wrapping, and mukluks stuffed with hay." Unfortunately, no matter the cold, when sledding "the part of the face around the nose and the eyes cannot be covered."[49] To his sled Stuck attached his treasured Native-made moosehide sled bag, edged with red cotton and white seed beads and fringed with trade beads and wool tassels. The Episcopal shield with cross and anchor in the center were overlaid with the Latin word, "Haereo," the archdeacon's motto: "I Stick."[50]

⁓

Efficient and effective as dogsleds were during the long winters, they couldn't cover all of Stuck's territory, nor could they be extended throughout the year. After the river ice broke up each spring, Alaska's waterways were the main means of travel in those pre-bushplane times. Stuck, determined and creative as ever, found a way to exploit this fact of Alaskan life.

"A knowledge of the Yukon River system," Stuck wrote, "is the key to the knowledge of the greater part of Alaska." He pointed out that "it is possible to get very near to almost every human habitation in the interior of Alaska by water." That meant that with a good gasoline boat Stuck would be able to visit "an enormous area of country and a large number of scattered people in the course of one open season, which lasts from June to September, inclusive."[51]

On a summer day in 1908, Stuck, "Hap" Burke, and Arthur Wright stood on the bank of the Yukon in Whitehorse, Canada. They watched intently as a wharfside derrick prepared to drop a thirty-two-foot gasoline launch, the *Pelican*, into the water. Burke had just arrived in the North, joining Stuck as a medical missionary at Fort Yukon after completing his medical training.

Wright was a half-Native youth beginning a two-year stint as Stuck's interpreter and assistant. The boat had been designed by Stuck himself, then "built on the Hudson, taken across the continent by train and up the Inside Passage to Skagway on a steamer, and then over the White Pass to Whitehorse by train again," Stuck wrote. Now, the crane operator lowered her into the river, "so gently . . . that had a glass of water stood on her cabin roof it would not have spilled a drop." Having survived her 5,000 mile journey and her many handlings "almost unscathed," the boat and crew began the *Pelican*'s maiden voyage, "through Canadian territory to the American waters for which she was built."

The *Pelican*, named in honor of the Louisiana church members who had raised the funds for the boat, became an integral part of Stuck's work across the interior of Alaska. By 1920, the boat had made twelve seasons' cruises, ranging from 1,800 to 5,200 miles each summer. Stuck described "the mail she carried to trappers and wood-choppers along the rivers she traversed, the store of magazines she distributed, the scattered Indian camps she visited," as well as "the constant calls upon the doctor's services that were made, and his glad response to them; of the medicines she carried and left here and there."[52] The *Pelican* was "a good boat, and as comfortable to live in as any craft may be in which a man can get no walking exercise. And there is nothing pretty or fancy about her."[53]

Reveling in the freedom afforded by the *Pelican*, Stuck fairly crowed, "The Tanana is my wash-pot, over the Koyukuk will I cast my shoe, upon the Iditarod will I triumph! I am sometimes tempted to vaunt."[54] The vast river systems of Alaska offered unparalleled avenues for travel and exploration: "Where else do waterways open such vast country to travel? where else could one be so footloose and free?"[55]

❦

Before long, Stuck's almost ceaseless travel made him a well-known figure across Alaska. By 1910 the *Iditarod Pioneer* described him as "famous throughout the North for the deep interest he takes in the welfare of the Alaska Indian and for his wide knowledge of Alaskan affairs."[56] His circuits made a profound effect on his work, and on his relationship to the land and people of Alaska.

"In the wilds at 50° below zero there is the most complete silence," he wrote of an early winter journey. "All animal life is hidden away . . . in the absolutely still air not a twig moves. A rare raven passes overhead, and his cry . . . reverberates like the musical glasses." He saw "the bold, shapely peaks of the South Fork of the Koyukuk turn their snows to pink fire" at dawn, which "stirs one's spirit with . . . keen delight." He learned that in winter "it takes time and care to make a comfortable camp, and time and care in the wind and cold involve suffering."[57]

Aboard the *Pelican* he enjoyed "the excitement of shooting rapids in the swift upper reaches of the tributary rivers . . . of bears in the brush along the banks and bears fishing in the streams, of eagles swooping down into the water and bringing up salmon in their claws." Like a bard of the Far North, he intoned, "I could tell of distant lofty mountains . . . of great canyon-like walls through which the rivers flow . . . I could tell of wonderful sunsets and sunrises." He was particularly intrigued by the northern lights, and devoted an entire chapter of his first book to the phenomenon. From the *Pelican* he saw "one [aurora borealis] that is fixed in my memory. It waved and gleamed around a clear crescent moon in all manner of fantastic banners and streamers," while "the whole fairy-like scene was reflected and exactly reduplicated in the still, smooth water of the river."[58] The Alaska Native boys, Walter Harper and Arthur Wright, who accompanied Stuck on the river matched the English and Native names of the native and migratory birds they spotted, including *ch'izhin* the golden eagle, *daagoo* the ptarmigan, *chalvii* the widgeon, *kikii* the goldeneye, *deedzaii* the loon, and *tl'aanii* the bufflehead duck.[59]

His perceptions of the people of the territory were similarly keen. He described the Kantishna River as a highway where Natives return home from spring hunting in 'boats of the hides of the moose they have killed," while "down its stream come also the gentleman hunters from New York and Boston with trophies 'for the Smithsonian.'"[60] At Rampart House on the Alaska-Canada boundary, Stuck spoke with an ancient Native woman who remembered the coming of the first white man to the Porcupine River, John Bell, in 1842. Reaching "the most northerly gold fields in the world," the Koyukuk fields north of the Arctic Circle, after the "long, weary journey, walking every step of the way, half the time on snowshoes," Stuck wrote, "I shall never forget that gathering of men from almost every civilized nation on earth. I shall never forget their warm-hearted and respectful demeanor."[61] The Inuit of Alaska's coast were "essentially navigators; they are as aquatic as ducks; the centaur was not a more intimate union between a man and a horse than the Eskimo is between a man and a boat," while the Natives of the lower Koyukuk were "noted for turbulence and for mighty men of magic."[62]

Stuck was attuned to the tragic story, repeated again and again, of mining-town boom bust, rise and fall. In Circle City he had once seen "a gorgeous silken banner and a circulating library of several thousand volumes." Returning only a few years later, he found the gorgeous silken banner "covered with dust and mildew," while "the books, injured by flood-water, were anybody's that cared to take them away." Circle City, at its height home to 3,000 people, at that point held only twenty-five whites and sixty to sixty-five Natives. "Circle," Stuck wrote, "shares the fate of all placer-mining towns, which after their brief period of expansion and feverish prosperity, sink into a steady decline from which there is no revival."[63]

∽

Whether "standing for hours at the wheel of the launch *Pelican*, slowly grinding upstream, or slipping swiftly down with the current,"[64] or trudging on snowshoes ahead of the dogs in winter, beating out a trail for them through the snow and ice, Archdeacon Stuck benefited tremendously from these trips across the interior territory. They furnished him material for two other books: *Voyages on the Yukon and Its Tributaries* (1917) and then *A Winter Circuit of Our Arctic Coast* (1920), both filled with insight, literary merit, and attention to detail. The trips allowed him to learn the ways of miner and trapper, roadhouse keeper and saloon girl. They gave the missionary a priceless education in the cultures and situations of the Athabascan and Inuit Alaska Natives throughout the region as well as much of the Arctic, deepening his respect and concern for the indigenous people of the North. Finally, they gave Stuck the opportunity to engage in collaborations with young Alaska Native men, who served as guides, assistants, translators, mechanics on the voyages. One of these young men was Walter Harper.

By early 1906 Stuck could claim, "I have met [Natives] now from Eagle, near the British border, to St. Michael at the mouth of the Yukon; and from the upper waters of the Koyukuk at Bettles and Bergman to the upper Tanana at Goodpasture; that is, over twenty degrees of longitude and three and a half of latitude."[65]

∞

At 1 A.M. on July 9, 1907, a young woman from the lower forty-eight arrived at the landing at Fort Yukon. Claire Heintz had accompanied Miss Carter, deaconess at the Allakaket mission of St. John's in the Wilderness, and had chugged up the Yukon to the Allakaket with the deaconess and Bishop Rowe. There to greet them was "a light, red-bearded man in well-cut sport clothes who looked as though he had stepped out of a shop window instead of a Koyukuk tent." She had been reading Stuck's articles in *Spirit of Missions*, and expected to see an erudite-looking middle-aged gentleman of slightly seedy appearance.

Instead, the Archdeacon looked like a youthful college professor, slender and wiry, with a narrow sensitive face and sharp blue eyes. His movements were nervously abrupt, and though his voice was well modulated and his enunciation flawless, his manner of speech was brusque, sometimes to the point of gruffness.[66]

Her less-than-positive impression wasn't lightened when Stuck asked her if she was a teacher, whether she had any training, or even whether she could cook. Hearing all negative answers, he turned to the deaconess and said, "I don't understand why you brought this inexperienced girl up here, Deaconess. This is not kindergarten, you know."[67]

Before long, though, she would temper her view of the Archdeacon. "I realized that this irritable Archdeacon had much more to him than a nervous temperament," she wrote. She began to understand Bishop Rowe's glowing praises of this "dynamo of determination," of both his work and his character. She also learned that "his bristly manner covered the gentlest of natures." Later, she would marry Dr. Grafton Burke; the lives of the Burkes would be closely braided with Stuck's for the rest of his life.[68]

6

WALTER HARPER
& THE NOBLER IDEAL

The Archdeacon did not traverse the 250,000 square miles of his mission territory, year after year, solo. From the day of his arrival, Hudson Stuck was determined to cover as much Alaskan ground as possible, and to learn as much as he could in the process. He was also intelligent enough to understand how best to achieve those two goals. "There are good reasons," he wrote in his diary, "why it would be much better that I travel with an Indian: I could get a good insight into the

Indian character, perhaps learn something of the language, and be able to make investigation into Indian conditions on the Koyokuk and elsewhere," goals which "with a white guide will be out of the question."[1] For his first dogsled trip he hired Charley Pitka, a Native from Rampart "of whom I have heard excellent accounts."

Eventually he began employing Native youth in their late teens. In doing so, and especially in the case of Walter Harper and Johnny Fredson, he would forge one of his deepest connections with the indigenous people he served. By supporting Harper and Fredson in their education and later careers, Stuck created a lasting and positive impact in the Alaska Native community.

∽

Three decades before Stuck's arrival in Alaska, and two decades before the discovery of gold in the Klondike, Westerners who were interested mainly in neither trade nor God began traveling up the Inner Passage to Alaska. They were, instead, the first consumers of scenery. As historian Robert Campbell has described, the steam engine allowed these first tourists, including writers such as John Muir and Rudyard Kipling and industrialists like Edward Harriman, to shift Americans' cultural attention to Alaska as the next stop for the nation's manifest destiny. "If," Campbell wrote, "in the minds of late nineteenth-century Americans, the western frontier had closed, then an alternative was found in the North, their last frontier."[2]

The significance of these Gilded Age sightseers lies in the mindset that they encouraged and helped to foster in the lower forty-eight states. As in the western United States, the existence of indigenous people was given little or no weight, nor were there any qualms about to whom the land properly belonged. Campbell again: "those who followed the tourists—the gold seekers, the miners, and settlers—trooped north certain of one thing, that Alaska was theirs for the taking . . . Alaska was a scenic bonanza before it was a mining bonanza."[3]

The Gold Rushes, wrought by those takers from outside, brought chaos to the ancient culture of Alaska Natives. They also brought disease. The 1900 influenza epidemic began in Nome and "spread like wildfire to all corners of Alaska, killing up to 60 percent of the Eskimo and Athabascan people."[4] The Great Sickness, as that year's wave of disease is called, combined influenza with measles, which reached Western Alaska for the first time that year.[5] The horrific losses sustained by Alaska Natives were not merely physical or economic, or even emotional. Native writer Harold Napoleon put the costs in deeper, more primal cultural terms: "Even the medicine men grew ill and died in despair with their people, and with them died a great part of *Yuuyaraq*, the ancient spirit world of the Eskimo."[6] He has even argued that the Native susceptibility to alcohol might not be a genetic trait, but rather a condition of widespread trauma in the wake of the epidemics: "I have come to the conclusion that the primary cause of alcoholism is not physical but *spiritual*."[7] [emphasis in the original]

༄

Arriving four years after the Great Sickness, Hudson Stuck had a clear sense of his vocation and of its worth. He referred to missionary work, "using that term in the way I always use it, as including all practicable improvement in habits and character and mode of life."[8] As to missionaries themselves, in 1898 Dean Stuck had preached at St. Matthew's Dallas on the topic. "The missionary joke . . . [with the] anthropophagous savage in the middle distance with the carving-knife and the cooking pot are commonplaces," he admitted, using a portmanteau word for "cannabilistic." However, he continued, "I know no modern hero that has half the claims to respect that a true missionary has. In an age of self-seeking and self-indulgence . . . amid the mad race for wealth and place and power, the missionary is the one guarantee that remains to us that the rugged virtues and resolute endurance of the first ages of the faith still persist in the church."[9]

Nor did he have any doubts about his priorities. "White men come and go, but the natives remain," Stuck was known to argue. "So far as the interior is concerned our permanent work . . . is amongst the natives." A recurrent theme of Stuck's was the corrupting influence of white Alaskans. As an example, he wrote in 1906 of approaching "a group of three or four half-grown [Native] boys" and trying to make friends with them:

> Did they "sabe minister?" "No sabe." Did they "sabe church?" "No sabe." And then I asked a question that I hope The Spirit of Missions will print, even at the risk of shocking its readers . . . Oh, it was eloquent! Pointing upwards, I asked, "You sabe God?" And one

of the little chaps looked up to me in perfect inno-
cence and said, "Me sabe God-damn!"[10]

He considered St. John's in the Wilderness, in Allakaket, one of
the most hopeful missions in Alaska, "due largely to its isolation."
The Natives there "are not brought as much into contact with the
dissolute white man as are the natives of the Yukon. And there is
practically no whiskey here at all."[11] That last point was crucial to
Stuck: "For the chief worry and trouble, the chief drawback and
hindrance, the cause of sleepless nights and depression of spirits
to the Alaska missionary, is the illicit whiskey trade which white
men of the baser sort ply with the natives."[12]

Unsurprisingly, this didn't endear the Archdeacon to some
white Alaskans. Not that that bothered him. "It is the easiest
thing in the world for a missionary to be popular in Alaska. He
has merely to shut his eyes and be pleasant," Stuck wrote. "If you
could show me a missionary who is popular with the riff-raff of
the river towns, I would show you a man out of place, who ought
to be presiding gracefully over the decay of some small parish
'outside.'" In fact, "I will almost gauge the usefulness of a missionary in Alaska by his unpopularity with a certain large and
influential class."[13] The archdeacon, who had little experience
with shutting his eyes and being pleasant, stood little chance of
being popular with the riff-raff.

∞

Stuck wasn't always on the dogsled trail or the waters of the
Yukon watershed. In 1907, for example, he left Alaska at the end

of the summer to attend the church's general convention in Richmond, Virginia. Stuck volunteered to stay in Alaska, but it was Bishop Rowe's desire that Stuck "come out" to recruit men.[14] A notice in *The Churchman* announced that "Until Sept. 1 he should be addressed in care of the Rev. Herbert H. Gowen, Eighth and James streets, Seattle, Wash.; after that date at the Church Missions House, 281 Fourth Avenue, New York."[15]

By October 7 he was in Richmond, addressing a mass meeting in connection with the General Convention on "The Church's Work in the Land of the Midnight Sun." November found him in New Orleans, where on Sunday the 24th he preached at Christ Church Cathedral, and on Monday addressed the Women's Auxiliary in the afternoon and that evening "delivered an illustrated lecture to a crowded house at the Sophie Newcomb Hall."[16] On January 5, 1908, Stuck was in Baltimore for two addresses in the diocese of Maryland.[17] Two days later he was back in New York for two addresses to the Mission Society. By January 20 he was in Minneapolis to address the Church Club of Minnesota.[18]

All of these lectures and presentations had one goal: promoting the work of the Church in Alaska. And it was that cause that found him, at 11 A.M. on February 5, 1908, being welcomed to the White House by President Theodore Roosevelt. After a "pleasant five minutes," Roosevelt insisted that Stuck meet with Interior Secretary James R. Garfield, son of the former president. Their forty-five minute meeting about the Native matters was, Stuck wrote, "very useful."[19]

March found him back in New York, to speak to two branches of the Girl's Friendly Society of the Episcopal Church on the 5th and the 12th. By April 1908 he was in Sewanee, and from there sailed for England for the first time since he left in 1885. He then visited France and the Swiss Alps, returning to the United States after two months and bringing Grafton "Hap" Burke and the *Pelican* with him to Fort Yukon,[20] where Stuck had decided to relocate from Fairbanks. He had realized that "the river plays a great part in the maintenance of our missions" as it "furnishes the only means of communication with distant villages in summer, and feeds us at all seasons." The Yukon, as another Alaskan missionary had written, "is the missionary's firm and steadfast friend—even if it does sometimes menace his life."[21]

⁓

As noted in chapter 1, the Church of England had been among the more enlightened missionary groups in Alaska in the mid- and late-1800s. To Evon Peter, Vice Chancellor for Rural, Community and Native Education at the University of Alaska Fairbanks who is also Neetsaii Gwich'in and Koyukon, Hudson Stuck followed in the missionary tradition established by the Anglican Archdeacon Robert McDonald,[22] a one-fourth-Ojibwe Anglican priest who was the first Protestant missionary ever assigned to work among indigenous peoples of the Arctic. From 1862 to the early 1900s, McDonald became known for his missionary efforts and for his translations of the Bible, the Book of Common Prayer, and hymns into the Gwich'in language (for which he invented an alphabet). Hudson Stuck would write of McDonald that his "remarkable labors and extensive evangelizing journeys" had "never received the recognition they so richly deserve."[23]

Judge Wickersham told of attending an Indian burial near Eagle City in 1900. The judge, new to the region, was not known for enlightened views of Alaska Natives. He was "interested in how these apparently ignorant and certainly poverty-stricken creatures would conduct a burial service and in what view, if any, they might have of life after death." Wickersham was surprised when "a young man, probably twenty-eight or thirty years old, came forward to conduct the funeral ceremonies" from a book in the Indian tongue, and even more amazed to discover that it was a Christian service, "conducted as decorously and with the same ease and intelligence as if a Bishop were carrying on the service in his cathedral." The young man told Wickersham that he had read from an Anglican book of common prayer, translated by Archdeacon McDonald and printed a quarter-century before in 1873, and still "generally used in the region on all proper occasions."[24]

McDonald and Stuck shared a commitment to supporting the perpetuation of at least parts of Gwich'in and Koyukon culture and language—though that commitment did not extend to traditional spiritual ceremonies and ceremonial practices. Peter noted that as a result of Alaskan missionary work, "among the Gwich'in nation, all but one tribe lost the traditional drum songs. And that was my tribe . . . and even among my tribe, Gwich'in songs went dormant for probably 30, 40 years." This highlights a bifurcation, or contradiction, in the actions and beliefs of missionaries like McDonald and Stuck. They approved of some Native practices and ways, and sought to perpetuate them; on the other hand, they seemed to think that others, as deeply ingrained and inculturated, could be summarily dismissed while somehow not damaging the whole fabric of Native culture. As Mary F. Ehrlander writes in her biography, *Walter Harper: Alaska Native Son*, "Even those [missionaries] who urged Alaska Natives to maintain traditional lifeways encouraged at least partial acculturation in mainstream American society." Though far less destabilizing than the influx of gold miners or later policies mandating English-only schooling, the missionaries' presence—even that of someone as open-minded as Stuck—inherently undermined the ancient ways of Alaskan Natives.[25]

Shamans, for example, were important figures in traditional Gwich'in spirituality. They would adopt a companion animal, and carry totems symbolizing that animal, such as its head. Shamans were believed to have the power to bring bad luck or death to their enemies, to cure sickness, and to help with difficulties in childbirth.[26] To Stuck, though, Native animism was "a gloomy and degrading superstition" which "lived in a constant dread of the baleful activities of disembodied spirits." In his eyes, "The people, without exception, cowered under this sordid tyranny, a prey to its panic terrors."[27]

On the other hand, Stuck was not totally unsympathetic. He wrote, "I can declare with Wordsworth that

'I'd rather be
    a pagan suckled in a creed outworn'

than go about this beautiful and mysterious world with no religion whatever, as so many people with eyes and ears in their heads do to-day." He would "rather believe in the power of the medicine-man than in no power at all beyond the blind forces of nature," and (in at best a backhanded compliment) "rather hold to his venal and sordid and self-deluded supernaturalism than deem myself caught in the wheels of a cosmic machine without brains or bowels or consciousness."

> For there is this much truth in the old primitive animism;—it recognises that the world and life are full of deep mysteries, that there is something in man superior to himself and to his environment that does not die with the death of his body, and it seeks, however crudely, if not to penetrate these mysteries, at least to lay hold upon them, to keep in touch with them, to give new glimpses of them that shall make men less forlorn; it feels out, blindly, groping towards them; and I have a tenderness and compassion for the infant gropings of mankind that will not let me treat them with harshness and contempt.[28]

At any rate, Stuck wrote, "My own feeling is that in the process of time and education and persistent Christian teaching the thing is bound to come around and right itself." In his eyes, "A primer of elementary physics is a good antidote to a belief that the shaman can conjure storms," and "a modern hospital is the best rival to the witch-doctor," while "the teaching of the love of God will ultimately abolish the childish terror of evil spirits."[29]

Stuck was opposed to the banning of Native language in mission schools; doing so would create a "danger of the real misfortune and drawback of natives growing up to live their lives amongst natives, ignorant of the native tongue." He thought that "by and by all the Alaskan natives will be more or less bilingual, but the intimate speech and the most clearly understood speech will still be the mother tongue."[30] Stuck doubted that "the substitution of a smattering of broken English for the flexibility and picturesque expressiveness of an indigenous tongue" is anything to be desired, even though "to suggest such a doubt is treason to some minds." He foresaw a time "when all the world will speak two or three great languages, when all little tongues will be extinct . . . and all strange customs abolished." The world would be a much less interesting place then; "the spice and savour of the ends of the earth will be gone."[31]

Not even all Episcopal missionaries shared Stuck's tolerant views. Six months before his arrival in Alaska, Edith Pritchard wrote in *Spirit of Missions* about the mission children of Ketchikan, "They are really clean, but are untidy in their dress. The cassock and cotta would be a great contrast to their native attire, and the Indians are ready for the improvement."[32]

Stuck, though, couldn't be bothered with such primness. "Most white people have such a prejudice against dirt that they find it hard to get fond of the native childen in Alaska. Yet I never knew healthy, hearty, natural children of any race who did not love to get dirty," Stuck wrote. "When one can overlook the dirt and ignore the smell, there are no more attractive children anywhere than the children of the Alaskan natives."[33] Stuck constantly hoped for what today would be called multiculturalism, for an Alaska in which "different races . . . perpetuate themselves, with their special cultures and their special tongues."

Ironically, Stuck may have succeeded better than he hoped in blending Native culture with Christianity.

In 1932, Cornelius Osgood, Curator of Anthropology at the Yale Peabody Museum, left New Haven for the Yukon Territory and Alaska. After traveling hundreds of miles on the Yukon River, which he called "delightfully navigable," in a small boat, he spent the summer doing extensive ethnographic work among the Gwich'in, much of it from Fort Yukon.[34] He later wrote that "it sometimes appears that the Christian theology has been superimposed upon, rather than substituted for, the aboriginal point of view."[35] Shamans, for example, sometimes became lay readers in the Episcopal Church. A modern scholar has argued that the Gwich'in "embraced Christianity as a means of preserving and maintaining their lifestyle, values, and overall worldview," using the new religion "as a mode of cultural preservation," and even of "resistance to the cultural assimilation and destruction anticipated by Hudson Stuck and addressed so eloquently in his . . . writings."[36] To the extent that these scholars are correct, Stuck's hopes for a blending of old and new ways of thinking came to pass.

Stuck always felt the worst outcome, for Native culture and for individuals, was for Alaska Natives to be caught halfway, acculturated fully in neither direction.

> To the ordinary government school-teacher in Alaska
> . . . [civilization] seems to mean chiefly teaching the
> Indians to call themselves Mr. and Mrs. and teaching
> the women to wear millinery, with a contemptuous
> attitude toward the native language and all native

customs . . . so, occasionally, the grotesque spectacle may present itself, to the passengers on a steamer, of a native woman in a [large-brimmed, flowered] "Merry Widow" hat and a blood-stained parkee gutting salmon on the river bank.[37]

Instead, "the nobler ideal," Stuck wrote, "is to labor for God-fearing, self-respecting Indians rather than imitation white men and white women." A Native who was "honest, healthy and kindly, skilled in hunting and trapping, versed in his native Bible and liturgy" would be preferable to a re-educated Native as envisioned by the government, "even though he be entirely ignorant of English and have acquired no taste for canned fruit and know not when Columbus discovered America."[38]

Away from theory and back in the field, Stuck continued with his work of "improvement in habits and character and mode of life." Deaconess Clara Carter described for *Spirit of Missions* a typical Stuck visit in 1908 to the mission of St. John's in the Wilderness in Allakaket: after baptizing seventeen Kobuks and one Koyukuk baby, "He settled matrimonial difficulties and various disputes; arrested a troublesome and dangerous native and sent him to Coldfoot; took our choir boys in hand and trained them [to] sing their Christmas hymns; held service, besides Sundays . . . every Wednesday and Friday evening; and played with the boys until they think him the greatest man in the world."[39] Stuck kept candied almonds in his pockets for the children he met on his travels. Seven decades later, Susie Williams recalled that students in her mission school were excited to see him because he always brought a big sack of candy.

"Yeah, we liked him. He used to play with us. He was so nice to us."[40]

On these visits to mission schools Stuck would notice young men of promise, and select them to assist him in his travels. As in Dallas, he would further their educations and serve as a mentor. Here, though, he was serving not only individuals; by helping the boys create pathways for themselves through the modern world, he was also serving the greater Native community. Arthur Wright was the first of these proteges; he later would attend Mount Hermon School in Massachusetts, return to Alaska as a missionary, and produce two sons who were active in Alaska politics and another who was prominent in dogsled racing.[41] The next was another half-Native: Walter Harper.

∽

Stuck first met Walter Harper, then fifteen, at a fish camp on the Yukon. Seeing the boy's promise, Stuck sent him to St. Mark's School, a new Episcopal mission and boarding school at Nenana. Unlike those schools to which Native children were often forcibly relocated, St. Mark's, like all Episcopal schools in the territory, was voluntary. Stuck believed that "for a long time there had been need of a native boarding school situated in the central part of the interior of Alaska," and had sent Annie Farthing there to be the anchor of this enterprise on the bank of the Tenana River, just above its confluence with the Nenana, in the fall of 1907.[42] Within a year of their meeting, Harper was in charge of Stuck's dogsled on winter trips and Stuck's boat the *Pelican* in summer.

Jan Harper-Haines, Walter's great-niece, described the Koyukon people from whom his mother came:

> "Through the centuries, those who lived along the Yukon learned ways to heal themselves with the help of nature. They knew ways to protect themselves from danger. They understood that making love under the Aurora Borealis, when nocturnal light thrummed the sky, could result in the birth of a special child—one who was a bright light to the Dena, the people."[43]

Walter's father, Arthur Harper, is generally considered the first Westerner to reach the Yukon valley in search of gold. The "Irishman with a square face, shrewd eyes, and a great beard that later turned white and gave him the look of a frontier patriarch"[44] established a trading post at Tenana in 1874, and that same year married Seentahna Bosco, whom he called Jenny.[45] Harper, who had prospected in California, insisted on sending their first six children to schools there, against Jenny's wishes. Then, after Arthur and Jenny were married for eighteen years, Walter was born. Arthur didn't believe the boy was his and disowned him, to Jenny's relief. According to Harper-Haines, Jenny no longer grieved; instead, she said, "This is one chilt that old bastard won't get!" Walter's parents soon separated, and when Arthur came down with tuberculosis, he left Alaska for Arizona, where he died in 1897.[46] Walter was four.

Walter, the youngest, was raised in Native ways:

From his mother and her people, he learned how to honor nature and the spirit world; how to burn sage and spruce boughs to clear the air of bronchial coughs and influenza germs; how to use tree sap and the pulp from devil's club plants to clear the skin of cuts and rashes. He became skilled at interpreting the dialects of Indigenous Alaskan villages. He could handle boats and dogs, and he knew how to survive in the forest. He could find safety in a whiteout and start a fire in any weather.[47]

Hudson Stuck admired Harper's woodcraft and knowledge of Alaskan fauna. "He was adept in all wilderness arts," Stuck wrote. "An axe, a rifle, a flaying knife, a skin needle with its sinew thread—with these he was at home." When a cast-iron bracket on the engine of Stuck's boat the *Pelican* broke, Harper had fashioned a new one from the wooden stock of a shotgun.[48] Stuck desired to pair Harper's Native resourcefulness with a modern Western education. He tutored the young man in Shakespeare and the Old Testament, *Treasure Island* and American history. By 1913, this odd tutor-pupil combination—one English-born, cultured, and trained in the seminary; the other born to the Alaskan bush, unable to read or write until the age of sixteen—had been sharing dogsled trails, winter camps, and Yukon river voyages for three years.

As to Harper's views of Stuck, of his own future, or of the conditions for Alaska Natives, very little is known. As his biographer Mary Ehrlander writes, "The comparative dearth of . . . accounts in Harper's hand hindered my ability to discern his own perspectives on his life." However, he seemed to respond eagerly to the opportunities Stuck presented him. Piloting the *Pelican* with Stuck and Bishop Rowe in Alaska's interior gave him wide experience of Native life as well as white society. Harper spoke of dedicating his life to mission work, through which "he could contribute to the health and well-being of his people, while remaining immersed in the culture and homeland he loved."[49]

Harper in turn aided Stuck immensely, as the archdeacon was quick to acknowledge. In Ehrlander's words, "As an intermediary he fostered trust between Stuck and the Athabascan people," while Harper's translations "effectively endorsed Stuck's views and gave them credence among Athabascans." By Stuck's side on the trail and on the river, Harper "enhanced Stuck's reputation in Interior Alaska, in Episcopal Church circles, and in the general public."

This was in part because, as Harper's sister Margaret recalled, "Walter had personality—scads of it. Everybody liked him. The girls were crazy about him." Stuck valued Harper for his likeability, character, and intelligence as much as his woodcraft. Upon him, the missionary put his hopes for the future of Native Alaska, as the two of them planned Harper's future as a medical missionary. Stuck saw in Harper's education and life path a possible way forward between the inevitable loss of past ways and the perils of assimilation into white culture.

On the cusp of departure for Denali, Walter Harper was twenty-one years old and six feet tall. To Stuck, "no more need be said than that [Harper] ran Harry Karstens close in strength, pluck, and endurance."

7

THE SEVENTY-MILE KID

O n August 5, 1906, two men stood gazing at the great
massif of Denali from a promontory off to the northeast,
likely near the spot known today as Stony Hill, twenty
miles away. Although the pair could not have been less alike in
background, in many ways they were kindred spirits.

One, Charles Sheldon, was a visitor to Alaska, and an inde-
pendently wealthy member of the East Coast elite. A member
of the prestigious Boone & Crockett Club, author, hunter,
and conservationist, Sheldon was "our most famous big-game
hunter," according to a contemporary.[1] He had come north to

hunt mountain sheep in the Yukon in 1904–5 and then returned for his first expedition to Denali and its environs. Photos invariably showed Sheldon cleanshaven, healthy and trim, neatly dressed, his dark hair groomed and parted.

The man beside him had lived in Alaska for a decade. He had ridden the wave of the Gold Rush north as a teenager, and then made a life, and a name, for himself beyond the prospecting camps. Harry Karstens, having established himself in those ten years as a full-fledged Sourdough, was Sheldon's assistant guide on this trip; in time, thanks to Sheldon, he would fill a more prominent and historic position.

The two men were of similar size, though Karstens at six feet was about two inches taller than Sheldon. Beyond that, they shared a quiet, no-nonsense manner and a fierce sense of perseverance and fortitude.[2] Sheldon thought Karstens "a splendid fellow, thoroughly efficient . . . inventive and resourceful." Karstens in turn described Sheldon as "one of the best men [I] ever roughed it with."[3]

Now, looking at the great mountain, they discussed a possible route to its peak. Following the Muldrow Glacier upward with pointed fingers, they glimpsed another glacier above the Muldrow, and rocky ridges on either side of it leading to the two summits. That was the way. "A glacier descends between the south and the north summit-domes," Sheldon wrote in his journal that day. "I believe that if the top of this glacier can be reached along its south edge the mountain can be ascended."[4] (Today, Stony Hill lends its name to a scenic overlook on the nearby Denali Highway where visitors can have Sheldon and Karstens's view of the mountain.) They spoke then, and often thereafter, of making an attempt at the summit together some day.

❧

Henry Peter "Harry" Karstens would be a major figure in Alaskan history even if he had never teamed with Hudson Stuck to attempt Denali's summit. His adventures and achievements during Alaska's frontier epoch, his epic feats of backcountry travel, and his role as the first superintendent of Denali National Park would have secured his place for posterity.

He had run away from his family's Chicago feed store and livery in 1895, aged seventeen, and headed west. He then bounced around the northern prairies working on farms for two years. In July 1897, stories from the North sent Karstens and a fellow young adventurer, Tom Cavanaugh, hurrying out of Montana toward Seattle. They boarded the dilapidated steamer *Al-Ki* on August 2 and headed up the Inside Passage, bound for the Klondike.

❧

The late nineteenth century had engendered waves of Americans washing westward. What Gregory Crouch has written about Gold Rush California was true of the West in general: "In the eastern states, most men earned a living, nothing more. For farmers, laborers, clerks, and others in the emerging middle classes, it took years of drudgery to gain a yard of advantage." But there was a way out, a place of hope and possibility.

"California promised more. California offered a man the opportunity to enlarge himself, to escape the pigeonhole of his eastern existence, to aim for heights beyond his previous imaginings."[5] The Industrial Revolution had created a permanent underclass, it seemed; but it also created yearnings, appetites, demand.

Newspapers and the telegraph helped to create and stimulate those appetites; cheap sources of news and information fired the imaginations of tenement-dwellers and dirt farmers, giving them unprecedented glimpses of a (perhaps) better world Out There. First in 1849 (California), then after the Civil War (Texas), and then in the Far North, claims of greener pastures, dreams of better lives, accounts of new starts and bonanzas for the diligent and hardworking caused mass migrations.

In few cases were those media accounts accurate.

Or, to be more charitable, those accounts and the dreams the dreamers brought with them to the West lagged sadly and definitively behind the reality. As in the cliche concerning amateur investors and stock tips, by the time gold had been announced in the Klondike, those who would make money had already done so. The real profits were made long before a million people made their way to Alaska beginning in 1897, the year Karstens stepped onto the *Al-Ki*. "It should have been obvious that the locals had long since staked the best claims," wrote one of Jack London's biographers. "It should have been obvious that by leaving the lower forty-eight in mid-summer, the survivors of that terrifying overland trek would arrive in the gold mining region just in time to confront the greatest terror of all, the Arctic winter," requiring all their resources to endure and survive "before even thinking of prospecting for gold in the spring."[6]

But the Gold Rush, after all, was less about rationality, even rational greed, and more about dreams. "Gold rushers . . . lived contradictory lives," historian Robert Campbell has argued. Their urgent journeys to the Far North were "at once a rejection of modern technology, a return to a primitive economy, [and] a nostalgic putting on of the modes and masks of the frontier past," while at the same time they themselves were "the emblem of modern market culture, buying tremendous amounts of goods and services to get themselves into the northland, the land of their dreams." In short, they "yearned to escape the very culture that they most exemplified."

The throngs reading the headlines of the *Seattle Post-Intelligencer* (GOLD! GOLD! GOLD! GOLD! the July 17, 1897 edition proclaimed; STACKS OF YELLOW METAL!) may have thought they would find an almost utopian society with, in Campbell's words, "collective relations, rigorous and masculine enforced codes of conduct, and the law of the trail." If they expected to be part of "an older moral economy,"[7] the harsh realities of a raw free market would soon make a shambles of those assumptions.

Later, Hudson Stuck admitted to daydreaming occasionally about following the path of the Klondike prospectors. "I have often purposed crossing the mountains on foot from Dyea as the pioneers did, following the traces of their track and seeing for myself the difficulties they faced"[8] he wrote in 1918. He imagined the "heavily laden men toiling painfully up the rocky path in a continuous procession, their backs bowed under their burdens but their hearts buoyed with the expectation of wealth." Though the Klondike gold was in Canada, the only feasible routes to it ran through Alaska, along ancient Native trading paths between the coast and the interior.

Cavanaugh and Karstens disembarked in Dyea in mid-August, gathering their meager supplies and preparing for the Chilkoot Trail. The Chilkoot was the shorter and steeper of the two prospectors' routes to the Klondike, and had historically been used only by the Tlingit tribe. Its steepness and height—year-round snow covers its almost-vertical 3,525-foot summit—would kill an average of three or four stampeders a day at the height of the Gold Rush. As Hudson Stuck wrote, "It is moderately estimated that not less than ten thousand men . . . were upon the trail at one time. For miles up the hillside [along Chilkoot Pass], wherever it was not too steep, the trail was lined on both sides with tents, containing gambling games and tables of hucksters of all sorts."[9] In a black-and-white 1898 photo of the trail, an unending line of hundreds of loaded-down, bent-shouldered bodies, nearly touching as they seem to shuffle along between spans of steep white snowfield on either side, head single-file toward a shallow notch up above.

Badly underfunded, in need of more than the scant supplies they had brought, Karstens and Cavanaugh hauled other miners' supplies in fifty-pound backpacks over the Chilkoot Pass for pay, walking with the others in single file. The Royal Canadian Mounted Police, after the deluge of underequipped gold-seekers in the original rush, began requiring each "stampeder" (those who intended to stay and mine) to bring in two tons of supplies to provide for himself for a year, half of it food. Karstens and Cavanaugh made it over the pass days before the rule went into effect.[10]

As it happened, another runaway, nineteen-year-old Jack London, was on the Chilkoot Trail at the same time that year, also en route to the Klondike. The future author of *Call of the Wild* and *White Fang* would, like Karstens and Cavanaugh, spend the winter at Dawson City and Henderson Creek, and they all had claims on the same branch of the Henderson. Although there's no firm evidence that Karstens and London ever met, the main character in London's novel *Burning Daylight* is said to be modeled after the young Karstens:

> He was a striking figure of a man, despite his garb being similar to that of all the men in the Tivoli. Soft-tanned moccasins of moose-hide, beaded in Indian designs, covered his feet. His trousers were ordinary overalls, his coat was made from a blanket. Long-gauntleted leather mittens, lined with wool, hung by his side. They were connected in the Yukon fashion, by a leather thong passed around the neck and across the shoulders. On his head was a fur cap, the ear-flaps raised and the tying-cords dangling. His face, lean and slightly long, with the suggestion of hollows under the cheek-bones, seemed almost Indian. The burnt skin and keen dark eyes contributed to this effect, though the bronze of the skin and the eyes themselves were essentially those of a white man.[11]

Scurvy eventually chased Jack London out of Henderson Creek and out of prospecting; by July 1898 he was back home in Oakland, bringing with him less than five dollars' worth of gold. His time in Alaska spent listening to the tales being swapped between the Sourdoughs and the newcomers to the North—who were starting to be called *cheechakos*, from a Chinook term—would pay other dividends.[12]

Karstens, meanwhile, ended his partnership with Cavanaugh and in February 1898 struck out with another partner to Mission Creek and Seventymile River, in Alaska. (In a typical digression, Stuck explained in one of his books that the Seventymile was seventy miles from the mouth of the Fortymile River, a Yukon tributary which was itself forty miles from the trading post at Fort Reliance. As Stuck put it, "'Twas a vicious custom this place-naming by miles, and the cause of much confusion.")[13] At a miners' meeting, according to Karstens, "they voted me the Seventy Mile Kid, which stuck to me for a good many years."[14] A Fairbanks newspaper article in October, 1911, listed among a steamship's passengers "Kid Karstens," by then thirty-eight years old.[15]

∽

In the hierarchy of Alaskan hardiness in the early twentieth century, even miners fell below the mail-carriers. Those who met the growing demand for letters and packages in the interior were essential and important figures. Stuck, having shared winter trails with these men, praised them: "So far as there is anything heroic about the Alaskan trail, the mail-carriers are the real heroes. They must start out in all weathers, at all temperatures; they have a certain specified time in which to make their trips and they must keep within that time or there is trouble."[16] Judge Wickersham focused on the more attractive aspects of the position:

> All other vehicles are required by the United States laws to give the right of way to mail teams, and so the mail driver is the most important personage on the trail, in the mail station, or at the overnight roadhouse. He is given the best seat at the table, the first service of hotcakes for breakfast, and the best bunk at night. He sports a striped denim parka trimmed round his face with wolverine fur which does not gather frost, and a gaudily beaded pair of Tena gauntlet gloves, often prepared for his special use by a beautiful Tena girl resident in the Indian village on his line.[17]

So it was fitting that Harry Karstens would end up in this vaunted position, although he became a mail-carrier almost by accident. When he returned to Eagle City from a season's prospecting, he learned that a mail route was being planned connecting Eagle to Valdez, an ice-free port on Prince William Sound 120 miles east of Anchorage. The man selected to take the first mail for Valdez and meet another carrier at Tanana Crossing [present-day Tanacross] gambled and drank away the money he had been paid for supplies, and hanged himself. As Karsten wrote, "This left no one to take out the mail . . . Not thinking of the future, I held up my right hand and signed on." His only experience with mushing to that point had been "one dog and a sled on the Seventy Mile, and four days with a nine-dog team on the Yukon." Karstens eventually discovered that his contract kept him from leaving to tend to his mining claims, and as I result "I lost all my mining ground."[18]

This first stint as a mail-carrier lasted about a year and a half. It deepened Karstens's understanding of the Alaskan winter, and began his education in dogs, dog care, and dogsled travel. He had survived, in Tom Walker's words, "howling storms, bitter cold, treacherous overflows, deep snow, and reluctant or recalcitrant dogs."[19]

In the winter of 1901, a young lieutenant in the Army Signal Corps arrived in Alaska, charged with constructing the telegraph line between Valdez and Eagle. Billy Mitchell, later famous as the father of the US Air Force, "found Alaska to be more uninviting than he imagined," according to his biographer, with winter temperatures that dipped to fifty or sixty degrees below zero. Mitchell's mission involved "moving several hundred tons of supplies to complete 420 miles of telegraph lines,"[20] which he soon realized would have to be done by dogsled. Karstens later wrote, "I guided [Mitchell] and his outfit [as guide and teamster] over the route, which entailed some exciting times,"[21] though the laconic Karstens didn't elaborate. In little over a year, Mitchell's solders completed the 420-mile Eagle-to-Valdez segment of the line in spite of the brutal conditions. Within two years, WAMCATS, the Washington-Alaska Military Cable and Telegraph System, stretched 1,396 miles, connecting fifty-four Alaska locations.[22]

After a brief, disappointing trip home to Chicago ("everything was strange, and I didn't fit in"),[23] Karstens returned to Alaska, and to the mail service in the winter of 1903–04. In Valdez he was hired to team with Charles McGonagall, pioneering a new route and helping to build many of the first roadhouses along the way. "Our run was from Gakona on the Copper River to Fort Gibbon [near Tanana] on the Yukon at the mouth of the Tanana via Fairbanks—a 900-mile round trip each month," Karstens, and "we could find no maps to guide us." The two considered themselves lucky to be alive after a very hazardous season. Karstens wrote of his partner, "Mac, losing the trail over the summit, got caught in a storm in green willows. He went snowblind, cut the handlebars off his sleigh to start a fire, couldn't see, burnt his snowshoes trying to get the ice off them." After randomly encountering the seriously hurting McGonagall ("the wildest looking man I ever saw"), feeding him, and adding one of his own dogs to McGonagall's sled, Karstens had his own mishap. Making camp after thirty miles of hard mushing, he dozed off while cooking dog feed on the stove. "I woke up with a start; the whole tent was ablaze. I managed to save the front and back part, and a strip two feet wide which I laced together." He and McGonagall considered themselves, after that hazardous winter, to be living on borrowed time.

Karstens would sum up his time as a mail carrier:

> I travelled in all kinds of very cold weather, breaking
> through overflow, fording open streams, breaking trail
> in deep snow—going ahead a few hundred feet and

bringing the dogs up, the trail blowing full after me in a very short time; trying to go through a canyon in extreme cold, with a gale of a wind to face, freezing nose and face and unable to make the dogs face it, so go back several miles to timber, and camp.[24]

By 1910, a newspaper could refer to Karstens as a "well-known dog musher, mail carrier and real-estate dealer of the Tanana Valley." But he wasn't always, or only, a serious, hard-bitten Alaska backwoodsman. An item in the Valdez *Alaska Prospector* recapped a 1904 baseball game between Liscum and Valdez. Although Valdez lost 11–0, "Bishop and Karstens, the new talent of the Valdez team showed some clever playing."[25] Six years later found him in Fairbanks claiming prize money thanks to a pony named Toklat as a "large crowd" witnessed "our first attempt at real racing" at Model Park.[26] And in late 1910 he was touted as an entrant in a big January 1 dogsled race in Iditarod, though he later dropped out.[27]

In 1914, E. Marshall Scull arrived in Fairbanks with a hunting party, and began asking around about local conditions.

Inquiries about the game of the neighborhood all led back to Harry Karstens. When one tried to locate a person in this, as in other towns, the answer frequently was, "You'll find him at the Northern, or the Palace," or one of the other bars. But not so with Karstens: "You'll probably find him at Hall's bookstore." Finally we tracked him down; a tall, strong, clear-eyed young man.[28]

In December 1887, twenty-nine-year-old Theodore Roosevelt had returned from a hunting trip to the Dakotas concerned about the future of American game animals, having seen with his own eyes the drastic reductions in their numbers. Back in New York, he had gathered "a dozen wealthy and influential animal lovers to dine with him at 689 Madison Avenue." Among them was George Bird Grinnell, editor of *Forest and Stream* and "a crusader against the wanton killing of wildlife on the American frontier." The Boone and Crockett Club was formally organized the next month, with Roosevelt as president.[29] Other members included General William Tecumseh Sherman, Gifford Pinchot, and "twenty other visionaries comprised of outdoor sport enthusiasts, scientists, military and political leaders, explorers, artists, writers and industrialists."[30] Charles Sheldon had been elected to the club's membership in 1905 and was later elected vice-president.

Sheldon had been born in 1867 into a Vermont family involved in marble quarrying and manufacturing. After attending Andover and Yale, he entered the railroad business. He moved to Mexico and in 1898 became general manager of the Chihuahua and Pacific Railroad. Sheldon's investment in one of the richest silver and lead mines in Mexico made him wealthy enough to retire at age thirty-five. A hunter-conservationist in the Roosevelt mold, Sheldon could now pursue his true interests: exploring wilderness, pursuing large game, and writing informative and evocative descriptions of the animals he hunted and the habitats in which they lived. His first book, *The Wilderness of the Upper*

Yukon, was an account of his experiences hunting Stone sheep in the Canadian Yukon Territory in 1904–05.[31]

The following year brought Sheldon to the area around Denali, and into contact with Harry Karstens. After his second mail-carrier stint, Karstens in 1905–06 had worked claims with McGonagall in the Kantishna area north of the Alaska Range.[32] Karstens decided to set up a freighting company, while McGonagall chose to continue prospecting. In the summer of 1906, as Karstens was leaving the Kantishna, Sheldon arrived in Fairbanks. Rejecting Judge Wickersham's suggestion of a guide, Sheldon hired Karstens. "As I look back on my experiences in Alaska and the Yukon Territory, I recall no better fortune than that which befell me when Harry Karstens was engaged as an assistant packer," Sheldon later wrote. "He is a tall, stalwart man, well poised, frank, and strictly honorable."[33] In addition, Sheldon noted, "Karstens had the reputation of being one of the best dog drivers in the North. He always took the best of care of his dogs, taking no end of trouble to prepare ample food, and arranging the best available spots for them to rest."[34]

Karstens returned the admiration, as he watched Sheldon spend long days in pursuit of game through all weathers, followed by hours of thorough and often nearly-poetic logging of his experiences. Sheldon's *The Wilderness of Denali: Explorations of a Hunter-Naturalist in Northern Alaska*, would be published in 1930, after his death. A reviewer found that it "reads like a logbook, with entries written nearly every day, sometimes as late as midnight after exhausting days of tramping for miles in deep snow, across ravines, or waist deep in frigid water fording streams tracking white Dall sheep." In these entries, Sheldon "meticulously documented the health of his specimens, down to the fleas and ticks he found on them, and sent many sheep, birds, squirrels and more to the U.S. Biological Survey for further study."[35]

He also spent time looking at the great mountains, and the region around them, pondering how he and his Boone & Crockett friends might safeguard this wild and scenic area. By 1907 Sheldon would be sketching out possible boundaries for a national park, to include territories suitable for a game refuge.[36]

And of course, Sheldon and Karstens were keenly interested in climbing Denali. On August 1, 1906, Sheldon had written, "I could now view its double summit from the east and distinctly see the great Muldrow Glacier falling down its eastern side from the snowfield between its two domes."[37] Four days later, he and Karstens had eyeballed the second glacier above, and talked about climbing the mountain via the long northeast ridge, which would ultimately bear Karstens's name.[38] Karstens encouraged Sheldon in the idea: "With time and careful study we can do it like a charm . . . in my opinion you're the man."[39]

Having spent four months in the area, Sheldon decided to return in 1907, this time with plans to stay for a year. Karstens gladly signed on, and Sheldon was more than pleased to be teamed up with the Sourdough:

> Karstens had proved himself a splendid fellow, thoroughly efficient in all that pertained to practical life in the northern wilderness—a skilful packer of horses, a good traveler and woodsman, inventive and resourceful in any kind of constructive work,

from sewing to mechanics and carpentering, and an excellent camp cook. And what counted more than anything else, he was brimful of good nature, thoroughly companionable, and agreeably interested in all that I was doing.[40]

On January 14, 1908, Sheldon's party visited the cabin of Tom Lloyd, who within two years would become part of Denali's mountaineering history. The cabin had what Sheldon called "a magnificent unobstructed view, reaching along the Alaska Range east and west of Denali." He recalled that "while standing there with Tom Lloyd, I told him of the double ridge summit and of the great ice fall descending easterly from the basin between them." Sheldon shared with Lloyd his belief that "if no technical difficulties should be found below the upper areas, the great mountain could be climbed from the ridge bordering the north side of the glacier." At that time, Sheldon noted, "no one had suspected the course of the Muldrow Glacier or had identified it with the ice fall I had observed."[41]

By the time the trip was over, Karstens hoped and expected that Sheldon would return, and that they would mount an attempt at the summit of Denali. For his part, Sheldon wrote of Karstens, "When we shook hands before he started up the creek to take the horses to the Tanana River, over the mail route trail, I felt as though I were parting from a good friend."[42] But their summit expedition was not to be.

On March 10, 1909, the first item in the *Tribune*'s "New York Society" column announced the engagement of Charles Sheldon and Louisa Walker Gulliver, who was "well-known as a four-in-hand [carriage] whip."[43] The wedding, along with a downturn in Sheldon's finances, killed off the idea of another Alaska trip. "Sheldon spoiled it by getting married," was Karstens's laconic judgment. Still alive, however, was Sheldon's intense desire to create a park including and surrounding the great mountain. And to Sheldon, there was only one man in Alaska who should become that park's first superintendent.[44]

Karstens meanwhile began to be courted by another man with eyes on Denali's first ascent: Archdeacon Hudson Stuck.

∽

"Long ago," Stuck would write in *Ascent of Denali,* he had picked out Karstens as "the one colleague with whom he would be willing to make the attempt." After recounting Karstens' career in the North, Stuck described his "full vigor of maturity, with all this accumulated experience and the resourcefulness and self-reliance which such experience brings." In short, Karstens was "admirably suited to this undertaking."[45]

According to Karstens, "Bishop Rowe gave me permission to stop at any of their missions and in this way I met Archdeacon Stuck." In his recollection, Stuck had been eager to enlist Karstens in a Denali climb since 1907.[46] By 1911 Stuck and Karstens were in serious talks about the project. "Harry Karstens at dinner & a long and interesting consultation about our attempt on Denali,"[47] reads Stuck's diary in June 1912; in another entry a month later, Stuck persuaded Karstens "to stay over & he spent the night & we had opportunity to discuss further the Denali enterprise."[48]

In Harry Karstens, Hudson Stuck found one who seemed an ideal co-leader for the Denali expedition. Karstens's life in the North as a miner, pioneer, and wilderness guide—the very personification of a Sourdough—made him a perfect choice for the attempt on Denali. Karstens, for his part, knew of Stuck's time in the Alps and Rockies, as well as his travels around interior Alaska. As David Dean wrote, "Their partnership was straightforward: Stuck agreed to finance the venture, do the cooking, keep the records, and read the scientific instruments," while Karstens was to contribute "nothing more than experience" to the expedition.[49]

As it happened, however, while Stuck would explicitly rely on Karstens as the physical leader of the party, early conflicts between the two men foreshadowed the much deeper rift to come.

∽

Karstens, for his part, didn't really want to climb Denali with Hudson Stuck. But after Sheldon's marriage, Karstens realized that his best chance to get to the top of Denali was with the missionary's expedition."I did not care to join [Stuck] in such venture because he was not liked very well by the gentry of the trail," Karstens would later claim, after the expedition and years of enmity toward Stuck.

If he actually felt that way before the attempt, as opposed to when he wrote those words long afterward, Karstens may have acquired his opinion of Stuck from the Sourdoughs in Alaska, who resented Stuck's attitude toward many whites in the North. The archdeacon did not hide his scorn for the drunkenness, lack of respect for the law, and mistreatment of Alaska Natives from many of the whites that he regularly witnessed. His fellow missionaries had feared for their lives from drunken white reprisals; they had placed themselves bodily between whites and Native women. Stuck could not have been popular with the fraternity of mushers, miners, and trappers—Karstens's "gentry of the trail."

Harry Karstens' Denali ambitions were no less worthy, if less lofty, than Stuck's. He sought and expected financial rewards from the feat—a belief which he believed Stuck reinforced in their discussions about the expedition. He wanted to vindicate the Sourdoughs of the 1910 expedition—one of whom was his old friend Mac McGonagall—with whom he shared a common background and outlook, by showing that they had indeed reached the South Summit as they claimed. Having someone of Stuck's reputation, a priest and missionary, would add credibility to the expedition after the plausibility problems of the Cook and Sourdough attempts. In addition, as his friend Charles Sheldon had stressed to him, the publicity of an ascent would lend momentum to Sheldon's goal of making Denali and its environs a National Park.

And finally, the challenges of the climb captured Karstens's imagination: "After the failure of all those other parties I was very curious to know how come."

6

THE GREAT MONARCH
OF THE NORTH

T he first quarter of the twentieth century is considered a Golden Age of exploration, when men became national heroes by scoring historic firsts, reaching new lands, and making new discoveries. AMUNDSEN FINDS THE SOUTH POLE announced the *New York Tribune* on March 8, 1912, in its front-page headline. "The news of the brilliant achievement was received at a late hour last night." It seemed that the entire world had followed the race between Norway's Roald Amundsen and England's Robert Scott for the polar prize. The same wave of cheap mass media and instantaneous sharing of news via the telegraph which had triggered the Gold Rushes also brought exploration into the view of the larger public, and made celebrities of its outsized personalities.

Scott became an unlikely British hero. His team had made it to the Pole only to be stunned by the sight of Amundsen's tent already there. Attempting to return, Scott and the other two remaining men of his party died of starvation and exposure just eleven miles from their cache of food and supplies. Three months later, when news of the tragedy reached England,[1] Scott became an object of adulation and sympathy, his grit and determination in failure somehow transmogrified into quintessential national attributes.

In 1914, Ernest Shackleton forged his own way into the history of Antarctic exploration with his travails on and around his ship the *Endurance*. Like Scott's, Shackleton's was another of those British sagas which turned failure into glorious personal survival, overcoming wildest nature and personal setbacks. After the *Endurance* was trapped and crushed by Antarctic ice in 1914, Shackleton's leadership delivered his crew to safety, guiding them in lifeboats over 700 miles to South Georgia Island. Eventually Shackleton's image would surpass Scott's in the eyes of the British public.

For the other pole, there was no dramatic, simultaneous dash to be the first. Frederick Cook, fresh from his claimed first ascent of Denali, added the North Pole to his supposed achievements in 1908, accompanied by two Inuit men, Ahwelah and Etukishook. A year later, Robert Peary claimed to have reached the pole with Matthew Henson and four Inuit men, Ootah, Seegloo, Egingwah, and Ooqueah, a claim which was generally accepted for decades. Like the Antarctic explorers, these men were lionized, celebrated, and paid handsomely for lectures and endorsements—at least, the ones who survived. In a full-page ad in the *Saturday Evening Post*, Peary endorsed the Howard pocket watch, shown being held in a fur mitten: "Dear Sir: the movements . . . which I used on last year's trip to the northern extremity of Greenland enabled me to return to my point of departure . . . with a deviation of a trifle less than five miles." The aura of the rugged outdoors, then as now, was savvy marketing to city-dwellers with disposable income.

One modern historian of exploration has written,

> Arctic explorers . . . were men of consequence in the nineteenth century. They captured the attention of the nation's scientific and political elite and shaped the ideas and institutions of geography at a time when it dominated American science. Their voyages kindled the fires of the Romantic imagination as settlements overran the American frontier . . . Explorers were also the darlings of the world's most powerful publishers, who fell over each other trying to secure rights to their stories. Arctic voyages thrilled-and sometimes galled-those who read about them in personal narratives, newspapers, papers, school geographies, family atlases, and dime novels.[2]

In the *Boston Globe* in October, 1901, J.W. Smith wrote, "today . . . the chief interest in the polar regions is not commercial . . . One might cite numerous reasons why polar exploration has been and will continue to be of great value and importance. The fact that polar explorations are not valuable from a purely commercial point of view is no reason for abandoning them." *The San Francisco Call*'s lead editorial for March 25, 1909, was "The Assault on the South Pole." The quest to attain the pole, the *Call* claimed, "has an attraction all its own, although to average humanity it might seem a futile and ineffectual pursuit. But the adventurous quality still asserts itself and will not be discouraged." That pursuit indeed "offers fresh evidence of the unconquerable spirit animating the peoples that inhabit the temperate zone."

Not all agreed, of course. *The Chicago Chronicle*'s November 23, 1900, editorial, "The South Pole Will Come Next," declared, "America, Italy and Norway are rivals for the somewhat doubtful honor of reaching the north pole. The attainment of that object will accomplish nothing for mankind . . . It will add nothing to the resources of science . . . The moment the pole is found it will cease to be interesting."

Mountains had their heroes, too, in this golden age. In 1921 the British Alpine Club and Royal Geographic Society would together underwrite the first expedition to Mount Everest, sending a party that included a young George Mallory. In 1924, Mallory would die on Everest's slopes, and become immortal for having answered, sincerely or not, the question "why" with "Because it's there."

Hudson Stuck was no more immune to this exploration craze than Mallory, Shackleton, Scott, or any of the men who flocked to join their teams. From childhood, he sought out wild places, pored over his uncle's leatherbound accounts of polar exploration, and spent his youthful days exploring in the Lake District. In the Texas plains, he had reveled in the wide-open spaces and open skies near Junction City. At the University of the South, he had left his name in carbide-lamp soot deep within Wet Cave. And while serving the church in Dallas, Stuck made his first forays into American mountaineering. Stranded on the Muldrow Glacier on Denali, Stuck wrote in his diary, "I remember the August weather when I was camped at 12,000 ft on the Sierra Blanca in Colorado and the number of different kinds of weather we could see obtaining at the same time in different parts of the wide prospect stretched before us."[3] He took three trips to those Colorado Rockies, and also climbed Mount Rainier before heading to Alaska. In Europe in the summer of 1907, Stuck and two companions spent several days climbing in the Alps.[4] A decade later, while dogsledding along the Alaskan Arctic coast, Stuck would recall "a wretched experience in crossing the Albula Pass," in the Swiss Alps near the Italian border, when snow turned rain turned ice left their clothes stiff with frost. The experience, he wrote, was "trivial in comparison with . . . winter travel in the Arctic regions.'[5]

Stuck's exploration library of several hundred books included works by both Scott and Amundsen. His Arctic selections included Peary's *The North Pole* as well as *My Attainment of the* [North] *Pole,* by Frederick Cook. Stuck's collection spanned all epochs and nations, from the sixteenth-century Englishman

Richard Hakluyt to Stuck's Scandinavian contemporaries Fridtjof Nansen and Knud Rasmussen. Stuck hoped to follow in these explorers' footsteps by writing about his experiences with the land and people of the North. He had written John Wood while still in Texas, "I shall go to Alaska prepared to attempt to add something to the world's knowledge of that region, as occasion may serve me . . . The miner has gone far ahead of the geographer."[6]

In the dim dawn light of July 25, 1904, Hudson Stuck peered westward from his seat in a canoe on Canada's Lake Louise, keen to spot the Victoria Glacier. Along with two guides and three other climbers, he hoped to scale Mount Victoria, at 11,365 feet one of the most picturesque of the Canadian Rockies.

On his way to the Far North to assume his new post as Archdeacon, Stuck had routed himself through Banff National Park, founded twenty years before. His diary entries for the visit show Stuck's determination to exhaust his mountaineering options in the area. He had been charmed with "the chalet & the scene" when he reached Lake Louise on July 22; that same day he had rowed across the lake with a guide, and "climbed part way up the Victoria glacier." Below that line in his journal Stuck had written the single word "glissade"—he probably had learned the technique of sliding seated down low-angle snow slopes, or at least become familiar with the term, that day.[7]

The next day, Stuck and "a 'professor' from the Smithsonian Institute who is measuring glacier movements" had climbed the Victoria glacier and Abbott Pass.[8] Not one to sit around the chalet, the following day, July 24, Stuck had climbed Mt. Fairview, an easy 9000-foot Class I scramble on the south side of Lake Louise, "in the afternoon with the Rev Dr Bushnell and his wife and Mr. Slattery's mother—the old lady did greatly."[9]

Now on the 25th he found himself at the Victoria Glacier yet again, this time planning to proceed beyond Abbott Pass to the top of Mount Victoria. Although the previous night's weather hadn't been promising, Stuck's party was awakened by the Swiss guides, brothers Hans and Christian Kaufmann, at 3:30, "which in this latitude is but a little before sunrise," for a breakfast of meat and bread by candlelight. Then the guides rowed them across Lake Louise to the glacier's moraine.

Though Stuck gave no indication that he knew it, the Kaufmann brothers came from a notable lineage of Swiss guides. Their father, Peter Kaufmann, and brother, also Peter, led pioneering climbs in the Alps and squired notables, including a former British prime minister and a Rothschild, into the mountains. Hans and Christian earned a place in North American climbing history when, in 1901, they came to Canada to promote climbing and tourism for the Canadian Pacific Railway. Christian was part of a team recruited by Edward Whymper, whose first ascent of the Matterhorn and 1871 book *Scrambles Amongst the Alps in the Years 1860–69* had made him one of the first famous mountaineers in Europe. The brothers would notch more than a dozen first ascents in the Canadian Rockies between 1902 and 1904.[10]

What Stuck described as "the long grind up the glacier and over the avalanche snow to the top of Abbott Pass" took the party until 8:30, followed by two hours "amidst the shale and the disintegrating granite" before reaching the snow. (The famous Abbott Pass Hut would not be built until 1922.) "When the snow slopes were reached they seemed quite impossible, and I learned for the first time the skill of the Swiss guide," Stuck wrote. Cutting steps up the 60° slope, along the ridge which forms the Continental Divide, the guides led the party on, although one of Stuck's team seemed to have a harder time. "Christian Kaufmann had Dr Bushnell in charge; Hans had Theodore and me," Stuck noted. The doctor "kept his guide fully occupied, especially in rock corners and walls," where "a lack of confidence rendered him specially helpless."

At 3 P.M., eleven hours after leaving the chalet, Stuck and the others stood on Victoria's summit, with its views of nearby Mount Lefroy and Mount Huber, and blue Lake Louise below. Six more hours found them back at the chalet at 9:30.[11] The route taken by Stuck's group, from Lake Louise across the Victoria Glacier to Abbott Pass, is known today as the Death Trap, viable for only the most experienced and skilled alpinists. The Alpine Club of Canada today warns that the glacier has become more crevasse-ridden since Stuck's time, and that a large bergschrund across the route makes it "practically impassable."[12]

On July 26, Stuck left Lake Louise and reached Glacier House, at what is now known as Revelstoke. The next day he "climbed about ⅔ way up the Great Glacier [now known as Illecillewaet Glacier] with a guide." Stuck left Glacier House that afternoon for Seattle, and Alaska.[13]

Stuck's first sight of the mountain with which he would be forever linked might well have happened on September 1, 1904, the day he arrived in Fairbanks. Describing his journey up the Tanana River in his diary, he noted "glimpses of the mountains of the Alaskan range in the distance."

The mountain was a constant in his travels around the interior. In *Ten Thousand Miles With a Dog Sled*, Stuck wrote about seeing Denali from the winter trail,

> It is not a peak, it is a region, a great soaring of the earth's crust, rising twenty thousand feet high; so enormous in its mass, in its snow-fields and glaciers, its buttresses, its flanking spurs, its far-flung terraces of foot-hills and approaches, that it completely dominates the view wherever it is seen at all.

"How my heart burns within me whenever I get view of this great monarch of the North!" he continued. "Yet how its apparent nearness mocks one; what time and cost and labour are involved even in approaching its base with food and equipment for an attempt to reach its summit!" He considered how he had for seven years schemed and dreamed about climbing Denali. "Some day time and opportunity and resource may serve, please God, and I may have that one of my heart's desires."[14]

Even a summer boat-trip on the Kantishna River could lead Stuck to find ways to connect his location to Denali. The Kantishna, Stuck wrote, receives the Bearpaw, which receives the McKinley Fork, "which drains the Muldrow Glacier . . . which brings down the ice from the northeastern face of

Denali . . . so that the Kantishna . . . [derives] its ultimate waters from a greater height than any other river in North America."[15] On Lake Minchumina, with "its bright blue waters as a foreground," Stuck described "the noblest view of mountains in North America, and one surely of the noblest in the world," with "the sheerest, most precipitous face of Denali and Denali's Wife . . . companion peaks, rising by escarpment upon escarpment to jagged pyramids that thrust themselves . . . into the 'stainless eminence of air'; with their buttresses and ridges, their connecting arcades, their steep slopes, and awful headlong pitches, all glittering in perpetual snow." The sight was, to Stuck, "the finest that Alaska has to show."[16]

From childhood, Stuck had been mesmerized by explorers' accounts, and considered them "as fine a body of real chivalry as Christendom has ever known." He admitted that one reason for coming to Alaska was "that it contained an unclimbed mountain of the first class"—Denali, "the Tall One." Stuck's motives for attempting the summit were both altruistic and very personal. He wanted to publicize the work of the Church in Alaska, and have a platform from which to argue for Native rights—including having the mountain bear its Native name, which had been called Mount McKinley by white Alaskans since 1896. On the other hand, Stuck had eagerly (and unsuccessfully) applied to be a Fellow of the Royal Geographic Society in 1904, before he even arrived in Alaska. He was ambitious to place himself in the ranks of those who had staked out new territory on the edges of the known world. What better way to earn the letters "F.R.G.S." than to be the undisputed first to ascend a continent's highest peak?

By the summer of 1912, he had put together a team to do so and begun planning in earnest. On June 20, he met with Billy Taylor, "one of the party that climbed Denali two seasons ago. He gave me interesting & valuable information, but said that $5000 was the least fee he would consider for taking a party up."[17] Taylor wasn't taken up on his offer.

But that season also held uncertainty. Stuck was well aware that Belmore Browne and Herschel Parker were then on the mountain for the third time since 1906. In fact, on June 29, the day that Stuck was in Tanana running errands and taking a group of ladies "to a stupid moving picture show," Belmore and Browne awoke to a morning "as clear as crystal." They eventually found themselves peering up at the summit, only a few hundred feet away, rising "as innocently as a tilted snow-covered tennis court." In that moment, according to Browne, "we *knew* the peak was ours."[18]

Stuck waited anxiously for word of the attempt. Would Browne and Parker reach the top, and deprive Stuck and Karstens of their prize?

ABOVE: The oldest known photo of Hudson Stuck, 1890 or 1891. Inscription on the back reads, "The original staff of the *University of the South Magazine*, precursor of the *Sewanee Review*." Stuck is second from right. BELOW: St. Matthew's School football team, c. 1896. Stuck is center, back row; Ormond Simkins, who would later attend Sewanee as a star of its storied 1899 team, is directly below Stuck, holding the football. *Both images courtesy of William R. Laurie University Archives and Special Collections, the University of the South.*

Photo of Hudson Stuck, taken in Sewanee, Tennessee in 1904. The ridiculously young-looking thirty-one-year-old was about to leave Texas for Alaska. *Courtesy of William R. Laurie University Archives and Special Collections, the University of the South.*

TOP: The campus in Sewanee, as it looked when Stuck attended. CENTER: Convocation Hall at the University of the South was completed in 1890, the year after Stuck arrived in Sewanee. BOTTOM: St. Matthew's Episcopal Church and St. Matthew's Hospital, Fairbanks. Note the sign for the reading room, Stuck's initiative to offer men a place to spend evenings besides the taverns. *Courtesy of University of Alaska, Fairbanks.*

ABOVE: Stuck loved children, and the feeling was mutual. Here, playing with Alaskan Native children. BELOW: Stuck with his favorite lead dog, Muk.

ABOVE: Stuck on the trail. The caption reads, "Rough ice on the Yukon." Note Stuck's sled bag on the back of his sled. BELOW LEFT: Stuck's Native-made moosehide sled bag, featuring his motto, "Haereo"—"I stick." *Courtesy of University of Alaska, Fairbanks.* BELOW RIGHT: Stuck was once described as "a light, red-bearded man in well-cut sport clothes who looked as though he had stepped out of a shop window instead of a Koyukuk tent."

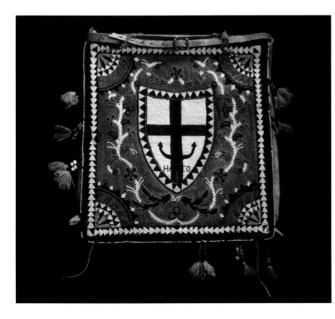

Stuck's boat the *Pelican*, with which he traveled thousands of miles on the Yukon River and its tributaries in summer.

Walter Harper in Alaska.

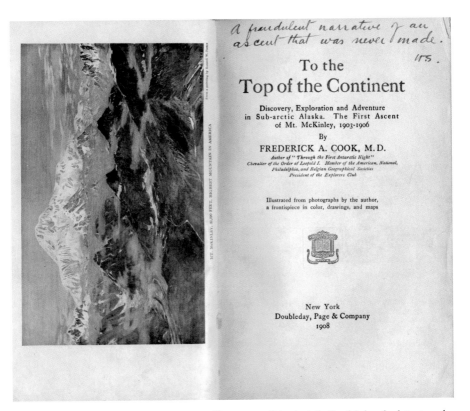

a fraudulent narrative of an ascent that was never made.

175.

To the
Top of the Continent

Discovery, Exploration and Adventure
in Sub-arctic Alaska. The First Ascent
of Mt. McKinley, 1903-1906

By

FREDERICK A. COOK, M.D.

Author of "Through the First Antarctic Night"
Chevalier of the Order of Leopold I. Member of the American, National,
Philadelphia, and Belgian Geographical Societies
President of the Explorers Club

Illustrated from photographs by the author,
a frontispiece in color, drawings, and maps

New York
Doubleday, Page & Company
1908

MT. McKINLEY, 20,390 FEET, HIGHEST MOUNTAIN IN AMERICA

From a painting by Russell W. Porter

Stuck's inscription on the frontispiece of his copy of Frederick Cook's book claiming the first summit of Denali—"fraudulent narrative of an ascent that was never made." *Courtesy of William R. Laurie University Archives and Special Collections, the University of the South.*

ABOVE: Bradford Washburn's photo detailing the routes taken by the 1910 Sourdoughs, the 1912 Brown-Parker expedition, and the 1913 Stuck-Karstens expedition. *Courtesy of the Museum of Science.* BELOW LEFT: John Fredson at Denali base camp. The sixteen-year-old was left to fend for himself for a month, two weeks longer than expected. BELOW RIGHT: Fredson a few years later, at Sewanee.

TOP: John Fredson in Native dress. *Courtesy of the National Park Service.* CENTER: Harry Karstens running the mail into Fairbanks c. 1905 on Birch Lake, Alaska. *Courtesy of the Karstens Family Archive.* BOTTOM: Robert George Tatum, commencement photo, 1917. *From Northfield Mount Hermon archives.*

HARRY KARSTENS AND HIS FAMOUS DOG TEAM.

TOP: Stuck and Karstens at the group's camp on Clearwater Creek. CENTER: Stuck took this photo at Clearwater Creek before beginning the ascent. From left: Robert Tatum, Esaias George, Harry Karstens, Johnny Fredson, Walter Harper. BOTTOM: Harry Karstens on the Muldrow Glacier, the "Highway of Desire."

ABOVE: Karstens and Harper navigating a crevasse on the Muldrow Glacier. BOTTOM LEFT: Double-exposed photo of Tatum hoisting his handmade American flag on the summit of Denali. BOTTOM RIGHT: The American flag sewn by Tatum while on the expedition. *Courtesy of the family of Robert Tatum.*

Saturday 7th June 1913

min - 14 : at start 4 am. - 4 .
a bright clear cloudless day.

I remember no day in my life
more full of distressing toil and exhaustion.
I had no sleep all night and at 4 o'clock, when
we sallied out, I had an headache in addition
to the malaise upon any exertion due to the
great altitude. But yet this 7th June will always
be a red letter day in my life, for we reached
the summit of Denali.
                    Although the sun was shining when
we started - it has shone all day - it was
intensely cold at 4 below zero and a keen north
wind made it impossible to keep warm. Very soon
everyone's toes were nearly frozen. I had no
sensation in my feet at all until nearly noon;
and even my lynx mits could not keep my
hands warm.
                    We look right up the enormous
steep snow ridge rising S. of our camp,
and then around the peak into which it
rises; both ridge & peak showing signs
of earthquake cleavage. K. was unwell,
his stomach as usual out of order, & so
Walter led all day cutting every step that was
cut. I was sick last night, so that
altogether we were a somewhat feeble folk.

ABOVE AND OPPOSITE: Stuck's diary pages for the summit day, June 7, 1913.
Courtesy of the American Geographical Society.

But we kept on at it. When we had rounded the N. summit of the S. peak, catching it well up, it had been so broken down by the earthquake, we came to the horseshoe curved ridge which is Denali's culmination. Here the climbing grew steeper & steeper, and when the ridge was reached, & the N.T.S. summits were passed overpassed in height and it was very evident that we were well above the great N. peak of the mountain, still there stretched ahead of us another ridge with a couple of little snow summits. This is the real top of Denali. It is a little basin about 60 or 65 feet long by 20 or 30 wide with a snow peak or turret at each end, the S. one being the higher. We entered this little basin with the excitement & the enthusiasm that had sustained us on this adventure. Walter, who had been in the lead, was the first to set foot on the highest point of N. America. Karstens & Tatum were quick behind him, but I had almost to be hauled, puffing & panting, into the secret place of the greatest mountain of the continent. There was no doubt about it. We were well above everything in sight: beyond us lay Denali's wife, or Mt. Foraker as the white men call her, the second largest of the Alaskan range. For awhile I could do nothing but point: then presently I gathered the others and said a short prayer of thanksgiving. This prime duty attended to

After the Denali climb, Harry Karstens became the first superintendent of McKinley (later Denali) National Park.

Walter Harper, c. 1916. *Photo from Yvonne Mozee Collection, University of Alaska, Fairbanks.*

Statue of Stuck, All Saints Chapel, University of the South, Sewanee, Tennessee.

The 2013 Denali centennial climbers, posing on the McKinley River on June 8. Left to right: Dustin English (AMS Guide), Hunter Dahlberg (AMS guide), Sam Tatum, Sam Alexander, Dana Wright, Ken Karstens (in mosquito net), Ray Schuenemann, Dan Hopkins, Paige Brady (AMS guide), Elliot Caddy (AMS guide). *Courtesy of Tom Walker*

9

THE "FRAUDULENT NARRATIVE," THE JUDGE, AND THE SOURDOUGHS

W hen Stuck and his companions launched their expedition in March of 1913, they followed in the wake of a short but tumultuous history of attempts on the mountain's peak. In one short decade, Denali had attracted exploratory parties led by an esteemed member of the Alaskan establishment, by sheer amateurs, and by one of the most famous frauds in the history of exploration.

Fort Yukon, Alaska, 1909. Hudson Stuck is reading, his pencil close by. The book before him, *To the Top of the Continent,* by Dr. Frederick Cook, had been published the previous year. (This copy, Stuck wrote at the time, is "the only one in Alaska.") Bound in green cloth, with an oval medallion on its front cover featuring the silhouette of a mountain, it describes what its author claims is the first ascent of the tallest peak in Alaska, and in North America. Cook refers to the mountain as Mount McKinley.

When Stuck gets to page 198, he writes two words in pencil along the left margin. The handwriting is sharp, clear, and old-fashioned, the letters pointed. The lines of the letters resemble calligraphy, as though the pencil was sharpened with a knife, not a modern machine. The two-word phrase he writes is flavored by the vocabulary of his home nation: *What rot*

This comment is not the only or the most severe reaction he will scribble in the margins of this book. Four pages later, he will add this:

> *here or hereabouts the true narrative ends. This at 8,000 ft. on the glacier or a ridge not much above it, is the highest point reached. The rest is grandiloquence & vague "fine writing" to cover up imposture. HS.*[1]

In 1903, Judge Wickersham, having established Fairbanks and set up his court there, decided to lead a group of five on the first known attempt to climb the mountain. "He had recently moved his court from Eagle, Alaska to a ragtag mining camp on the Tanana River called Fairbanks. From there he could look south to a great peak shimmering in the distance. He would recall that, 'From the moment we reached the Tanana Valley the longing to approach the mountain had been in my mind.'" Alaska historian Terrence Cole wrote, "The Judge's physical endurance was legendary, as befitted a man not afraid to walk twenty-five miles a day at forty degrees below zero."[2]

To raise funds for the expedition, Wickersham's climbing crew, who "had youth, hope, and climbing experience, but no money," decided to publish a newspaper and sell advertising space. The *Fairbanks Miner*, Vol. 1, No. 1, all eight pages, was published on May 8, 1903.[3] In it a small story announced, "Within a week a party consisting of Judge Wickersham, M. I. Stevens, George A. Jeffery and Johnnie McLeod will leave Chena on the Tanana Chief for the Kantishna River on a trip to Mt. McKinley."[4]

"On May 16, with flags flying and a band playing, Wickersham left Fairbanks, provisioned with flour, bacon, beans, dried apples, and prunes along with a hundred pounds of rolled oats for the mules he hoped would help his men bushwhack their way to the base of the mountain."[5] The steamer *Tanana Chief* was, according to Wickersham, "the first to enter [the Kantishna's] waters."[6] They traveled up the Kantishna River to the north side of the Denali massif.

The party "woke one morning to find fifty Indians and a hundred malamute dogs staring at them. When the Indian leader asked if they were climbing the mountain to find gold,

Wickersham said, 'No, we merely go to seek the top, to be the first men to reach the summit.' Great laughter ensued as the Indian told him, 'You are a fool.'"[7] "The old [Native] hunters who are acquainted with the caribou hills near Denali have drawn us a map with charcoal on birch bark, showing the rivers falling away from the high one, and giving us distances from point to point in that direction."[8]

From there the party headed directly to the base of the mountain. Unfortunately, as Stuck would later point out, Wickersham's party "attacked the mountain by the Peters Glacier and demonstrated the impossibility of that approach, being stopped by the enormous ice-encrusted cliffs of the North Peak."[9] After an ineffective week of climbing, Wickersham's group turned back, having concluded that "there is no possible chance of further ascent from this side of Denali at this season—or any other for that matter." The judge wrote, "Thus happily ended the first attempt to scale the mighty walls of Denali. We returned to our normal labors with a glow of satisfaction that we had done so much with so little . . . No lover of nature, of mountains, glaciers, and high places, can have any sense of defeat after such a journey."[10] In reality, Wickersham was barely on speaking terms with the rest of the expedition at the end. Tensions were so high, Wickersham was worried that two of the others would take the party's raft and leave him stranded, and so he insisted on keeping his gun and ammunition close at hand.[11]

Wickersham was given the dubious honor of having his name bestowed on the sheer face of rock and ice that had stymied him. The Wickersham Wall, rising over fourteen thousand feet from the Peters Glacier, would not be successfully climbed until

1963, by seven young Harvard students whose route has never been repeated. According to Stuck, the judge "was always keen for another attempt and often discussed the matter" with him, but Wickersham's judicial and political business kept him from following through.[12]

Later that year, Dr. Frederick Cook, already famous for his participation in Robert Peary's Arctic expedition of 1891–2 and the Belgian Antarctic expedition of 1897–99, arrived at Denali. Like Wickersham's group, Cook's was blocked by the steep north wall, but his expedition accomplished the first circumnavigation of the Denali massif, an incredible feat that wouldn't be duplicated for another seventy-five years.[13] Three years later, Cook returned for his second attempt—the one that would cement his infamy. Cook had in the interim helped to found the American Alpine Club and been elected president of the Explorers Club. Roald Amundsen himself had described Cook as a "man of unfaltering courage, unfailing hope, endless cheerfulness and unwearied kindness."[14] Cook's ascent to these heights of renown and reputation have been suggested as a possible reason for his ensuing behavior concerning Denali—and later, the North Pole. As Hudson Stuck would write, "Indignation is . . . swallowed up in pity when one thinks upon the really excellent pioneering and exploring work done by this man," whose "immediate success of the imposition about the ascent of Denali" led to the even "more audacious imposition about the discovery of the North Pole—and that to his discredit and downfall."[15]

Cook's second expedition on Denali included Belmore Browne and Professor Herschel Parker, who would later make their own attempts on the mountain. From May to August 1906, the party searched along the southern and southwestern sides of the Alaska Range without finding an avenue of approach. Returning to Cook's Inlet, the party broke up. Then, after Parker and Browne left him, Cook sent a telegram to a New York sponsor that he was making one last attempt. With only one companion, Edward Barrill, Cook ascended what he had named the Ruth Glacier (known to Athabascans as *Dghelay Ka'a Li'a*)[16] after his youngest daughter; from there, Cook claimed, he had reached the summit.

Belmore Browne later wrote, "At this time we heard the rumour that Dr. Cook and Barrille had reached the top of Mount McKinley. We knew the character of the country, and we knew the time that Dr. Cook had been absent was too short to allow of his even reaching the mountain." The entire original party having regrouped in Seldovia, on Alaska's southern coast, Browne then took Barrill for a walk up the beach, and asked him about McKinley. "After a moment's hesitation he answered: "I can tell you all about the big peaks just south of the mountain, but if you want to know about Mount McKinley go and ask Cook." This was all the corroboration Browne needed; "I had felt all along that Barrill would tell me the truth." Browne said he knew Cook hadn't summitted Denali "in the same way that any New Yorker would know that no man could walk from the Brooklyn Bridge to Grant's Tomb in ten minutes."[17]

Two years later, Cook published *To the Top of the Continent.* His critics, including Browne and Parker, suspected that Cook's "summit photos" were fakes, and later would provide substantial evidence to support that view.

As for Hudson Stuck, his reaction was unequivocal, as we've seen. In his copy of *To the Top of the Continent*, Stuck at some point would write across the top of the title page—with fountain pen, as though he wanted to render a more formal and final verdict:

> *A fraudulent narrative of an ascent that was never made. H.S.*

⚬

Nor did Stuck confine his opinion of Cook to the privacy of his library. In a letter to the Royal Geographic Society dated October 20, 1909, Stuck wrote that "as an Englishman by birth and breeding and jealous for the honor of English institutions" he hoped that the Society would "look very narrowly into the facts" before endorsing Cook's claim to have reached the North Pole. "It is the very general opinion in Alaska, in which . . . I share, that Dr Cook did not climb that mountain."[18] The Society's respondent replied, "All I can say on the subject is, that this Society has never taken any notice of Dr Cook."[19]

The rest of Alaska seemingly thought as Stuck did. In the taverns, rest houses, and hardscrabble settlements, the miners and packers, the loggers and hunters were unconvinced. Their consensus about Cook: impossible. Years in the bush had taught them that Cook could never have done what he claimed, in the time he claimed. Eventually, their indignation would launch one of the oddest summit attempts in the history of mountaineering: the Sourdough Expedition of 1910.

The Sourdoughs were Billy Taylor, Peter Anderson, Harry Karstens's friend Charles McGonagall, and their leader, Thomas Lloyd, described by alpinist and author Jonathan Waterman as a "Welshman-cum-Utah sheriff-turned Alaskan mine promoter and rake."[20] In 1908, Lloyd and Charles Sheldon had stood gazing at Denali, discussing routes to its top. Now, he and his group of Alaskan backwoodsmen, totally untrained in mountaineering, aimed for the top of Denali in their quest to prove Cook a fraud.

They came astonishingly close. Establishing a route which would be followed by those after them, including Stuck and Karstens, they found access to the Muldrow Glacier. On April 10, leaving the out-of-shape Lloyd in camp, the other three ascended, ropeless but with crampons, toward the lesser North Summit. After McGonagall stopped five hundred feet shy of the top, Taylor and Anderson completed the climb. There they planted a fourteen-foot flagstaff—naively believing it would be visible from Fairbanks. (As it happened, it would be three more years, until Stuck's expedition, before the Sourdoughs' pole would be spotted, and their story verified.) Unfortunately, Lloyd couldn't help exaggerating afterward, telling the New York Sunday *Times* that he himself had reached both summits of Denali. This not only detracted from what was, in Stuck's words, "a most extraordinary feat . . . unique in all the annals of mountaineering;" it also cast doubts on whether the Sourdoughs had even reached the north summit.[21]

∽

Two other attempts took place in 1910. The Mazamas was a climbing club founded in 1894 on the summit of Mount Hood to promote climbing and conservation in the Pacific Northwest.[22] The group, which took its name from a Nahuatl (Aztec) word for mountain goat, launched an expedition led by C. E. Rusk to try for Denali's summit. According to Rusk's account in *The Pacific Monthly*, "On the Trail of Dr. Cook," the group was also disgusted with Cook's claim, or, as Rusk described it, "Dr. Cook's little break into the domain of *fiction*" (emphasis his). "Had we a Magic Carpet or a good airship we might have duplicated the doughty Doctor's feat of photographing McKinley's summit," he continued.[23] The Mazamas party made it only as far as the Ruth Glacier before running out of time and abandoning the attempt.

The next attempt on Denali belonged to Belmore Browne and Herschel Parker, the former members of Cook's expedition. Browne, who according to Bradford Washington "personified the ideal of what an explorer and mountaineer should be,"[24] had spent time in British Columbia and Alaska since 1902. In 1906 he was enjoying a pipe in a Canadian Pacific Railroad smoking car when he struck up a conversation with a man "whose eyes never left the rugged mountainsides as they flew past the window." Browne saw that the man's interest "came from a deeper feeling than the casual curiosity of a tourist." In fact, the man, Professor Herschel Parker, was planning an attempt on Denali the next year. By the time Browne left the smoking-car, "I had cast my lot with his."[25]

When Browne and Parker learned that Cook was also planning an attempt at Denali in 1906, they joined him on the expedition in a marriage of convenience, but left Cook before his supposed final summit attempt. Now, in 1910 Browne and Parker had returned to Denali with two main goals: proving Cook's falsehood and mapping "the impressive mass of peaks and glaciers that guard the great mountain's southern flanks."[26] The first they accomplished by finding and photographing the "little outcrop of rock" that Cook had labeled "The Top of our Continent." It lay twenty miles from Denali.[27]

Now they were determined to finally claim the first undisputed ascent of the mountain. And in Stuck's opinion, "It is morally certain" that if Browne and Parker "had approached the mountain from the interior instead of the coast," they "would have forestalled us and accomplished the first complete ascent."[28]

Delayed by the long trek around the base of the mountain, and not beginning their ascent until June 4—more than a month later than Stuck's party and nearly three months later than the Sourdoughs—Browne and Parker were turned back by blizzard conditions almost within sight of the top. As Hudson Stuck would write in his account of the Browne/Parker attempt, "Only those who have experienced bad weather at great heights can understand how impossible it is to proceed in the face of it."[29] Continuing bad weather and dwindling provisions forced them off the mountain before they could reach the top. Browne, however, was able to take photos on Denali which proved, to almost everyone's satisfaction, that Cook had not in fact reached the top.

On July 29, 1912, Stuck wrote in his diary, "I have just learned that Prof. Hershell [sic] Parker & his party were in town last week for a few hours, on their return from their ascent of Denali. It is a great disappointment to me to have missed them.

They got within 300 ft. of the summit & were compelled to desist from the attempt by storms."[30] That sober retelling was not Stuck's only reaction; by one account, "At the news that the way still lay open, the Archdeacon was as jubilant as anyone of his age and dignified demeanor could be."[31]

The belief that an outsider like Cook had lied about Denali, and had in the process robbed Alaskans of something valuable, a piece of their birthright, an honor which should have been theirs to claim for themselves or to bestow upon a worthy hero, had united onlookers as disparate as the Sourdoughs in the taverns, Cook's disgruntled former expedition members Browne and Parker, and the Episcopal clergyman in his book-lined, pipe-smoke-filled library. Now, it would fall to an expedition led by Stuck and another Sourdough, Harry Karstens, to set the record straight, and attempt to claim the prize.

10

TO THE FOOT OF DENALI[1]

The March 17, 1913, edition of the Fairbanks *Alaska Citizen* reported on Page One that Major J.F.T. Strong would be appointed the next governor of Alaska by President Woodrow Wilson. Other front-page stories included the conviction of Julian Hawthorne, Nathaniel Hawthorne's son, on stock fraud in New York; the hearings of a US Senate Vice Committee, which had interviewed "society women, actresses, department store girls . . . and girls who are now living lives of shame"; and an article datelined Cleveland, Ohio, declaring "Side Whiskers and Tight Pants the Thing" in men's fashion.

On page seven of the *Citizen*, an article headlined "Will Attempt to Scale Highest Peak" described a party "under the leadership of Archdeacon Stuck, of the Episcopal missions." The expedition was leaving Nenana, heading for "the Mount McKinley district" to scale the peak "that has heretofore been inaccessible to . . . many famous mountain climbers." The group was "well equipped" with "numerous instruments with which to make scientific observations," as well as "specially made boots and spurs"—those would presumably be crampons—and several cameras, the pictures from which "will be turned over to the geographical societies." The expedition was "one that the archdeacon has long cherished," but he had "been from time to time delayed by the rush of his work." Accompanying the archdeacon would be Harry Karstens, "thoroughly competent and experienced," who "will act as a guide;" Robert Tatum, "connected with the mission at Nenana;" and Walter Harper, "whose experience and hardihood in mushing is known throughout Alaska."[2] Thus one of what Stuck called the "hungry stupid little Fairbanks papers" had depicted the expedition as Stuck's, with Karstens relegated to a guide's subordinate role, at the outset. It would not be the last such description.

Robert Tatum was the last person added to the expedition. Stuck had invited two different army officers to be the fourth member, but neither of them could leave duty long enough for the attempt. One officer's younger brother, Robert Tatum, happened to be volunteering at St. Mark's Mission in Nenana while studying for the Episcopal priesthood.[3] Tatum, from Knoxville, Tennessee, was a Sewanee graduate who had done some climbing and caving on the Mountain.[4] His main role would be as cook for the expedition; during his time on Denali, he would have problems of his own with the cold, and altitude, and the oppressiveness of the mountain landscape.

Left unmentioned by the *Citizen* were the other two members of the team: two Alaska Native youth, Johnny Fredson and Esaias George. Stuck would write that the two, who had been "picked out from the elder boys of the school at Tanana, all of whom were most eager to go," were "of great help to us."[5] They would go with the team as far as base camp, helping to haul supplies and to hunt for food. Once there, Esaias would drive one dog team and an empty sled back to Nenana; Johnny would maintain the base camp while the men scaled the mountain. Stuck had given each of the boys a brand-new Winchester rifle, one of the best sporting models on the market at the time.[6]

For Hudson Stuck, the inclusion of three Alaska Natives in the expedition was intentional. Of all the ways in which Hudson Stuck went against the grain of his time, one in particular stands out. In his age, as too often even today, exploration narratives glorified the heroic, solitary, white explorer—sometimes with a faithful Native assistant by his side, as in W. A. Percy's erroneous description in *Lanterns on the Levee*.[7] Many today can name Edmund Hillary as the first to summit Everest; fewer know his Sherpa partner, Tenzing Norgay. Stuck, however, did something unique. In fact, it is entirely possible that Hudson Stuck was the first to do what is commonplace today: seeking to climb a mountain or reach a pole specifically to draw attention to a cause.

For Stuck, of course, that cause was the Native people of Alaska. As writer and mountaineer Art Davidson, who claimed the first winter ascent of Denali in 1967, has written,

> [Stuck's] quest was not to claim 'the top of the continent,' or make any sort of 'conquest.' For Stuck the summit was not so much an end in itself as a means to a greater goal. He hoped his ascent would bolster respect for Native Alaskans by having several of them participate in the climb . . . Stuck also hoped to restore the name 'Denali,' by which Indians of interior Alaska knew this mountain that was such a physical and spiritual presence in their lives. For Stuck this was not an ancillary issue to be taken up with a board of geographic names. It was symbolic of everything that had been stripped from native people. And it went to the heart of why he climbed.[8]

∽

We are fortunate to have the journals of all four of the Denali expedition's members, revealing as much or as little as they chose to share about the journey. Tatum's is hinged at the top, with fine red lines printed vertically on the pages as though for a ledger-book. His entries, typically about a page long, focus on his family and his homesickness as much as they do the landscape and events of the day. Harper's is a duplicate of Tatum's, "just a small, beat-up, once-blue notebook."[9] Like Tatum, Harper wrote about a paragraph a day, with correct grammar and punctuation. Athough Harper's has the occasional misspelling, the writing is impressive when one remembers that only four years before, when he first met Stuck, Harper could not read or write.

Harry Karstens' journal is tiny, only 2½ by 4 inches, a cloth-bound diary with dark brown leather edges.[10] The most laconic and least grammatical of the four, Karstens often dispenses with end punctuation altogether. On the other hand, his rare commentary could be pointed. Karstens, a keen reader, included in gear & equipment listed on the inside front cover of his journal two books, Prescott's *Conquest of Mexico and Peru* and Fisk's *Discovery of America.*

Stuck's journals are those of a writer. Both the larger diary and the smaller journal—almost a notepad—which he took onto the final slopes of the mountain contain multipage passages, detailed accounts of each day's activities, his typically blunt opinions on various topics, and keen accounts of each member's physical and emotional condition.

∽

In the age before airplanes, long journeys by boat and/or dogsled were required just to get to the base of Denali. (Today, aspiring summitters are usually dropped off by plane on the Kahiltna Glacier, only fifteen miles and 13,320 vertical feet from the summit.) The 1913 expedition left Nenana facing 120 miles and three weeks' worth of travel merely to arrive at the start of their climb. Art Davidson has written of this era, "Just reaching Mount McKinley required the skills of a Meriwether Lewis.

One faced flooding rivers, quicksand, muskeg bogs, and grizzlies before ever setting foot on uncharted glaciers and ridges."[11]

Tatum described Stuck as "very nervous" the first day out, but didn't elaborate. After reaching their first stop, Twelve-Mile Roadhouse on the Nenana River, at 7:00 P.M., Stuck cooked dinner. Tatum: "Every time [Stuck] wants water some one had drunk it. Slept on floor with spruce bows. Very comfortable."

As they continued southwest over the Kantishna Trail, Stuck noted that "the country grows more diversified . . . and we have had frequent glimpses of the great mountain." The party traveled mainly on overflow ice, their sleds moving smoothly over "a continually renewing surface of the smoothest texture." Stuck called the following day, March 19, "one of the most enjoyable days of travel that ever I remember. The sky has been clear, the sun bright and there has been no wind." That afternoon "the scenery became more picturesque," with the foothills of Denali, "much broken & deeply sculptured, stretching to our right." March 20 was equally fine; "we had superb views of Denali & his wife, our best yet," Stuck wrote. He ended that entry, "One of my best days."

The next day they reached Eureka Creek, which was to be their base for a time. The 22nd was spent traveling to Glacier City, and Easter Sunday, March 23, was for rest and for repairing sleds: "Karstens is an ingenious mechanic and will get them I think in good shape." Tatum noted, "A d.s. [Archdeacon Stuck] preached very impressive sermon on the flowers. What they mean to man. Even the Crocus that is found in the early Spring the pleasure it gives to man and its value and the love flowers create in man." The next day they reached Diamond

City, "another of these abandoned mining towns, this one with out a single inhabitant," Stuck wrote. They found their cache in good shape except for thirty pounds of casa meal and fifty pounds of rolled oats that mice had taken care of—"This is getting out pretty easily," Stuck remarked. The following day, March 25, they returned to Glacier through three inches of new snow with most of their goods; an additional three inches greeted them the following morning. They sent Walter, John, and Esaias for the remainder of the stash while Karstens fashioned heel-pieces for the "creepers" (crampons) and Stuck and Tatum cooked ham, beans, and doughnuts.

A notable part of that day: "Pete Anderson, one of the two (Billy Taylor is the other) who claim to have been to the top of Denali in Lloyd's party, is here & he and Karstens have had a long confab," according to Stuck. "Anderson maintains that he and Taylor actually got to the top, and set up a 14 ft flagstaff there, which they maintain is there yet. Karstens believes him and I do too, though the task of carrying a 14-ft pole up that mountain must have been enormous & the feat sounds incredible."

On March 27 the three young men returned, and "all our stuff is now here." Stuck finished writing "Photography in the Arctic Regions" and "The Natives of Alaska," two of the last chapters in *Ten Thousand Miles with a Dog Sled*, "for dispatch to John Wood at the first opportunity." Saturday the 29th was "a long hard day," the team rising at 5 A.M. and fighting through and around overflow water on the trail. Fredson and George, in the second sled, didn't arrive until nine that evening, and Stuck noted that he was writing his journal entry at 11:45, "all very tired, but all well."

Monday, March 31, found Stuck concerned about the expedition's gear—more specifically, their footwear. They had met up with Mac McGonagall, Karstens' old friend and former partner, here at Eureka, had dinner, and visited his quartz mine. They had also picked his brain about the 1910 climb. Stuck wrote, "McGonnegal's [sic] experience shows that mocassins with the great creepers under them are the only footwear for the mountain, & we are now skirmishing around to find mocassins." On April 1 Walter played an April Fool's joke on Stuck, pretending that Muk, his favorite Malamute, had been injured in a fight. Meanwhile, Stuck wrote, "the men of this district are very good to us, & have been digging up old big mocassins until I think we shall be supplied."

The next day they borrowed a tent, a gallon of alcohol ("a relic of Parker's expedition"), and a 6mm rifle from Fred Hausman, a Kantishna miner. Karstens put on his snowshoes and "went off to Lloyd's tent, still standing" from the Sourdough expedition three years before, "to hunt for creepers." On April 3 the party left Eureka for Clearwater Creek, a sixteen-mile day. Stuck observed, "The vicinity of these great mountains has a climate all its own subject to sudden changes. All day yesterday the clouds were struggling to pass the mountains; in the night they evidently succeeded." After "beating trail through the heavy snow through the canon [canyon]," Stuck said of their stopping point, "'Tis a pretty place and we have made a good camp. The Clearwater runs open through a break in the ice a few paces from the tent; there is good wood & shelter around; right in front Denali rises; and tonight the skies are clear again & the stars shining." Stuck took a photo of the other five at the Clearwater camp, their long-sleeved shirts buttoned up to the neck. Tatum, clean-cut, could be a young Knoxville banker or lawyer on a campout. Esaias George and Johnny Fredson, dark-skinned and dark-haired, both a head shorter than the others, stand on either side of Karstens. Karstens, holding a rifle, wears a long fur-trimmed parka and a billed cap, while Harper, the tallest and fittest-looking, stares at the camera.

That night Tatum wrote, "Camp tonight was very nice Mr. K. angry with ads."

∞

Karstens was more than angry; he was forming an unfavorable opinion of the Archdeacon. After almost a decade on the trail, Stuck had formed routines as eccentric as he was, including leaving Harper to do much of the camp-work while Stuck wrote, or prepared Harper's lessons. Harper, having been with Stuck for half of that decade, was accustomed to Stuck's ways, but Karstens almost immediately disliked the established dynamic between Stuck and the Native youth. Karstens and Sheldon had taken on all of the daily tasks of the camp, in spite of Sheldon's elite background; Karstens assumed that Stuck would do the same. As Harper's biographer Mary Ehrlander put it, "[Karstens] certainly had not planned to serve as one of the archdeacon's trail boys . . . The respect that the four younger team members showed the archdeacon likely annoyed Karstens as well . . . Tension thus mounted between the project's co-leaders."[12]

Harper's personality, as well as his physical prowess and sturdiness, would be crucial to the success of the expedition. Ehrlander points out, "The traditional Athabascan values of nonconfrontation and nonintervention had fostered harmony and promoted survival within Athabascan bands for millennia. Harper's personal charisma, congeniality, and stocism deescalated tension, while his strength and stamina moved the project forward."[13]

Neither Stuck nor Karstens mentioned the conflict in their journals. Meanwhile, the party had brought themselves near enough to Denali to begin truly sensing its immensity.

‿

The mountain itself, alpinist and author Jon Krakauer wrote, "is so big that it beggars the imagination."[14] Its size—occupying 120 square miles of the earth's surface—and position as the Earth's northernmost peak of more than 6,000 meters elevation make it one of the world's deadliest mountains. Although its height from base to top is greater than Everest's, it is weather, not altitude, that have caused most deaths—over a hundred since 1903. Krakauer described "conditions more severe than the North Pole, with temperatures of forty below zero and winds that [howl] at 80 to 100 miles per hour for days at a stretch."[15]

By comparison, sixty-four climbers have died on the north face of the Eiger in the Swiss Alps since 1935, and Everest has lost close to three hundred since 1922. About half of those who attempt to reach Denali's summit, even in the twenty-first century, are turned back short of the top due to extreme weather which in a sense acts as a buffer, saving climbers from mortal peril closer to the top. "To all but the deluded or psychotic, the climbing season in the Alaska Range is roughly restricted to the last week or so of April, all of May and June, and—if it has been an inordinately cold spring—the first few days of July," according to a 2001 account. On average, 1,200 men and women will attempt to summit Denali during that period. "As a rule, half will succeed, 100 will need medical attention, and 12 will require major rescues."[16]

Permanent snow and ice cover over 75 percent of the mountain, and enormous glaciers, up to 45 miles long and 3,700 feet thick, spider out from its base in every direction. It is home to some of the world's coldest and most violent weather, where winds of over 150 miles per hour and temperatures of -93°F have been recorded. The self-registering thermometer that Hudson Stuck would leave at 15,000 feet on Denali was found nineteen years later. The minimum temperature reading of -95° apparently was surpassed, as the indicator was forced back into the bulb of the device.[17]

Weather on Denali can quickly change from sunny and clear to blizzard conditions with fierce winds, intense cold, and heavy snowfall. Climbers must understand and pay close attention to warning signs of changing weather, and use their observations to plan when to climb, when to retreat, and when to dig in.[18]

"The air on Denali is considered to be thinner than any mountain of similar height that is located closer to the equator. Due to its close proximity to the Arctic Circle, the barometric pressure is lower, leading to a much higher "real feel" at any given elevation. The effects of AMS—acute mountain sickness—can range from a mere loss of appetite to death."[19]

∽

On April 4 Stuck spent "a lazy day occupied chiefly in reading Thorold Rogers's *Economic Interpretation of History* while Karstens and Tatum "went out in the morning cutting wood . . . and in the afternoon Karstens took the rifle and went up the hill looking for caribou." It's easy to imagine how Karstens might have felt about Stuck spending the day reading.

The next day Karstens "found an easy way across to the Glacier," Stuck wrote, where the group would establish the Willow camp. "We lay around singing for a long time this evening & then to bed after prayers. So far it has been a very pleasant party & I think it will so far continue." Tatum that night wrote, "Arch deacon & I went up on the hill and had a noble view of the Mountain."

April 6 was a Sunday, so "All hands & the dogs enjoyed the day of rest today & I was very glad that it could be so."

The following day they began carrying loads from the Clearwater camp south to the Willow camp, where "we entered the valley that leads to the Muldrow Glacier, and to the heart of the mountains." Their strategy from the start had been to haul huge amounts of food, gear, and firewood with them onto Denali, eschewing the fast-and-light tactics of the Sourdoughs. It would take them three weeks to shuttle supplies to the head of the Muldrow. (Modern guided climbs cover the same distance in two weeks. In 2019, Ecuadorian-Swiss alpinist Karl Egloff reached the summit using the West Buttress route, on the western side of Denali but of similar difficulty to the Muldrow, in under eight hours—making the entire round trip from and to the 7,200-foot base camp in 11 hours and 44 minutes.)[20]

Stuck again took the opportunity to describe the weather systems created by the mountain's mass. "Denali's head has been shrouded in cloud-masses ever since we reached this spot: it is interesting to watch the clouds rolling up from the coast country, striving to pass the barriers of the mountain," he wrote. "For hours they are unable to pass; then, having deposited most of their moisture, one supposes, on the Southern flanks of the mountains, wisps of attenuated vapour stream across the sky & pour down the mountain gullies."

April 8, Stuck noted, was a "bright clear day," with a temperature range of "Min -8 at noon in direct sun 40." He continued to document his observations of nature: "I have been interested in the water-ousels (such I feel sure they are) that live in the stream that flows in front of our tent. They dive under the ice & even sing under it. In the water-bucket today was a minute creature resembling a crawfish in structure upon which we think the ousels live. The snowbirds made their first appearance today. Denali is entirely clear—the first time in several days." Meanwhile, Tatum recounted, "I spilled sourdough and was given the name 'Sourdough Kid.'"

Almost a month of travel had brought the six men via dogsled over rugged, wild terrain, through mining ghost towns—Diamond City, Bearpaw City, Roosevelt City, all of which had been built "with elaborate saloons and gambling-places, one, at least, equipped with electric lights," Stuck had written—and finally to the base of the Muldrow Glacier on the northeast side of the mountain. There, they repacked their gear, considered their route to the summit, and felt awe at the momentous Denali massif, and at the task ahead of them.

11

THE HIGHWAY OF DESIRE

The more popular approach from Wonder Lake descends to the McKinley River and then follows the East Fork of Clearwater Creek to Cache Creek and McGonagall Pass, a distance of 22 miles (35 kilometers). Depending on the loads being carried and the difficulties encountered in fording the McKinley River, the trek may take from two to four days.

—Mt. McKinley Climber's Guide [2020][1]

F rom the beginning, Stuck and Karstens had determined to follow the route pioneered by the Sourdoughs in 1910 and followed by Browne and Parker in 1912. Belmore Browne had described how the Muldrow Glacier "rises in steps, like a giant stairway" from the northeast corner of the mountain; it led up and southwest, then turned to the south, continuing until, in Stuck's words, "it is interrupted by a perpendicular ice-fall of about four thousand feet by which its upper portion discharges into its lower." Upon reaching the head of the lower glacier, they would climb onto what was then named the Northeast Ridge in order to circumvent the icefall, at around 11,500 feet; then, ascending the upper portion of the glacier to a shallow basin between the North and South Peaks, the group would turn left, or south, and climb above 20,000 feet to the top of Denali.

The glacier (Athabascan name, *Henteel No' Loo'*)[2] was named for Robert Muldrow II, a geologist who in 1899 was part of a U.S. Geological Survey crew sent to make a reconnaissance of the nearby Susitna River area. The crew had used transit instruments to shoot different lines of sight to the mountain's summit; then, by triangulation they had arrived at an average height of 20,464 feet for McKinley's height—higher than the current accepted elevation by 154 feet. For this first measurement of McKinley, Alfred Brooks named the glacier for the young scientist.[3]

On April 11, Stuck and Karstens had their first view of the Muldrow. "Today has been a very interesting one," Stuck wrote in his diary. "Karstens and I went up the long winding gulch, rising steeply at each turn for about 3½ miles, until we reached its head and looked out on the great Muldrow Glacier, describing a splendid curve to the West & South, with the peak of Denali closing the view . . . We sat on the ridge in the warm sunshine & enjoyed the magnificent view & ate our dry biscuit lunch." Then the two looked for and found a sled that Lloyd had cached during the Sourdoughs' climb. Looking through binoculars, Stuck was astounded to see a rabbit track going right up the glacier. "What on earth can Brer Rabbit find to interest him on this glacier? Perhaps he was trying to make the first rabbit ascent of Denali." Then they headed down the gulch to camp—"K. got on the sled & tobogganed for a mile while I followed on snowshoes."

In *Ascent of Denali,* Stuck would write,

> That day stands out in recollection as one of the
> notable days of the whole ascent. There the glacier
> stretched away, broad and level—the road to the heart
> of the mountain, and as our eyes traced its course our
> spirits leaped up that at last we were entered upon
> our real task. One of us, at least, knew something
> of the dangers and difficulties its apparently smooth
> surface concealed, yet to both of us it had an infinite
> attractiveness, for it was the highway of desire.[4]

∽

The next day brought Stuck's first disparaging words about Tatum in his journal: "Tatum was at his interminable slow cooking & I was sewing canvas rucksacks all the morning." That same day three Alaska Natives arrived at the camp:

"Manchúmina John," along with his wife and child. "About 1 o'clock . . . three Indians arrived . . . bringing a baby to be baptized, and hauling two small loads of wood for us." They had followed the group from Lake Minchumina, almost a hundred miles, for the purpose. "When I had baptized the child, it transpired that the parents had not been married—so I married them." Two days later, they took the first loads onto the glacier itself. Stuck found time to work on his chapter about the dogs of Alaska for *Ten Thousand Miles with a Dog Sled*.

Stuck had brought scientific instruments with him on the expedition, including a mercury barometer, a boiling-point thermometer, and two aneroid devices: one a barometer, the other an altimeter for measuring heights. On this day, using the aneroid barometer, he estimated the surface of the glacier at 6200 feet "above the sea."

Preparing food for the group's time on the mountain was a priority at this camp. Stuck and Karstens knew that one of the reasons the Browne-Parker expedition had failed was that it had relied on canned meat, hauled by the team from the coast to the mountains. This expedition would make use of local food sources. On April 15, with caribou killed by Karstens and Esaias and a sheep of Walter's, they made pemmican. Stuck wrote, "Tonight I have a large number of meat balls compounded with butter, and these, with the jellied liquor in which the meat was boiled, will be our chief food dependence at the high level camps." That same day, Esaias and one of the dog teams was sent back to Nenana.

At the bottom of Stuck's page for April 16 he wrote "Henry IV–Part II." He had continued his practice of tutoring the young

Natives in the evenings after supper; perhaps Shakespeare was that day's reading for Walter, Johnny, and Esaias. That same day, Walter Harper, "Johnnie and I took each a load of freight over the divide on the Muldrow Glacier, each having three dogs to one sled, and while Mr. Karstens and Mr. Tatum went on up the glacier breaking and marking out trail we came home." Karstens and Tatum returned without having found a spot for the next camp. As they prepared to move to the glacier camp, Stuck was still worried about their footwear. "I do not see how we will keep our feet dry in mocassins or felt shoes, for surely the sun will melt the snow at noon even on the high levels."

Stuck's journal for April 18 has the headline "1st Muldrow Glacier Camp." "The surface of the glacier for four miles is smooth, with very gradual grade & no crevasses; then it turns sharply to the left and is more broken up. Passing the point K. and T. reached two days ago, we had to go slowly, leaving the dogs behind. We rose over several ridges, and at length reached a wide deep crevasse . . . so we returned" and made camp on a bench in the middle of the glacier. High winds made their camp cold and uncomfortable until the boys returned from below with caribou hides, making the camp much more comfortable. "After a good supper are going early to bed to save fuel." Tatum called it a "low and uncomfortable camp."

Stuck's description of the Muldrow Glacier matches a photo he took. Denali looms at the top of the picture, while Karstens is a lone, tiny figure in the foreground, wearing long snowshoes and holding a sounding pole. The broad, flat expanse of white ice stretches before Karstens before curving to the left and out of sight. Ridges and shadows disrupt the glacier's surface near the curve, and rock walls slope up and away from either edge of the glacier.

Now the men began three weeks of hauling load after load of food and camp equipment across the glacier. Building snow-block bridges and dodging deadly crevasses which revealed, in Stuck's words, "hundreds of feet of blue ice with no bottom visible at all," the group pushed their way over the glacier toward the Northeast Ridge and the route to the summit. To carry the heavy firewood supplies, they used sled dogs and small Yukon sleds, with two teams of three dogs, and two men with each sled.

After lunch on April 19, Tatum, Karstens, and Stuck roped up with Karstens leading the way. Just above camp they encountered their first crevasses—some of them enormous, yawning breaks in the ice, others hidden by drifted, crusted snow. Before each step, Karstens gingerly probed ahead with his sounding pole. As the climbers trudged upward, winding around crevasses and house-size chunks of ice, they marked their trail with willow sticks. In midafternoon Stuck switched places with Karstens. "I had led for about an hour," he recalled, when "while prodding . . . the pole slipped out of my hand and went hurtling down into unknown depths." Karstens and Tatum stared in dismay. Without the sounding pole, there was no alternative but to turn back. By the time they were there a snow storm was blowing bitterly cold. "Read all the instruments and boiled the thermometer. We are about 7,800 above the sea level." That night Tatum recorded a telling observation in his journal: "Archdeacon Stuck through his desire to display his knowledge and authority, which he did not happen to have, twice took Mr. Karstens place and lost our only good pole." Back in camp,

Karstens fashioned a poor substitute out of a tent support. His entire entry for the day read, "Stuck Tatum and I prospected glacier. first use of rope. deacon tried lead & lost sounding pole crevases numerous some very large."

∞

Most climbers force a way through the Lower Icefall along its right margin and pass along the base of Pioneer Ridge beneath a potentially dangerous hanging glacier. From this point, the route regains the left center of the Muldrow and zig-zags upward to the 8,500-foot level opposite the base of Mt. Carpe. Here, at the base of the Great Icefall, turn left and proceed south along the flanks of Mt. Carpe and Mt. Koven toward Karstens Notch at 10,930 feet.

—*Mt. McKinley Climber's Guide*

∞

On Sunday, April 20, after "a wild stormy night gave way to a bright warm day" in Stuck's words, Johnny and Walter were sent down to base camp for firewood, while the other three continued up the glacier. Suddenly, Karstens broke through a snow bridge, and would have fallen into the deep chasm of the crevasse if he had not been roped to Stuck and Tatum. Once past the crevasses just above the camp, they found better conditions, and made about three miles and 1400 vertical feet of progress. They then turned back, reaching the camp at a little after six P.M. Karstens noted that night, "I broke through snow bridge but was yanked out," while Tatum's thoughts were elsewhere: "Have been thinking of Home, M & Beth a great deal the last few days."

In an unlikely glitch the next day, Karstens suddenly developed painful ingrown whiskers, having not shaved since Fairbanks. Tatum, who tried to help Karstens by plucking them out with a magnifying glass and a pair of tweezers, "was taken sick while thus engaged & had to go out & throw up his breakfast," according to Stuck. "He continued to be dizzy & faint though he resumed the process." The others realized that Tatum wasn't fit to rope up and go on the glacier; this presented a problem, as they considered three to be the smallest safe number on the glacier, and Walter had left to meet Johnny and bring a load of wood to camp. "So we lay around all the afternoon & the day was wasted so far as the mountain is concerned," Stuck wrote. However, "I wrote a few more pages of my chapter on 'dogs' & finished reading 'Hamlet.' All my books are read now, & I must start them over."

Karstens, for his part, was not really fit for roping up either. He wrote that night, "my Face in awful condition had to cut beard no more whiskers for me. I was sick in after noon Eyes hurting & stumich bad."

Harper had his first chance on the rope the following day. He considered it "very interesting and exciting for a while but after standing around and getting one's feet cold one gets very weary." After a morning of continual snow, the glacier valley had filled with mist, making travel slow and risky. Stuck's feet in the mocassins and six pairs of socks "grew intensely cold, waiting and standing about so much, & I was glad when we turned back." Harper described that evening's routine: "We got home and Mr. Tatum set to work making stew while I set to work making pie and some dumplings for the stew. Right after supper we went to bed with intention of rising early."

The men did in fact awake at 3:30 A.M. the next morning, April 23, but didn't get underway until 7:30—and even then it was -2° as the team's progress began toward the top of the Muldrow. They turned around short of their goal, the base of the Northeast Ridge at 11,000 feet; Stuck wrote, "The day was an interesting one, but not without discomfort. . . . We begin to have some notion of the work that lies before us now. I fear it will be at least the middle of May before we reach the top." It would in fact be three weeks longer than that.

After that twelve-hour day, Karstens, Tatum, and Stuck spent April 24 in the tent all day after sleeping in. Stuck "wrote some good pages of my chapter on dogs," while Tatum noted that he "had a lecture from Ad.s. on the 'Mercurial Baromater' discovered by 'Torri Chelli' (Tony Chily) [actually, astronomer Evangelista Torricelli] an Italian."

Bitterly cold wind greeted them as they left camp in the early hours of April 25 and "pursued the Muldrow Glacier to its source and end at about 11,500 ft," in Stuck's words. (The head of the Muldrow is actually 10,800 feet, not 11,500 as the party thought.) He found himself unable to carry his share of the work at this altitude: while Karstens, Tatum, and Harper took turns in the lead, feeling for crevasses, "The thrusting of that heavy pole as deep as it will go into the snow at every step is labour that soon exhausts me, and Walter was kind enough to take my turn." The archdeacon suddenly knew that for him, attaining the summit was far from a given: "Realize already that the climbing of this mountain is going to tax my strength to the uttermost, & that I am fortunate in having those with me who will save me all they can."

The group could now see what lay ahead for them, what Stuck described as "an amphiteater of mountains and ridges . . . To it from far above, comes the discharge of a great hanging glacier that drops down from the big basin between Denali's two peaks." They gazed at "the final cirque of the mountain . . . strewn with blocks of ice in wild confusion," while the Northeast Ridge, "by which we must pursue the ascent of the mountain rose jagged & rugged before us, and we saw that we have hard work in store." They turned around and dropped from sunshine into clouds and heavy snow, only reaching their camp by following the willows staked to the obliterated trail. Karstens, Stuck, and Tatum all noted the ptarmigan they had seen at 10,000 feet, and Tatum pointed out that "the try today was the highest I have ever been. Was 10,000 feet in the Rockies at Leadsville on my way to Alaska." Karstens added an enigmatic comment about Stuck. "The deacon is taking his siwashy [touristy] pictures in important positions which means? I plan everything & will get the bunk." Was the Sourdough already nursing thoughts of being cheated of money and due credit for his role in the climb?

Stuck was happy to stay behind the next day, drying out canvas and blankets and cleaning up the camp. The others returned with stories of Snowball "falling down a crevasse and Walter being let down by a rope to rescue him," and of a second sled dog "dangling over another [crevasse] suspended only by his harness, and squealing." Before they had set out on the glacier that morning, however, there had been what Stuck called "an unpleasant incident between K & Walter, the latter, in his careless way, leaving things just where he had used them, and K. very roughly reprimanding him with threats." Karstens made no mention of the incident, nor did Harper or Tatum. Stuck added, "I am sorry the boy's feelings were hurt, but he needed the calling-down." As for Tatum, "I have been thinking of home & mother all day."

The following day, a Sunday, Walter and Johnny took one load up to the next cache to take advantage of the nice weather; otherwise, the group had a restful day at the camp, with Stuck leading services at six that evening. Harper noted how "The sun has been shining all day and Mt. Denali stood out in the clear blue sky splendidly." Karstens also observed "McKinley peaks absolutely clear."

Stuck, typically, wrote in his diary at longer length about the environment in which they found themselves:

> I think I have never seen any other region where the weather changes with such frequency & suddenness as it does here. The Muldrow glacier seems to have a climate of its own . . . so far I have been unable to detect any connections between its movements and the changes of the weather . . . Sometimes the peaks are clear while we are in a perfect smother though which they loom ghostly . . . Bitter cold winds spring up suddenly and as suddenly cease. I remember the

August weather when I was camped at 12,000 ft on the Sierra Blanca in Colorado and the number of different kinds of weather we could see obtaining at the same time in different parts of the wide prospect stretched before us. Probably all mountain regions share this peculiarity & it is possibly even more marked where there are great masses of ice and snow.

On April 28 Stuck left Tatum in the tent and went up with the teams, "a rope over my shoulder pulling up all the steep places and holding Walter up as his team & sled crossed the crevasses. The dogs take kindly enough to the crevasses now they are used to them and go over them without any todo." Everything but the camp itself had now been moved halfway to the 11,500 foot camp where "the real climbing will begin."

"There was an unpleasant episode between K. and myself this morning," Stuck wrote. "His digestion is out of order & the cathartic pills I have with me do not seem to have any effect on him: furthermore he is sore, &, it seems, has been brooding all the trip over what he thinks is an unfair deal Betticher has given him over a wood contract for the hospital he expected to get—with which I have absolutely nothing to do." Karstens had "burst forth at me about 'lying in the tent' although he had himself declared that four were all that were required to get forward."

Karstens had reacted to what he considered laziness and imperiousness by Stuck. As he would later express to Charles Sheldon, Karstens had assumed that just as Sheldon had done in their sheep-hunting expeditions, Stuck would take equal shares of the camp work. By now Karstens had had enough, and so had confronted Stuck that morning. "O he was angry I shamed him to it as I never wish to shame another man, he got out that morning and worked." What Karstens wanted, he wrote Sheldon, was for Stuck "to live up to his agreement."[5]

Stuck, though, seemed incapable of seeing things from Karstens's point of view, or of imagining that in Karstens's eyes he wasn't pulling his weight. "However I am so dependent on him in this expedition that I have to put up with any bad temper he may show. I like him; have always liked him & he must be taken with his limitations. He brought up the wood contract matter & seems to hold me responsible." As for Karstens, his diary contains only another enigmatic phrase about Stuck: "deacon on rope relieved my depression."

Looking for ways to mitigate the cold, the team sent Walter & Johnny down to base camp the next day, to hunt rabbits for fur to line the team's mittens and mocassin socks. Stuck finished writing his chapter on the dogs of Alaska, "and am rather pleased with it." Karstens, Tatum, and Stuck spent several hours on the glacier looking for a cache supposedly left by the Sourdoughs three years before. They found nothing, "although we had exact directions by which to locate it." This led Stuck to speculate about the motion of the glaciers. "The crevasses below here seem very old ones with much weathered & discoloured walls . . . still in three years the ice must have travelled if it travels at all." The young men returned at 8:30 that evening with the news that the rabbits were shedding and useless for the purpose.

Cloudy skies and heavy snow greeted the men on the morning of April 30, as all five left the tent at 8:15, with two dogsleds. They succeeding in moving their loads of supplies "right through to the Lower Basin & picked a site for our next camp. It was a very long hard grind," Stuck wrote. Climbing 4,000 feet in about five miles on the ice, "I had to stop every few minutes until my heart ceased beating like a trip-hammer. The dogs feel the altitude too & it is necessary to take it slowly." Karstens noted acidly, "five of us with dogs made trip to 11500 with first load, dogs are the only means of transportation I guess Parker did not know how to handle dogs."

More snow—four or five inches—overnight was followed by bright sun on May 1. The thick soft snowfall made progress slow and difficult; the clear skies made for miserable heat, as it can in the thin air of altitude. It certainly was hard on Stuck: "I think I never worked harder in my life than I did today, the mercurial barometer & a heavy ruck-sack on my back, the rope on my shoulder. I shall long remember this Ascension Day." Realizing that reaching the new camp would take until very late and dangerously tax both men and dogs, they made camp at the halfway cache "& have pitched our tent in the lee of a great block of ice & are comfortably enough housed for the night." The men had an early supper and said Evening Prayer "& read the lessons for Ascension Walter the first and Tatum the second," while Stuck worried about the new snow: "It is likely to mean trouble on the heights." Tatum's entire entry for the day was, "Stove burn rather homesick today," while Karstens continued to vent his displeasure in his journal. "None of the others seemed to know a thing about [glacier travel]," Karstens grumbled, "and the Deacon worst of all." Then, the next day, disaster threatened the fate of the expedition.

∽

May 2nd dawned with part cloud and part sun, making the day by turns quite cold and very hot for the expedition members. Leaving Tatum at camp, the other four took both dog teams and shuttled a load of firewood to the camp at 11,500 feet. They paused there for hot cocoa from thermos bottles, and Stuck and Karstens decided to have a smoke. After returning to camp for lunch, the four started back up around 2:30 with a second load.

Stuck happened to be in the lead when he saw smoke rising from the cache they had left that morning. He later wrote that because "it is fixed in the mind of the traveller in the north beyond eradication that *smoke* must mean *man*," his first thought was, "had some mysterious climber come over from the other side of the mountain and built a fire on the glacier?" Immediately they left the sleds and dashed up to their supply tent, where they realized that a match from either Stuck's or Karsten's pipe had ignited the silk of the tents covering the cache. The fire was smothered, but not before significant losses. Stuck provided the melancholy tally:

> All our sugar was gone, all our powdered milk, all our baking-powder, our prunes, raisins, and dried apples, most of our tobacco, a case of pilot bread, a sack full of woolen socks and gloves, another sack full of photographic films—all were burned . . . Our carelessness had brought us nigh to the ruining of the whole expedition. The loss of the films was especially unfortunate, for we were thus reduced to Walter's

small camera with a common lens and the six or eight spools of film he had for it.[6]

Tatum was glad that "the sack with my things was saved . . . worst of all was the three silk tents." Karstens was, for him, eloquent on the events of the day: ". . . when we came in sight of cache with 2nd load we see cache was afire left loads & rushed to put it out losses—Fur Parkie all our new socks silk tents all sugar tea films clothes Mits underware axe & Grub. but still going on . . . Who would think of a fire on a glacier 11,500 feet in the air think of the months of labour getting those things up their even with the loss we are going on"

He also would claim that Stuck had lost control, shouting "All is lost!" Karstens's stoic response was to forget it, and start salvaging what they could. The team agreed, and continued with the expedition.

Stuck headed his diary entry for May 3 "Permanent Climbing Base" and below that "Head of Muldrow Glacier." Again that day, conditions changed from very to blazing hot; "it was a terribly rough grind . . . and we all suffered from it." Stuck declared himself "very much exhausted" when they reached the head of the glacier. However, "It is a great satisfaction to me to be here at last . . . I am sure no dogs in Alaska & I think no dogs in America, were ever higher above the sea than these dogs of mine."

The year before, Belmore Browne's group had camped at this same spot on the Muldrow near the icefall. "It was a wild-looking spot!" Browne wrote. "Great blue cliffs of solid ice, scarred here and there by black rock, rose above us, and while we staked down our tent a snow-storm whirled down from the upper peaks, blotting everything from view and wrapping us in a white mantle."[7] Now Stuck and the others made a wall of snow blocks around the tent, and a snow hut for a cache. He wrote, "We are certainly securely entrenched—as securely as men can be in the midst of a glacier basin, with hanging glaciers all around." Karstens, meanwhile, grumbled to himself about the losses from the fire. "Three weeks Provisions & wood sugar nearly all gone others believe in feast or famine"

In the Sourdough's defense, he almost certainly was in pain. The next day, he wrote, "I stayed home my face in awful condition." After the inflammation on his face spread to his forehead, Karstens decided that the cause was not ingrown hairs, but rather overexposure to the sun. Stuck insisted that Karstens stay in the tent, while the rest brought up the last loads from the cache below—after Stuck led the Morning Prayer service, with Harper and Tatum reading the lessons. The heavy loads and the heat and glare of the sun on the glacier ice caused Stuck to write, "Anyone who thinks that the climbing of Denali is a picnic is badly mistaken." After dinner, a survey of the fire-damaged gave them some cause for hope. They salvaged seven spools of film, protected by their cases; nine cases of tobacco—"three more are badly scorched but Harry says he can smoke them"; and six packages of raisins. The boys went down that afternoon to return the dogs to base camp and bring up canvas for tents, "& the little reserve of sugar & what socks can be found, for all our socks are burned."

The spectacular setting continued to enthrall the four men as they hauled supplies, made trails, or worked and rested at camp. Even the laconic Harper was moved to describe rushing out one day to take photos of the "finest avalanches this morning coming down from the north ridge of Mt. Denali one after another shaking the whole Muldrow Glacier as it struck it." Tatum called it "one of the grandest most magnificent avalanches I have ever seen. Some 500 feet of ice calved from the great hanging glacier and threw dense clouds 1000 or more feet in the air."

The altitude and weather had tested them as they moved slowly up the Muldrow Glacier. Not only would they contend with those two by-now familiar foes on the next section of the climb; but once they left the comfort of the glacier, the mountain itself would have an unforeseen complication to throw at them.

12

THE NORTHEAST RIDGE

From the notch, gain the knife edge of Karstens Ridge and proceed upward for 1.2 miles (1.6 kilometers) to the prominent step at 12,000 feet (3,688 meters). This is the only good campsite on the ridge itself. Continue along the ridge through the rugged Coxcomb section to Browne Tower at 14,600 feet (4,450 meters.)

The ridge is the crux of the climb. Early in the season, Karstens Ridge and the Coxcomb tend to be more icy than in late June or July when new snow sometimes requires climbers to shovel their way upward. As much

*as 1,800 feet or as little as 600 feet of fixed rope (600 or
200 meters) may be needed to safeguard difficult sections
of the route depending on conditions.*
                           —*Mt. McKinley Climber's Guide*

By May 5, the expedition was more than seven weeks out from Nenana, and had spent the last fourteen days on the Muldrow Glacier. At its head, the Muldrow dead-ended into what Browne and Parker had named the Northeast Ridge. Facing the ridge, the climbers had on their right the sheer icefall from the glacier above, which led up to the Grand Basin between Denali's two summits. They would have to find a way onto the ridge in order to bypass the treacherous icefall. Stuck felt strong enough that day to join Tatum on the first attempt to scout a path onto the ridge. With Harper and Fredson fetching supplies from base camp, Karstens was left alone at the glacier camp. After one foray stymied by unsafe rock and ice, Stuck and Tatum put on their "creepers" and made it to the top. From there they looked down into "a wild and savage valley," Stuck wrote, "filled with a glacier at least a thousand feet lower than the Muldrow."

Then, they turned and looked up the ridgeline. What they saw would shake their confidence about attaining Denali's summit.

∽

At the last moment before departure, Stuck had picked up a magazine article in which Belmore Browne described his climb.

The Northeast Ridge, he had written, was "a steep but practicable slope," which they had covered in a few days. What Stuck and Tatum beheld now was another landscape entirely. The top third of the ridge was as Browne had described, but at that point there was a sharp breakage, and the remainder below that was in Stuck's words "a jumbled mass of blocks of ice and rock in all manner of positions, with here a pinnacle and there a great gap." There were also, inexplicably, icebergs littering the floor of the glacier below.

Suddenly, Stuck had his explanation—"the earthquake!" Two days after Parker and Browne had retreated from the mountain, on July 6th, 1912, the mountain had been rocked by an earthquake strong enough to be recorded in Washington, D.C., as the worst since the San Francisco quake of 1906. Stuck realized the implications: had the Parker-Browne expedition not abandoned when they did, "they could never have descended that ridge . . . They would have been either overwhelmed and crushed instantly or have perished by starvation."[1]

Stuck and Tatum rejoined Karstens in camp about 3:30, and they were joined by Harper and Fredson at 8:30 that evening. "We now have everything here that we need, & save for the loss of our sugar & milk by the fire, would be well provisioned," Stuck wrote. "This is a comfortable camp and the weather the last two days has been glorious with wide views of the rugged mountainous country between here and the Tanana." For Karstens, "We have everything now freighting is over the real climb starts from here."

The next day was spent making supplies to make up those lost in the fire. In a wonderfully generous gesture, after breakfast

Harper took Fredson, who would be heading down to base camp soon, to the crest of the ridge so that he could "go as high up as we could let him and see all there was to see" before he left. Karstens and Harper began making the light tent which Karstens had designed, while Fredson and Stuck took the Jaeger camel's-hair lining from Stuck's sleeping bag to make a dozen pairs of socks. Tatum baked biscuits which, combined with eighteen packages of Zweibach, made the group's supply of bread. Using wood from supply-boxes and hides of caribou and mountain sheep, the team made themselves relatively comfortable.

May 7 dawned after Stuck spent a sleepless night due to altitude, just as he had experienced in the Sierra Blanca of Colorado at 12,000 feet. "I lie awake & toss about & am conscious of nervousness and sometimes of breathlessness." Nevertheless, "I seem to rest all right: I do not feel the lack of sleep." That day he and Tatum made another attempt to find a route to the ridge while the other three continued work on the tents. When the two reached the farthest point from the day before, "a great avalanche of snow & ice fell down from the sheer gully to the right of the great hanging glacier. It rolled in great clouds to the bottom & spread out over the glacier. I was glad that Walter, down at the camp, took a photograph of it." A small snowstorm turned Stuck and Tatum back after they had traversed across sleep slopes to the "gully up which, it seems, we must pack our stuff."

The next day, May 8, "K's face being much better & he tired of the confinement of the tent," Karstens, Harper, and Fredson went up the glacier and "made a direct ascent of a gully that led them to the top, cutting steps all the way." They came back having found "a difficult way around the break." The men were quite sure now that the ridge had been shattered by the earthquake of the previous summer. In Karstens's words, "ridge is all broken up from earthquake on July 6/12 [6, 1912] all the snow slopes are broken & the ridge is Honeycomed blocks of Ice with steep slopes on eather side." Meanwhile, according to Tatum, "Arch deacon and I stayed in today and talked all day." They "disgussed every thing & every body He aggres with me that I work on the survey party there this summer . . . Then next winter I hope to stay in Fairbanks and (read read read) . . . I hope to order lots of books also."

With the dogs' feed depleted and no further use for them on the glacier, Fredson was sent down to basecamp on May 9. Karstens and Harper wanted to continue cutting steps on the ridge, so Stuck and Tatum volunteered to go down with Fredson "until he should safely be over the crevasses." Once down, he would wait for the party with the sled and tend Stuck's dogs Snowball, Tan, Muk, Nenana, Hardtack, Bob, and Skeet. Fredson would be there alone for far longer than the fourteen days the team planned on. To keep busy, he would hunt to feed the dogs and himself, build a cache to store meat, and write in his journal. Heads of bighorn sheep shot by Fredson would eventually accumulate around the walls of the main tent. Stuck wrote, "We should have liked to keep the boy, so good-natured and amiable he was and so keen for further climbing; but the dogs must be tended, and the main food for them was yet to seek on the foot-hills with the rifle. So on 9th May down they went."[2]

Returning to camp, Karstens and Harper reported that "the whole ridge has been shaken to pieces; its edge consists of great blocks of ice heaped in confusion . . . and they say ahead looks worse than behind." Better news, Stuck noted, was that "the yellow glasses from A.&F. [Abercrombie & Fitch]" gave "the best protection for the eyes against the snow-glare that I have ever tried. I have suffered not at all with my eyes and this was what I dreaded most."

That same day, Karstens was moved to write his longest diary entry of the expedition, a description of the ridge in the wake of the earthquake:

> There is no doubt in my mind that the shake up of last year has broken up the snow slopes and left the ridge in the condition it is. great blocks of ice stand on top of ridge with shear drop on eather side other places honey comed blocks stand over one another which look as though they would tumble over by wispering at them. the slope of ridge to call is hard to describe in places it looks like hanging glaciers which are liable to break off any time. the shere walls of the north peak are covered with hanging glaciers which discharge great masses of Ice some of the discharges move the whole Muldro glacier the Ice falls between the two peaks is continualy discharging great masses of Ice which send clouds of fine ice Thousands of feet in the air

The four remaining members of the expedition—the summit party—were now ready to tackle the ridge which would lead them directly to the top of Denali. For almost three weeks, they would alternate days of tough work clearing a path through the earthquake debris, almost entirely by Karstens and Harper, with forced confinement in the tent, kept there by snow, fog, and wind.

∽

Time tentbound tended to bring out the differences in the team members' personalities, as expressed in their diaries. Here is merely the first third of Hudson Stuck's diary entry for Saturday, May 10:

> When I had begun to read the psalter for the day this morning, while Walter was cooking breakfast, the sun struck on the tent just at 7 o'clock; and the first verse of the 50th psalm was on my lips, "The Lord even the most mighty God hath spoken and called the world from the rising up of the sun even to the going down thereof." I stepped out and it seemed as though the words were a special message to us here. The great peaks were brilliant in the morning light: far away to the north the whole wide prospect of tangled mountain ranges was illuminated and even in the blue distance where the great flats of the Tanana valley spread out, the sun was lighting up the scene. I realized once again how "their voices are gone out unto all lands & their sound to the ends of the earth.

And here is Harry Karsten's entire diary entry for that same day:

> "Laid up Storm"

The next day clouds poured over the ridge as they made their way up the route Karstens and Harper had chopped out two days before. Once on the ridge the group began what Stuck called "the intricate twisting in and out amongst the huge blocks of ice of its crest: there is no longer any snow-slope on the ridge; it is a jumbled mass of rocks & ice with snow lying at an unstable angle on either side." Dropping their packs in the cache made on the previous journey, they proceeded up the ridge, Karstens and Harper doing the work of cutting steps. They reached "a flat place on the ridge from which the ascent becomes suddenly very steep" before turning and dropping back down to camp. Stuck wrote, "We are congratulating ourselves that we are halfway up to the Col [a mountaineering term for the lowest point between two peaks] where we hope to make our camp."

The dangerous precariousness of the severely disrupted ridge was driven home when the team encountered "an enormous block of ice, as big as a two story house, just poised on two little blocks & held in place by a flying-buttress of wind-hardened snow," as Stuck described it. It only took a few swings from Karstens's ice axe to dislodge the immense block and send it "hurtling down to the depths below & we heard it bound & rebound & then split with a report like a cannon though we heard nothing."

On May 12, continual heavy snow made the day dangerous for the expedition as they shuttled another load up the ridge. On the descent they found the trail wiped out by the blizzard, and even had difficulty route-finding back to camp. Once there, Stuck devoted himself to Harper's lessons—"I have put him through an examination & he is now writing out for me the states & capitals." Meanwhile, "K. allowed his temper to flare up this morning; this time at T. for his slowness. We have all of us now experienced his angry tongue. The delay tells upon him & he has no resources to pass the time." Karstens, for his part, stewed quietly at Stuck for not doing more of the work cutting the steps up the ridge.

Heavy snow falling almost all day meant two more days stuck in the tent. They began rationing wood, not knowing how long the rest of the climb might take. Stuck passed the time dictating Shakespeare's *Henry IV* to Harper, and writing "wildly and anticipatively about our ascent—which will probably be of no avail but it has served to occupy the time." He wrote late in the evening, "it grows too cold to use the pen. Harry, I am thankful to say, finds occupation in drawing plans for a launch he proposes to construct this summer."

On May 14 a new threat to the success of the expedition appeared, as Tatum suffered from "facial neuralgia" blamed by Stuck on the damp bedding; after "rubbing all day with the analgesic cream," Tatum's pain had at last passed, and the canvas, bedding, and caribou hides that had become damp from the ice were hung out to dry. Another tedious and uneventful day in the tent was relieved for Stuck by working on "Walter's dictation, some history & some geography."

Karstens successfully replaced the washer on the primus stove—"all we shall have to depend on for warmth as well as cooking up above," wrote Stuck—and thought of Fredson: "I wonder how Johnny is alone at the base camp Pretty lonesome." By five o'clock the temperature was -10°; Stuck guessed that up above it might reach "20 or even 30 below on a clear night."

(Stuck, who had known winter temperatures in Alaska's interior of well below minus-fifty, might have been shocked to learn that the thermometer he would leave behind would record a temperature of approximately -100°.)[3]

The next day Tatum's woes increased, as he began having trouble with his throat "(the neuralgia having turned to something like tonsilitis)," wrote Stuck. For the others it was a brilliant, clear day as they left for the ridge at 8:30. They attempted a lower route, then backtracked and resumed the already-made trail about 100 yards past their previous farthest point. There, reaching the "very difficult place beyond the flat . . . We think we see our way now up to the Col, but the difficulties still are great." The climbers could not identify any of the places on the ridge that Belmore Browne had described; "the 'Col 800 ft up in the air' from the glacier floor no longer exists." That evening they hoped that because Tatum had improved during the day, they could all four go up the next day. Tatum's mind once again was elsewhere: "I have thought a great deal of Ken. & Bertha today also Mildred and the home folks." Stuck, meanwhile, was hopeful. "God send that this weather last: this would have been a glorious day for the summit."

They would spend three weeks more on Denali before that day arrived.

Hope gave way to reality the next day, May 16. "I had expected that this climb would be a difficult and perhaps a dangerous one," Stuck wrote, "but I had not thought it would be so terribly tedious & laborious as it has been." The group had expected to reach the flat spot they had named the Parker Col; today, ten hours on the ridge saw them still a long way from it, "with difficulties that increase and multiply as we proceed." After six hours of chopping near-vertical steps to a height of 1,800 or 1,900 feet above the glacier camp, they came out upon a clear view of the ridge ahead—only to find it "still stretch[ing] away, even more shattered and broken" than the previous sections. (Karstens's comment in his journal that night was "Ridge looks easy from distance but 'O' my.") They turned around there, a few hundred feet from the point where the earthquake damage ended, hoping to reach it the next day.

Tatum had stayed behind in the tent, his tonsilitis having kept him awake the previous night. He "hope[d] to climb again tomorrow I slept a little this afternoon but have felt misserable all day." Stuck wrote, "What we shall do with him if he does not quickly recover I do not know."

Saturday, May 17 marked two weeks since they had pitched their camp at the head of the Muldrow Glacier. "The tantalizing and tedious nature of this undertaking manifests itself unbated," Stuck began that evening's journal entry. He had stayed behind to minister to Tatum while Karstens and Harper tried the trail. They were able to move almost all of the gear to the farthest cache on the ridge before being turned back by weather. Back in the tent, Stuck believed that "With the persistent use of cold compresses Tatum's throat grows better, & I think, when next the ridge is possible, he may go along." Tatum, meanwhile, was looking past the end of the expedition, like a sailor contemplating the horizon to ease his seasickness. "Archd complemented me on my work done on this trip. His plan is for me to work this summer & go to the states next winter and have a private tutor from the U.T. for 2 yrs. and enter some university."

The storm blew snow and shook the tent. Meanwhile, the primus stove began to leak after it overheated and some of the solder melted. Stuck added, "Later: K. with his usual ingenuity has repaired the primus stove." Harper wrote, "Just before we went to bed we heard an avalanche so we rushed out of the tent to see where it . . . coming from the hanging glacier at the head of the Muldrow Glacier." They watched it "rolling down the mountain side like a roaring thunder and afterwards raising a cloud one thousand feet or more up in the air."

The next day was one of the worst yet. Clouds and thick mist enclosed them in "a chilly damp tent in which we have not dared to light a fire other than the kerosene stove since breakfast, so low has our wood supply fallen," Stuck wrote. Tatum was sick again, this time with a bad headache, though his throat was improved. "He is certainly out of sorts," Stuck noted, "and I grow more & more uneasy about him." Stuck led Morning Prayer with the lessons for Trinity Sunday and sang the hymn "Holy, Holy, Holy." The sky cleared just long enough for Karstens and Harper to begin gearing up for the ridge, and then shut them down again. So they spent another dreary day in the tent. Stuck wrote until it grew too cold to hold the pen, and then cooked supper with Harper while the other two slept. "About 6 o'clock we are talking about going to bed as the warmest place—And so the days pass." Karstens wrote "'O' for one good day & the call will surely be ours wood very near gone, a few spoons full of sugar left." Harper noted that "It has been two months and two days since we left Nenana. It is very tedious staying in the tent all day waiting for the weather to clear."

May 19 was no better. "There is nothing for it but patience, and we are all trying our best to be patient," Stuck wrote. "Some reading aloud by Walter in the Pilgrim's Progress, an hour's dictation to him from Shakespeare, and some other studies are all that the day holds of occupation." He was pleased to see that Tatum seemed to have recovered, but worried about Karstens, who had "about exhausted the resources of boat-designing and sleeps a great deal." Stuck wished he could find something else for Karstens to occupy himself with in the tent. Meanwhile, "the sugar is all gone & we shall get no more til we go out. We shall soon be short of grub, for it is all cached up on the ridge." They spend most of the day keeping warm in their beds, getting no exercise; in the whiteout, they would be lost twenty yards from their tent. Harper sounded a little more upbeat than the day before. "We hope tomorrow will be a fine day, although that has been our hope for a week. All we want now is one good day to reach the col and we hope from there it won't be so hard."

But the barometer refused to budge, and a third day passed with little activity. Stuck reported that Harper had memorized the Presidents and their dates, and was memorizing "(for the second time I am afraid)" the books of the Bible. Tatum, who seemed to have recovered, studied his Prayer Book. Karstens, though, "is at a loss for any diversion; he sleeps a great deal," according to Stuck. As for the archdeacon himself, "What with dictating to Walter from some of the best passages of Henry IV, parts I & II, and explaining the history of it to him, hearing him read aloud from the Pilgrim's Progress, and a little more writing . . . the time passes not too unbearably tediously for me."

Stuck pondered the ridiculousness of their situation. "Think of four men deliberately pitching a camp on the ice of a glacier, 20 miles from the nearest wood, and then sitting down in it day after day, killing time as best they can." While down below, "the Yukon has gone out; navigation is now beginning; all the stir and excitement of the new season's life is on the river; the ducks & geese have come & gone on further north; the trees are in tender new leaf," and "the flowers are springing everywhere in the moss," they were "here on the ice with nothing but rocks & snow & ice in any direction when it is possible to see anything at all! And Heaven only knows how much longer we must remain just where we are. We are in mid-winter here, and one day's tramp would take us into summer!" The tedium was slightly relieved when Harper spotted a blackbird flying across the glacier over their tent. "Just think of a bird being up here at an altitude of twelve thousand feet," he wrote.

Finally, on May 21 they had a beautiful clear day. Karstens and Harper worked on the ridge all day, advancing about a hundred yards beyond their previous farthest before turning back. Harper wrote, "the sky was clear and the clouds managed to keep off the ridge till we were finished. But Oh! How hard the work was of clearing the steps. It took us six solid hours to make one mile." They reached camp about seven that evening, and by eight the mist had slammed down again, and once again snow fell. They all felt weaker after the days tentbound. Stuck "found myself so short of breath this morning & so dizzy upon slight exertion that I spent the day marching up and down a promenade of 35 paces or so." Although he considered himself to be "of no help up above, where only two can work at the step cutting," he could at least work on his fitness while in camp. That same day they were amazed to see and hear a "flock of tiny little black birds . . . What are they? whence come? whither bound?" Stuck wondered.

The day's success made the next day even more disheartening. Shut down by mist and snow, Stuck, Karstens, Tatum, and Harper were tentbound once again. "Walter & Harry constructed a checker-board & have spent some time playing games," Stuck wrote. "I have been out tramping up & down my promenade for exercise in which Tatum joined, whenever the wind dropped & the sun shone." They learned a lesson about digestion and diet at altitude when a pot of beans gave them all diarrhea and made Tatum vomit. "No more beans for us." Tatum's condition was also a concern. Stuck wrote, "K. & I have been uneasy about T. for a week and tonight we had a plain talk with him, offering to take him down to the base camp. But he feels strongly that it is just the altitude that is affecting him & wants to go up. It will be a dreadful business if he gets sick up there & may knock the expedition out." Tatum recorded that "Mr. K & Archd. asked me if I felt that I were able to make the top or return to the base camp. I hope to go up if possible." Meanwhile, "I have thought of Kenneth much today. Have thought of Mildred today and wish her much happiness on this her 23rd birthday." Karstens, as always, was terse and decisive: "Laid up Tatums illness to much confinement needs more exercise."

On May 23, though the Northeast Ridge was still shrouded in mist, Stuck suggested to Karstens that they take loads up to the flat place on the ridge where they had proposed moving the camp. Karstens, tired of inaction, accepted immediately, and the four set out at 11:30. Soon, however, as snow began falling "as heavily as I ever saw it," Stuck realized he could not lug his forty- or fifty-pound pack up the ridge. In their desperation to make progress, all of them had taken on heavy packs; according to Stuck, "even Karstens, who had packed his 'hundred and a quarter' day after day over the Chilkoot Pass in 1897, admitted that he was 'heavy.'" They were back at their tent by noon.

The next day, with better weather, went more smoothly. Wisely dividing the loads in two, the four left the tent at 8:15. In two hours they were on the ridge; two and a half more brought them to the cache. At the new campsite they dug out snow and pitched their 7 × 6 tent, securing it with a wall of snow blocks. Then they returned to the cache and brought a second load, so that all the gear was there except their bedding. Stuck wrote, "the new camp is just 1500 ft. above the old one: so that it stands at about 13,000 ft. All day the great cloud masses have poured over from the coast, but they seem to be condensing into cumulus clouds spreading over all the Tanana Valley & probably the Yukon." They were summer clouds; even as they climbed in the wintry landscape of Denali, the season was turning.

Stuck marked the day's events by switching to a smaller pocket diary for the rest of the climb. "Please God this is the last entry I shall make in this diary until we come down from the top of the mountain or definitely fail to reach it." Harper was determined. "Tomorrow," he wrote, "we will come up to it rain or shine."

No one bothered to record the weather the next morning, perhaps because they were eager to finally leave the Muldrow behind for their new campsite on the ridge. In his small notebook Stuck wrote, "having said Morning Prayer, Walter reading the first and Tatum the second lesson, we made up our packs & left the glacier camp for good." It was tough going for the fifty-year-old; the day before, there were pauses to clear the steps, but now they trekked on along the ridge without interruption—except when Stuck had to call a halt himself to regain his breath. They reached the tent by 10:45, and by 1 o'clock had eaten lunch. Stuck read his instruments and "boiled the thermometer" and judged their altitude to be about 13,150 ft. (In the 1950s, Bradford Washburn, alpinist and geographer who would become famous for his black-and-white photographs of Denali, established that the campsite was actually at 12,100 feet.) He recorded the temperature at 2:30 P.M. in direct sunshine: 35 degrees.

Stuck decided that they should have moved a week or ten days before, and believed that Karstens agreed. Stuck considered it "certainly the hardest work I ever did in my life, & my breath up here, under any exertion whaever, is terribly short." Karstens and Harper returned to camp about 4:00; they now hoped that tomorrow they would reach the cleavage where the earthquake damage on the ridge ended, "so our spirits are high tonight & the little tent is comfortable," Stuck wrote. Harper felt "a great deal of pleasure and satisfaction that we won't have to come down the old ridge which we were all tired of, and I specially for I am at the head always cleaning out the steps. I think I know every step of the way nearly." Karstens described the work chopping steps as "rather trying Very slow work & requires patience. caul a little nearer tonight."

The team found the new camp to be actually warmer than the lower one on the morning of May 26. "Apart from the abominable overcrowding . . . we were not uncomfortable, though no one slept much," Stuck noted. He pointed out that the sun hit the tent almost 2½ hours earlier than it had down below, and that cooking took longer, both because of the altitude and because they had left the larger pots down below. Because Karstens was not feeling well, Tatum took a rare turn chopping steps with Harper. The two were hidden by pinnacles and ice-shoulders from the rest below. There was little sun. The two returned at 6:30 having made progress but not as far as the earthquake cleavage, as hoped. Harper wrote, "I wanted to go on, no matter how late it was but Mr. Tatum got cold and so we turned." Karstens believed they would make the cleavage the next day, "though some of our worst climb before us."

They woke the next day to find the inside of the tent coated with frost from their breath, and a strong wind which shook the tent showered the frost all over their bedding and faces. Salt was getting very short—sixteen spoonfuls, according to Stuck. None of them had slept, except Harper, Stuck wrote, "I think none of us slept much save Walter who always sleeps. I envy that boy his splendid rugged strength and adaptability."

Stuck wrote at length in his journal that day about Karstens's state of mind:

> K's indisposition yesterday was mental rather than
> physical; the tedium of the undertaking is wearing
> on him & I seem to get upon his nerves particularly.
> For his sake as much as for my own I long for a speedy

conclusion of this ascent—but I want a successful one. So, to do him justice, does he, in quite equal measure. We are so situated that we must all stay together. One could not leave the party & return. But I think K. will never really give up as long as there is the slightest chance of success. He has that sort of dogged determination. But he is inured to putting the slightest restraint upon himself & the constant effort frets him.

Harper and Karstens had left the tent that morning around 8:30. At 11:00, Tatum, who was outside, called to Stuck that he could see the two men near the cleavage, but "before I could get out of the tent the whole ridge was obscured again—& so it goes." Back in the tent, Stuck was laying out chapters for his Denali book. "I think I shall permit myself digressions and excursions and let the thing be more frankly personal than my previous book—though some may think that personal enough." He had decided to dedicate it to Sir Martin Conway, "whose mountain-climbing books first excited my desire to head to the heights." Then he caught himself. "But—good heavens! here I am publishing & dedicating & the mountain to climb yet!"

At 4:00 Stuck left the tent for snow to melt. Glancing up at the ridge, he had a clear view of Karstens on the unbroken snow above the cleavage. "I gave a great hallo! which they heard and answered. I stood & watched while Walter went up also," then clouds returned and obscured his view. "This is the best thing I have been able to record for three weeks. It means that we can now advance to the basin, and gives new and invigorated hope of reaching the summit." Harper reported finding Parker and Browne's camp, "which looked as though it had been left yesterday. There were empty cracker boxes and raisin boxes." It was the first trace of the Browne-Parker expedition that they had seen. Karstens that night wrote, "We have practly conquered ridge to caul though we chopped our way over & around some very dangerous places I have not slept for two nights."

Tatum continued to struggle emotionally.

> I dreamed last night that we were living at 400 East Main Ave and Papa died. I was sitting in the sitting room & Bertha came & kissed me—or rather it's equivalent, in my dream—and after that I was alright. I cried also in my sleep, Walter said. And I feel very blue and ill at ease today Mr. K & W. have gone up the ridge today and Archd. & I are staying in camp It is rather clear on the ridge today but cloudy on the glacier I am reading Papas letter over today and feel rather homesick . . . I rather fear climbing the ridge with A.d. but will as it is my duty.

The following morning of May 28, Karstens and Harper started out at 8:00, followed at 9:30 by Stuck and Tatum, who continued to feel "very blue and ill-at-ease also nervous." They each hauled a pack of supplies almost to the cleavage. "My breath was awfully short & it took us 2¼ hrs. to make it," Stuck wrote. "We cached the grub as best we could on the very crest of a snow ridge just before a sensational traverse around ice-cliffs that leads to the bold cleft face of the ridge." The weather grew worse and canceled their plan to take another load up the ridge. While making lunch back in the tent, Tatum was cleaning the primus stove when he broke off a wire in the hole "whence the vapour issues." Without the stove the party could not have cooked food or dried clothes. According to Tatum, "Archd. was very much upset and I would have been to blame for the party's either delay or not reaching the top had such have happened. A.d. would not let me touch the stove after words." Unable to fix it, Stuck and Tatum sat shivering until a little after four, when the others returned and "Harry set to work at once to make a tool wherewith to unscrew the little tiny burner in which lay the broken wire." Karstens, "with his usual ingenuity," filed down the spoon from Stuck's pipe cleaner tool and was able to unscrew the burner and extracted the wire.

The mood was tense the next day as the team prepared for another push. "Mr. K dreadfully displeased about something," Tatum noticed, as did Stuck, who was perturbed that Harper and Karstens had not left early, during the clearest part of the day before the clouds and snow moved in. But "things are at such a pass however that I can hardly say anything. K's nerves are on their raw edge. I long for the conclusion of the enterprise, but it is not in sight yet, and I will put up with almost anything for a successful conclusion." Tatum unknowingly echoed Stuck, writing, "Every body A.d. & all are wishing it were all at an end but guess we will stick it out to the end . . . It makes me feel very blue when I think that it might take us until June 15th or after to reach the top. Have been thinking much of home and friends and will be very glad indeed to get some mail."

After lunch Stuck and Tatum took two loads to the cache just below the cleavage. Stuck again had to make frequent stops, but felt less distress than the day before. He took both the large aneroid and the mercurial barometer up to the cache, and reported that the aneroid showed a rise of 850 ft from the lower camp. Karstens and Harper had decided to pitch the next camp where Parker had, and Stuck gave Karstens the aneroid altimeter to take up to the new site. It showed the new camp to be at 17,200 feet. "I cannot reconcile this with Parker's 15,150 ft . . . I shall be curious to read the mercurial thermometer there." (Bradford Washburn placed this camp at 14,600 feet.)

Walter Harper found the distances among the vast peaks, valleys, and glaciers to be deceptive—"the comb which lay between us and the col seemed endless to me going up over it." Stuck noted another bird sighting, as "K. & W. report seeing a little bird (a swift?) between 14000 & 15000 ft, flying towards the basin. It is interesting to know that birds fly at this altitude." The group planned to move loads, and perhaps themselves, to the new upper camp the next day. Harper wrote, "We are all happier tonight than we have been for three weeks just because we reached the col."

The next day, May 30, marked four weeks since the tent fire. Stuck headed his journal entry "Camp at the Parker Col" and wrote, "today has seen what to me is the most important advance since we began the ascent of the mountain." They were camped at the Parker Col looking into the high basin between the two peaks. "We are perched amongst some granite slabs on the most conspicuous coigne [corner or angle] of vantage that I ever occupied in my life; higher than I have ever been in my life, with an uninterrupted view over more than half the compass, and I look forward with keen pleasure to the prospect that shall open when the clouds clear away."

The group had waited until 10:15 to start, due to signs of high wind on the ridge. Once they were over the cleavage, Stuck endured "the steepest longest climb over one continuous snow slope that I ever made in my life." He merely had to follow the steps already cut by Karstens and Harper, "but oh! how short my wind was and at times what a violent construction [sic] in my chest!" He hoped that the others would bring up the rest of the stash themselves: "I would give a good deal not to have to climb that ridge again & I am cherishing a hope that my companions will be so kind as to relieve me of that necessity." His fear of not being able to summit had returned with the exertion. "It is terribly distressing to my wind. At times I was near choking."

They had reached the Parker Col at 3:15, after five hours' climbing. "On the one hand," Stuck wrote, "we look into the basin where the much crevassed and broken glacier tumbles down, and on the other the prospect opens wide over all the foothills and the orography of the wide region." They were camped in the spot that Parker and Browne had chosen, and found a shovel they had left behind. "The great granite slabs afford a shelter & the sun must shine long hours (when it shines at all) upon this spot. This evening there is nothing visible but a sea of great clouds stretching as far as the eye can see." Stuck also noted, "It takes rice 50 minutes to cook at this altitude." Though low on bread, "the pemmican & erbswurst [German pea soup] make a substantial meal & thickened with rice satisfies us all—except Walter—who is hard to satisfy without plenty of solid substantial food. We have food for a couple of weeks with care, &, please God, shall not need half of it."

After almost three weeks, the team had fought their way through the upheaval of the quake-wrecked ridge. It can be argued that the successful ascent of the Northeast Ridge in 1913 was a unique achievement in the history of mountaineering. A year before, the ridge had given Belmore & Browne unhindered access to the summit slopes. By the time the next party attempted to reach the top of Denali, in 1932, time and the primal forces of wind, water, and gravity would have smoothed the edges, filled the ravines, and largely returned the ridge to its former condition. Only Karstens, Harper, Stuck, and Tatum would ever have the distinction of climbing the Northeast Ridge—which would be renamed, at Stuck's suggestion, Karstens Ridge—in the conditions of that May.

Now, although Karstens noted that the "least exertion causes heavy breathing," he was confident: "it seems to be an easy climb from 17000 ft. level."

13

A PRIVILEGED COMMUNION

Seven or eight camps are normally made in the course of ascending the Muldrow Glacier route. Parties prepared for high winds and a spectacular view sometimes camp at the base of Browne Tower (14,600 feet), while those preferring a secure night's sleep camp in the lower basin of the Harper Glacier at the 15,000-foot level.

—Mt. McKinley Climbing Guide

L ast night was a wretched night, one of the most miserable I ever spent in my life," Stuck wrote on May 31 from their new camp at the base of Browne Tower. They had left the caribou skins down below, to save weight, so the canvas and bedding were laid directly on the snow. "I was never warm all the night through and did not sleep at all . . . My breath troubled me somewhat also—as is the case more or less with all of us." Tatum had awakened with rheumatism in his left hand, but had insisted on going down with Harper to bring a load from the cache, in order to spare Stuck the trip. When Harper started up from the cache, "I had so much on my back that I had to make a head band to help my back."

About 10:00 that morning, Karstens and Stuck left camp to "make the traverse around the cliffs of the N.E. ridge to enter the basin" in order to find their next camp site, in the basin. Stuck's fingers grew numb as Karstens cut steps in the ice. When Stuck took over, "it grew warm and presently the sun came out from the smother which filled the basin and gave us a glimpse of the final ridge." Making their way into the basin, they chose a campsite about 800 feet higher than the Col camp, on the level ice of the upper glacier at around 15,000 feet, and returned to camp. "It is an 'easy traverse' as Browne describes it," Stuck wrote, "nearly all snow."

The team of climbers had decided to name the pinnacle of rock just above the pass onto the Grand Basin Browne Tower, and the pass itself Parker Pass. Stuck believed their names "should be permanently associated with this mountain they were so nearly successful in climbing."[1]

From the granite blocks of Browne Tower move up and right, north, through Parker Pass—the name Hudson Stuck gave the broad gateway to the stepped basins of the Harper Glacier—and find a passage through the first icefall at 16,000 feet (4,877 meters) along its right margin. Continue upward through the second icefall at 17,000 feet (5,182 meters). Once through the second series of ice blocks, continue in a southwesterly direction toward the prominent notch in the skyline, Denali Pass.
—Mt. McKinley Climbing Guide

On June 1 the team followed their typical Sunday routine, with Stuck leading the Episcopal church service. "We said Morning Prayer, and Tatum & Walter read the epistle and gospel for the 2nd Sunday after Trinity & I spoke a few words to them about St John the Divine, whose characteristic message the epistle carries, 'Love one another.'" Stuck felt rested and energetic. "I slept better than I have for a long time. What a difference a comfortable bed makes!" With all the bedding now brought up from the lower camp, Stuck could approvingly describe their sleeping arrangements: "At night it is always cold . . . But we always slept warm; with sheep-skins and caribou-skins under us, and down quilts and camel's-hair blankets and a wolf-robe for bedding, the four of lay in that six-by-seven tent, in one bed, snug and comfortable."

After the service, Tatum and Harper made their final descent down the Northeast Ridge for the rest of the supplies. Heading back up, according to Harper, "the wind was so strong that in several places on the narrow ridge I nearly lost my balance with the heavy pack on my back." With sheer drops on either side, a fall would have been fatal. Karstens and Stuck again moved packs up to the next camp on the upper glacier.

In the afternoon the other three took loads up while Stuck stayed behind to set up the barometer, for which he needed the tent to himself. Its readings convinced him that Parker's altitude of 15,150' was in fact accurate. "The aneroid itself is a poor dependence." The others returned by 4:00, so cold and battered by the icy wind that it was decided to wait until the next day to move camp. In the tent that night, Harper wrote, "while we were having our evening service it was so cold that had to ware our parkas." Tatum described how, around 8:00, "it began to clear off in the south and we saw the Alaskan range spread out like a great map before us."

Stuck, meanwhile, took stock of their position. "We are not as mobile as the Parker-Brown party. We have more comforts & conveniences with us, and more instruments, and that means more to pack." Parker and Browne, on the other hand, "were too mobile. They had not food enough to wait their chance of good weather." He predicted, "Probably two relays will move us on the basin." He summed up:

> The prize of this capital first ascent seems now within our grasp. Two more camp removes, and then a good day for the final dash are all that lie between us and our heart's desire. Pray God nothing intervenes to dash the cup from our lips at the eleventh hour, as happened to Parker & Brown. The difficult hard work is behind us and the way seems clear to the

summit. Our spirits are high . . . but a spell of very
bad weather could yet destroy our hopes.

∽

The next day, June 2, did nothing to dampen those spirits. Stuck
at the top of his journal wrote "Camp in Basin {Brightest day
in three weeks} {Cold Wind at intervals}" then noted, "This
promises to be the finest day in three weeks." For the first time
they could see the South Peak, their goal, with no cloud cover,
"and it looks, once more, like fair weather." Stuck took photos
before they left for the new camp, and Harper took one of Stuck.
Stuck's pack, now once again including the barometer, was "a
formidable burden & I had a great fight for my breath" as the
party crossed the basin. At 11:30 they reached the spot for
the new camp and had lunch. At 2:00 Harper and Karstens
headed up the basin. Harper wrote, "we used the creepers for the
first time on this trip . . . We made a good time on them on
the hard snow crest and we went up to seventeen thousand feet.
We saw Parker and Browne's tracks up one of the slopes which
had been tramped one year ago." Stuck and Tatum built a wall
of snow blocks and organized the food, while Tatum wanted
to talk of the future. "Arch deacon & I have had a pleasant talk
this afternoon and has offered to send me some books of refer-
ance if he gathers resources from any lectures he also promised
me a dictionary regardles of proccess of this trip which I shall
be thankful to have." Stuck believed that the team could "stick
it out two weeks & perhaps longer if we are economical." None
of them wants to be that long, however; they already found it

difficult to get their feet warm at that altitude, and "one fears that above the cold will be still more formidable. It is the fierce wind that ever and anon sweeps down from the heights, that is so bitter." Though impatient to finish the expedition, Stuck took time to appreciate their surroundings. "The view is most striking & extensive looking down from our camp. The glacier seems smoothly continuous with the Muldrow below, & no one would dream that there is an almost perpendicular drop of 4000 ft between the two."

Like Tatum, Stuck was also looking ahead. "If K. & Walter are successful today in placing our next (and, I hope, final) camp, and we can get moved to it in two relays tomorrow, it may be possible that we make our final climb on Wednesday," he wrote. "It makes one's heart beat high to think so. God send!—for I am much overstayed on this enterprise already & impatient to be at my work on the Yukon again."

The advance party returned about 5:45 having found a suitable spot for the next camp, though contrary to Stuck's hopes, Karstens thought one more would be needed before the summit. Stuck wrote, "With the continuous advance of the last week has grown a much better feeling amongst all the members of the party. There is no more of that irritability of temper which marked the tedium & suspense of the last glacier camp. Thank God for that."

∽

June 3 garnered a string of headings in Stuck's journal: "First Camp in the Upper Basin," "Second Basin Camp," "Bright Clear

Day," "bitter wind," "Fierce wind all last night," and "min.-10."
It was a day of further progress—and of a historic discovery.

The foursome took the tent, bedding, and supplies and pitched
a new camp about a mile and a half further up the glacier. Even
though Stuck carried only his instruments and the mercurial
barometer, "I had to call for such continual halts that K. insists I
pack nothing any more. My breath is so astonishingly short that
I pant and choke every half dozen steps. So hereafter I am to go
along without any loads." He later wrote in *Ascent of Denali*, "It
was some mortification not to be able to do one's share of the
packing, but there was no help for it, and the other shoulders
were young and strong and kindly."[2] After gaining about five
hundred feet of elevation and crossing to the right side of the
upper glacier, they decided to stop due to cold. Harper wrote, "For
the first time on this trip I suffered with my feet. They were so
cold that I thought they were going to freeze."

While resting, they began talking of the Sourdoughs, and
the flagstaff that Anderson and Taylor claimed to have planted
on the North Peak two years before. Stuck then recalled that
"much discredit has been thrown on their exploit, largely due
to the foolish conduct of the men themselves, & the thing is
very generally disbelieved." Suddenly, Harper pointed toward
the North Peak and cried, "I see the flag-pole!" Karstens then
saw it, and using the binoculars, each of them had a look at the
fourteen-foot pole. Stuck wrote, "It has weathered the storms
of three years, & I am very much pleased indeed to be able to
carry down confirmation of the exploit of Taylor & Anderson
(not Lloyd)." The team had actually discussed climbing the
North Summit after the South, if possible, "in order to verify

or disprove the planting of the pole. This will not now be necessary; all four of us have seen the staff still standing." Karstens's description of the event was terser: "'Hurrah' everyone sees flag staf on North Peak perfectly clear through glasses." He had vindicated his partner McGonagall.

After they made camp, Stuck stayed in the tent while the others went back down to shuttle their gear. Oil from the primus stove had leaked onto Karstens's sweater, saturating it, so Stuck washed it. The party returned at 5:40 and contemplated the next day, when Karstens and Harper would climb ahead for the next camp. "This thing draws near completion; if the weather holds we should reach the summit this week."

∽

The next day, June 4, Stuck's journal headline was "Bright Clear Day Fearfully Hot." Altitude and weather were draining all four of the men on the upper glacier. Stuck's thermometer at 3 P.M. read 50°—"the highest temperature of the whole excursion." Karstens that evening wrote, "Fine Clear Sunshinie day to hot to work 'O' it was torture in sun sat in shade of Ice block to cool off." He and Harper started at 8:00; the other two followed an hour later, Tatum with "a good load," Stuck with "nothing but the barometer which we arranged last night with a ruck-sack hitch. But in the hot sun I found the going very exhausting." Sleepless the night before, waking with a headache, Stuck also was nauseous, as was the rest of the party—thanks to Harper, who had dumped brine from a can of butter into the breakfast stew and "nauseated us with the extreme salinity." By this time, over a month since the tent fire, Stuck wrote, "We were burned as brown as Indians; lips and noses split and peeled in spite of continual applications of lanoline."

After reaching the top of the first icefall on the upper glacier, and taking photographs, Stuck "found myself so distressed for breath & so exhausted that I cached the barometer & said we must go back." He and Tatum returned to the tent, where Tatum had been making an American flag to hoist at the summit, while Stuck worked on a cross to erect there. Now, though, Stuck began "walking around & around the camp, for I will not go in and lie down." Within sight of his long-held goal, he was confronting a disturbing possibility. "I have realized for the last two days that there is quite a chance that it may be a physical impossibility for me to reach the top of this mountain—I remember Mr. Edwin [sic] Fitzgerald & Aconcagua." (In 1897, Edward FitzGerald, an American who had made first ascents in New Zealand, organized an attempt to summit South America's highest peak, but six times became too nauseated to continue to the top.)[3] "K. says I shall get to the top if he has to pack me. But I have felt so unwell today at 17,000 ft, that I do not know if I can possibly reach 20,000."

Karstens & Harper returned by 3:30 having reached what they believed was 18,000 feet (actually 16,800), where they proposed to put the next camp. This was higher than the Parker-Browne party's highest camp, but according to Stuck, "K. thinks nothing could have induced Parker's party to attempt the climb without another camp-remove except the shortage of grub." Karstens also felt much more certain of reaching the top from a thousand feet higher up on the glacier. "I dread the remove to the next camp, with its steep serac climbing, as much as the final ascent," Stuck confided to his journal. "Walter is sick tonight; the heat & the altitude together and his stomach on top of all, have knocked him out. He has done me yeoman's service."

Karstens noted that night, "Deacon having hard time breathing but we will get him there somehow."

∾

June 5 offered the climbers the gamut of high-altitude weather. The day began clear, and became intensely hot, then quickly became overcast. At 11:00 A.M. a heavy snowstorm raged, obliterating visibility and forcing them to make camp and have lunch. By 2 P.M. it was clear and intensely hot once again; and 5:30 brought yet more snow.

Karstens & Harper had left about 8:30, and Tatum and Stuck followed a half-hour later, Stuck carrying nothing, planning to pick up the cached barometer on the way up. He felt much better without his pack, even carrying the barometer easily, "without any of those blind smothering spells that alarmed me yesterday." They climbed the first icefall and traversed a long, almost level flat, scattered over with ice-blocks. Stuck called their view of "the abrupt final rise of the mountain to its South point, the glacier basin shattered by the earthquake," very impressive. He would use his description of the Northwest Ridge, ascending to the lower North Peak, almost word for word in *Ascending Denali:* "The great granite ramparts holding in place the final ridge-crests of black shale, swell out into the bellying buttresses with snow slope hollows between as they approach the glacier floor."

The overcast began as Stuck and Taum began climbing the second icefall. Karstens and Harper had stopped when the cloud descended, and when the other two arrived, stopped and made camp. The four ate lunch, and while Stuck wrote in his journal, "the sun came out hot again, & we were all simultaneously over-taken with heavy drowsiness, and slept a little." Then three went down to fetch gear while Stuck stayed behind to tend camp and cook some obstinate bacon, which had "boiled 3 hours already & is not done, though cut in small pieces." Karstens, Stuck noted, "has become very considerate to me now, as he recognizes that it is a simple physical impossibility for me to pack anything any further, and that there is some question whether I may be able to get myself to the top of the mountain." If allowed to go slowly, with rests every few slow steps, "I believe I can do it, but I am not sure. And if those blind choking spells come on me as they did yesterday & the day before, I may be unable to proceed at all."

Stuck pondered the effects of tobacco on his breathing:

> Ever since the last week in the last glacier camp I have smoked but two pipes a day; one in the morning & one after supper. Yesterday I stopped smoking alto-gether, hoping that my wind may be improved. I daresay my poor wind may be due in some measure to the heavy smoking of the last 20 years; though I don't know. Tatum's wind is poor also, though he has never smoked. Perhaps Walter has the best wind, perhaps K. Walter has never smoked; K. is a steady

smoker. All of them are in the prime of their health &
strength; Walter & Tatum about 21, K. about 31; but
I am in my 50th year. That must make a difference.

The other three were back about 4:00, and attempted to pass
the camp and move gear to the top of the serac, or even to the next
camp site. Rapidly deteriorating weather, however, sent them back
down. Stuck noted that he was unable to take readings, as the
instruments had been taken up, "but we regard this as a supernu-
merary camp anyway & tomorrow's camp as the important one."

Remarkably, Karstens reported, "Can see Parker Browne
route up ridge very plain following their description the Granit
slabs along ridge & last rock where they left thermometer." Reaf-
firming his choice of another camp, he wrote, "Their last camp
may look good to them but the next basin above looks better
to me 1000 ft. less climb at the final accent means a great deal
in this changable climate." Furthermore, "if they were camped
where we will make our climb from they would have made it.
Good luck to us in our final attempt."

૭૦

June 6th "Bright clear morning with wind in the N.
    Dense clouds below; all clear above.
    Intensely hot in sun.
    Last Camp of Expedition
    at about 18,000 ft.
    corrected mercurial thermometer 15.061"
                                        —Stuck's journal

Karstens and Harper left first that morning, with Tatum and Stuck following a few minutes later. All of them bore heavy loads except Stuck, who carried only his barometer, "& found it quite enough." Winding their way along the right side of the upper glacier at the base of the North Peak, they reached their last camp before the summit. Stuck congratulated Karstens on pitching the highest camp ever pitched on the North American continent.

After lunch Stuck stayed in the tent, finishing the inscription on the cross for the summit while the others went down to yesterday's cache for the rest of their supplies. When they returned Stuck set up the instruments "& I boiled the hyp. thermometer and afterwards set up the mercurial thermometer in the little tent made for it & read it." He was convinced they were above 18,000 feet, though Washburn would judge it to be around 17,500 feet.

They now planned to get up around midnight and head for the summit soon after. Karstens told them that if necessary he would put another camp on the summit ridge itself. "But all we need is one fine day now," Stuck wrote, "& the indications are that we shall get it, though we are trying not to be too confident, remembering how suddenly weather changes here." They had food for ten or twelve days—two weeks if need be, "but the little extra things like the chocolate & the sugared almonds, the figs & the raisins are very low." The only bread left was a few packages of zweibach, which was reserved for lunch on the mountain. In addition, "We boil a lot of flour paste in the stew and call it 'noodles,' but it is an heavy and I fear indigestible compound." The next day, his fears would prove correct.

Tatum was moved to eloquence that evening by the views from their camp. It "is located by a great bolder of ice and the scenery is most superb. To the south of us rises the great south summit of South Peak and by looking out our tent door we see the great Alaskan range spread like a map before us," he wrote, echoing his description of five days before. "The North peak also rises sheer up thousands of feet directly north of us and back of our tent rises another serac some 600 feet after which continues a smoothe snow slope that ends abruptly and Denali's children rise in all their majesty beyond."

Karstens that night wrote, "Weather fine. Moved all our camp to over 18000 ft. level the highest camp in America a weeks grub & good bedding will try Mt. tomorrow. around 2500 feet to climb." For the third straight day, Walter Harper left his journal blank.

❧

At the 18,320-foot (5,584-meter) pass . . . turn left and ascend the ridge that fishhooks to the southeast to reach the 20,320-foot (6,194-meter) South Summit.
—Mt. McKinley Climbing Guide

❧

"Saturday 7th June 1913—I remember no day in my life more full of distressing toil and exhaustion," Hudson Stuck wrote in his pocket diary. "I had no sleep all night and at 4 o'clock, when we sallied out, I had an headache in addition to the malaise upon any exertion due to the great altitude. But yet this 7th June will always be a red letter day in my life, for we reached the summit of Denali."

The day dawned brilliant and cloudless. After enduring eight weeks of bitter cold, severe altitude, and the loss of supplies to a camp fire, Stuck and his group had arrived here the night before. The camp lay within reach of the summit slope, 17,500 feet above sea level, but still three thousand feet below the peak. On this clear, windy, 4°-below day, they were so close. But would Stuck be among those standing at the top?

Only Walter Harper felt well that day, avoiding the stomach-aches that plagued the other three, most likely from the "noodles," as Stuck foresaw. Nor had they slept well. Karstens: "Everyone out of condition on last night & no one slept we tried from 7 to 10 but no go so we all sat around primus stove with quilts on our backs waiting for 4 Oclock." Even the tough Sourdough claimed, "If it where not the final climb I should have stayed in camp but being the final climb & such a promising day I managed to pull through." Even in the sun, a biting north wind kept the temperature below zero; all the climbers' toes felt frozen, Stuck's lynx mitts failed to keep his hands warm. Karstens had no doubt who should be, as climbers say, on the sharp end of the rope; "I put Walter in lead an kept him there all day with never a change. I took 2nd place on rope so I could direct Walter and he worked all day without a murmur."

"We took right up the enormous steep snow ridge rising S. of our camp and then around the peak into which it rises; both ridge & peak showing signs of earthquake cleavage," Stuck wrote. Although they were "somewhat feeble folk," they were determined to continue. "When we had rounded the N. summit of the S. peak, taking it well up, it had been so broken lower down by the earthquake, we came to the horseshoe curved ridge which is Denali's culmination."

Attaining a small plateau at 18,700 feet, they would at some point have crossed the path taken by Browne and Parker. "Here the climbing grew steeper & steeper," Stuck wrote; it was obvious to them that they were higher than the North Peak. Above them now stretched "another ridge with a couple of little snow summits. This is the real top of Denali. It is a little basin about 60 or 65 feet long by 20 or 30 wide with a short peak or turret at each end, the S. one being the higher."

Finding a respite on the south side of the mountain from the wind, the four men stopped for a lunch of hard, crusty zweiback bread, along with scalding hot tea made that morning on their kerosene stove and poured into thermos bottles. From here the climbing would grow steeper, seeming to Stuck to shoot straight up. Beyond lay a ridge with two small summits.

According to Stuck, not until then "did we all begin to have confidence that this day would see the completion of the ascent." But for Stuck, breathing became harder still as they rose. He would struggle upward twenty or thirty steps, and then "sink gasping in the snow again." Carrying no pack, reliant on the others, the man who had organized the expedition would have to count on them to finish the job.

Reaching at last the basin at the top, they saw "stretched ahead of us, and perhaps one hundred feet above us, another small ridge with a north and south pair of little haycock summits. This is the real top of Denali."

Walter Harper led the four across the basin, and up the ridge. Suddenly, finally, they were on Denali's highest point.

In Stuck's words, "Walter, who had been in the lead all day, was the first to scramble up; a native Alaskan, he is the first human being to set foot upon the top of Alaska's great mountain, and he had well earned the lifelong distinction."

Harper would wrote in his journal for June 7, 1913,

> Mr. K. had a headache and Tatum had another and the Archdeacon could not move without losing his breath and our spirits were all pretty low, for we knew what a tremindous task it was to get to the top and back in one day . . . It was one o'clock when we got to the top. I was ahead all day and was the first ever to set foot on Mt. Denali.

Karstens & Tatum were quick behind him, Stuck wrote, "but I had almost to be hauled, puffing & panting into the hitherto secret place of the greatest mountain of the continent." (Interestingly, Tatum would write, "Walter reached the top first Mr. K next Archd. third & I last.") Whatever the order, they were now, all four of them, above everything. "For awhile," Stuck wrote, "I could do nothing but pant, then presently I gathered the others and said a short prayer of thanksgiving." Then the four carried out their scientific measurements. "The little tent was pitched, the mercurial barometer set up & the boiling point thermometer set going." Tatum took angles with his prismatic compass, trying to take bearings of prominent features. The little silk American flag that Tatum had made from two silk handerchiefs and the cover of a sewing bag, with thirteen stars and thirteen stripes, was hoisted using a tent pole & photographed. Then Harper and Karstens made the cross, lashing the cross piece inscribed by Stuck to the upright and planting it in the snow. Around it, they said the *Te Deum*, the ancient Latin psalm: "We praise Thee, O God; Heaven and earth are full of the majesty of Thy Glory."

They took photographs, though haze prevented them seeing much of what was below. "Only the mountain maze in infinite complexity to the South and East stood out with dazzling distinctness, revealing their glaciations, their whole drainage system, and the great crescent sweep of the Alaskan Range for at least 200 miles," Stuck reported. They photographed Menlale, "Denali's wife," Mount Foraker, the second largest of the Alaskan Range, in dramatic misty shadow. It was too cold to linger, though, too frigid even to change the film in the camera. As a result of the difficulties caused by the cold, the images of the party on the summit were double- and triple-exposed. A ghostly Tatum holds the flagpole, like a golf caddy; indeterminate figures stand on a blank white plain against a blank grey background, around three repetitions of a small cross.

∽

After an hour and a half, they started down. Stuck described his emotions in *Ascent of Denali*:

There was no pride of conquest . . . no gloating over good fortune that had hoisted us a few hundred feet higher than others who had struggled and been discomfited. Rather was the feeling that a privileged communion with the high places of the earth had been granted.

The group decided to detour on the descent, looking for Professor Parker's thermometer, which he had left in a crack of the Western side of the last granite boulder of the ridge; "not stopping to think that this whole ridge bore the brunt of the earthquake last July," as Stuck said. They took the opportunity to collect some granite from the exposed rock of the ridge for souvenirs. The four were back at the 17,500-foot camp by 5:00, after thirteen hours' climbing. In his laconic Sourdough style, Karstens's response to the day in his journal was "Hurrah. The south summit of McKinley [note that Karstens did not call it "Denali"] has been conquered."

Tatum wrote, "Today stands a big red letter in my life as our party of four Hudson Stuck Harry Phillipp Karstens Walter Harper & my self reached the summit of Mount McKinley (Denallis) some 20600 feet above the sea level the highest mountain on the N. American continent." He was "Very tired but happy and expect to move back downward tomorrow." As he had done throughout his time on the mountain, "I thought of those at home and would have reread papas letter on top had it not have been so cold."

Tatum would later say, "It was like looking out of a window of heaven."

∾

As for Stuck, after considering the merits of various methods of glacier travel ("we have never had a slip with step cutting . . . but the creepers are much quicker") and a tribute to the amber snow glasses ("My eyes are weak; weakened by many Springs of sun on snow & many summers of sun on water while travelling on the Yukon & its tributaries. All kinds of glasses I have tried but none that ever gave the protection these have given") he soberly considered how close he had come to his limits. "My throat is hard and dry and my whole abdomen is sore with my continual panting & I twice lost consciousness for a moment at the end of yesterday's climb. How much further I could have gone I do not know."

∾

The next day, in Harper's words, "We took a last glimpse at the north and south peaks of Mt. Denali and turned our faces toward the lowlands."

After Morning Prayer, all feeling well-rested, they left at 9:30 and descended in the glorious sunshine of the Grand Basin. Stuck gazed around him at "the peaks standing crystal clear against a cloudless sky; the huge fragments of ice from the earthquake shock scattered all over the glacier, white in the sunshine, deep blue in shadow." They passed camp after camp, stopping at the first Grand Basin camp for lunch, then traversed to the Parker Col. There at 1:30 they stopped in the hot sun, lit the Primus stove, and boiled a big pot of tea. Stuck took the opportunity to stash his thermometer among the rocks, with a note stashed in a tin film case and an empty alcohol can with an inscription on it calling attention to the instrument. Stuck thought "it should stand there—the whole cache—for many years," and since the Col was such an obvious campsite, it would probably be eventually discovered.

(In 1932, the Lindley-Liek Expedition attempting the second ascent recovered a glass thermometer mounted in a hinged wooden case. A metal strip on the case was engraved with the words "No 11581 H.J. Green B'klyn, N.Y.," and the word "Stuck" was carved on the outside of the case, which was badly worn on one side.)[4]

There was one more task with regard to the glacier they had just re-crossed. In *Ascent of Denali*, Stuck would write, "Before the reader turns his back upon the Grand Basin once for all . . . I should like put a name upon the glacier it contains . . . I should like to name it the Harper Glacier." He did so not only for Walter, but also for his father Arthur, "the pioneer of all Alaskan miners," who had in 1878 made the first known written reference to Denali (the "great ice mountain to the south," he called it) after Vancouver's in 1794.[5]

Now the four turned from the Great Basin—or the Harper Glacier—and looked south, where the Northeast Ridge loomed before them. By 3:15, they had finished their tea, struggled into their packs, and roped up again. Harper once again relieved Stuck of the mercurial barometer—"I am grateful to the boy for his thoughtfulness and kindness"—and they began what Stuck described as "the difficulty & the danger, the toil and the anxiety" of the return trip down the ridge. Karstens led, followed by Tatum, each carrying forty- or fifty-pounds packs. Stuck was next with a smaller pack, perhaps twenty pounds, then Harper, with a heavy pack made even heavier by the barometer. They found two feet of new snow on the steep ridge above the cleavage, "but with Karstens ahead slowly and carefully descending, and with Walter behind me keeping the rope taut I felt perfectly safe," Stuck wrote.

An hour and a half brought them to the earthquake cleavage, as difficult and dangerous on the descent as it had been a week before on the upward climb. They had to cut out and shovel the steps they had made before, and then "pass most gingerly & carefully to the ice cliffs beyond." By six o'clock they had reached the ridge camp, and by nine they had reached the head of the Muldrow Glacier and their upper-glacier camp at 11,500 feet.

Snowstorms had covered their tent with snow, which the sun had turned to ice. They uncovered and cleaned the tent; then, Stuck wrote, "supper, with actually bread & then after thanksgiving to God, bed, thoroughly tired." He had nothing but praise for the others. "K. led most carefully & skillfully & is become already an accomplished mountaineer. T. & W. both did their full duty & did it handsomely."

⌒

The following day, June 9, was their last on the slopes of Denali. Impatient to be down at base camp, thinking of Johnny, they abandoned much of their gear and loaded the rest on the Yukon sled they had left at the camp. They started out at 10:30 that morning, even though as Stuck wrote, "It had been wiser to have waited until late in the evening." With all four guiding the sled with ropes, they made it easily down the first steep descents of the glacier. Down lower, however, the crevasses began to give them trouble. As on their ascent of the glacier, they were forced to take long detours to find safe passage, though the willows they had used to stake the trail were still standing and useful. Below that, the snow finally ended, and they abandoned the sled.

"When we got up to the pass," Stuck wrote, "we were greeted with the sight of little purple flowers amongst the rocks, & I do not know when any sight pleased me more." Then, however, they were greeted by fierce swarms of mosquitos, Stuck blaming himself for leaving behind the netting—"but we had all expected to be out long ago." Finally they came in sight of the Clearwater base camp, where "a load was lifted from every heart" at finding Fredson there. They were stunned and delighted to find that the fifteen-year-old had, as Karstens recorded, "saved sugar butter & milk & Coffee for us," having seen the fire destroy their rations.

Harper wrote in his journal, "When we got down about halfway to our first glacier camp the smell of the air was some what changed to our nostrels, and we supposed this to be from the green grass and flowers from the lowlands . . . When we got . . . to the base camp [we] found Johnny well and happy, and the dogs rolling fat. It is a wonderful transformation we went through today. This morning we were at the glacier camp in the season of winter and now we are at the base camp in the season of summer."

Karstens had made possible the physical attainment of the summit, leading young Walter Harper and almost dragging the fifty-year-old missionary up the final snow slope. But Hudson Stuck had been the prime mover; without him, the expedition would not have departed Nenana. Karstens had vindicated Mac McGonagall and the Sourdoughs; he had furthered his and Charles Sheldon's agenda of establishing Denali as a national park. Stuck, however, had accomplished what for him was a more transcendant goal.

He had often spoken about his desire to climb Denali, with a party of Alaskans, both Native and white, to win world attention for their cause. He hoped that their historic feat would somehow prevent the ruin of the land and its people by those who would wipe out Alaska's mineral—and cultural—wealth, leaving nothing behind but disease, poverty, and hopelessness. Stuck had seen how "they corrupt the rightful owners of the land," the people who had lived around and among these great mountains for millennia. The Church, Stuck believed, could only bind up the wounds; it was powerless to prevent the injuries.

The archdeacon had carried this message to Washington, D.C., to a President, a Secretary of the Interior, and anyone else in government who would listen. He couldn't tell what impression he had made on these men, but he knew that if he *were* successful, Washington and the entire nation would pay attention.[6]

14

"A LIAR AND A SNEAK"

For the expedition members, June 10 was a full day of what Stuck described as "lying around the base camp, resting & eating & writing," playing with the dogs and gorging on the hot biscuits and coffee that Johnny kept feeding them. While Karstens and Harper fashioned dog-packs for the trip out, Stuck turned to his account of the climb. "For myself, I am burning to write & impatient to be at it continually, turning phrases and descriptions, having for the first time in my life something entirely adequate to write about as I feel now. And I do not want the vividness of the impressions to pass 'ere I deliver myself."

The next day the party left their camp on foot, four of the dogs on leash and carrying packs, and began hiking north. "Again and again we looked back for a parting glimpse of the mountain," wrote Stuck, "but we never saw sign of it any more."[1] Hiking to the McKinley Fork, "with snipe & curlew whistling around us," thunderstorms drenched them, followed by heavy hail, then more rain. After a couple of wet, cold, miserable hours they reached their destination, Tom Lloyd's tent. There they took turns through the night tending a fire to dry out their wet clothes.

On June 12, they crossed the McKinley Fork, a mile-wide stream of rocks, glacial silt, and muddy water. "Because I was wearing mocassins," Stuck wrote, "the only one of the party not in someway dry-shod, Walter was kind enough to take me on his back across the running water." (This would not have improved Karstens's opinion of Stuck.) When they reached the deep main current, Tatum, following Karstens, was pulled into the water by his dogs. Stuck related the story:

> K. heard T.'s yells & hastily returned and found T. scared almost to death & wet through. Walter quickly joined them & it was all the two could do to bring the quaking, knee-trembling T. across. Arrived on the other side he lay and bellowed like a baby. He is a strange mixture of pluck & effeminancy, of cowardice & courage. When he had recovered from his scare, for it was scare pure & simple, we resumed our way, all bedding thoroughly wet again. T. lost his axe that he had carried to the top of the mountain, at the time of his ducking, & he mourns that.

Tatum described in his diary the river crossing "which I had so long dreaded," and the dogs who pulled him over and then "threw me on my back and splashed my face full of water and I lost my breath." Karstens "rushed to me and just before I was about to go under he grabbed my hand and saved me." When he reached shore, Tatum "fell on the ground and wept for thanks. We waited some time for me to gather strength and then traveled on to Eureka."

Through what Stuck described as the "increasing swarming torture" of mosquitos, that evening they reached Jack Hamilton's cabin near Moose Creek. As always, Karstens hit the main points in his diary: "Tatum got ducked in McKinley river Hamilton fed us at Eureka like a prince."

The following day, June 13, they traveled seven hours to Caribou Creek and the home of Joe and Fannie Quigley. Fannie Quigley was famous in the Kantishna, and around Alaska. A 2017 biographical sketch cited her reputation "as not only a renowned hostess and cook, but one of the finest hunters the region had ever seen." The profile continued, "Like the men around her, Quigley drank, swore, and shot bears—but unlike those men, she used her bear lard to create the legendarily flaky crusts of the rhubarb pies she served to her backcountry guests."[2] The arrival of Mac McGonagall that evening must have made for an even more interesting dinner, though the only detail Stuck mentioned about the evening was his conversation with the Sourdough about the 1910 expedition.

The next day brought the team to Glacier and what Karstens described as a "big feed"; they began the last land leg of their return the next morning. At a fish camp on Moose Creek, they loaded packs, dogs and men in a borrowed boat, reaching Diamond City around 8:30 that evening. "Mosquitoes very bad all day," Stuck noted; they spotted "Geese & young: moose & young: beaver: bear: Kingfisher." Tatum was homesick again. "Have been thinking of mama and all the family yesterday & today."

On June 17 they loaded onto the boat that Karstens nicknamed the "Getaway" and began their 300-mile float to Tanana. "Although the boat is a large one, it is badly crowded with five men & five dogs & all our stuff," Stuck wrote. "Dogs & men alike will be glad, I know, when the voyage is done." By the 19th they were almost to Tanana. As Tatum wrote, "This evening has found us so near our journeys end that we scarcely can believe that we are so near to civilization again."

After ten days of squishy, mosquito-bedeviled travel through the boggy plains north of the Alaska Range, the party arrived back at Tanana on June 20. Stuck waited for the telegraph office to open, then "sent a message of 175 words to Bunch, the city editor of the 'Seattle Times' with a summary of the results of the expedition, & a similar one to the Fairbanks 'Times.'" When the Seattle newspaper then asked Stuck for "five hundred more words on narrow escapes," the request was "left unanswered, for, thank God, there were none to describe."[3]

Stuck later received a message from Bunch "with congratulations & the statement that he had 'sent the news around the world.'" The Signal Corps office at the Tanana Army post told him that "by 11 o'clock the ships approaching home had received the news by wireless through the Associated Press." Stuck spent the day dealing with telegrams of congratulations and "an enormous mass of letters here, including one from Scribner's magazine asking for an article & offering to publish a book, & one from Colliers Weekly asking for pictures." While Karstens left for Ruby, the other four went to the Tanana mission.

"So ends the undertaking," Stuck wrote, "3 months & 6 days after it began with deep gratitude in my heart to Almighty God for vouchsafing the success and safety with which it has been attended." In the back of his own journal, Tatum wrote, "To Archdeacon I thank you for the kindness you have shown me in so many many ways. I can assure you that it is greatly appreciated I am very thankful indeed to have had been able to spend 3 mos with you It is one of the greatest privileges I have ever had."

∽

Less than a month after the ascent, on July 3, James V. Martin, an inventor and aviator, stood on a plowed strip of land outside Fairbanks. The 28-year-old, goateed and slightly chubby, posed for a photo with his Gage-Martin Tractor biplane and his wife Lily, who wore a long skirt and a large hat. Martin started the plane up, taxied down the makeshift runway, and on the second try wrenched it into the Alaskan sky. The plane cruised at 45 mph, 200 feet above the amazed and somewhat disbelieving crowd.[4]

By 1924, mail runs by plane had begun; three years later, the first Alaskan airline was founded. And on April 25, 1932, during the attempt of Denali's second ascent, Alaskan Airways pilot Joe Crosson landed a Fairchild 71 on skis at 5,600 feet on the Muldrow Glacier.[5] The age of the Alaskan dogsled as a way of life was coming to an end.

∽

On July 2, Stuck noted in his diary, "Karstens arrived from Ruby this evening & came up & spent the night." The next day, "Karstens left this morning with Johnny and five dogs of mine, the boy & the dogs to be taken to Nenana." Nothing in these brief entries indicated any tension between the men.

From the beginning, however, news accounts of the feat had stressed Hudson Stuck's name, with the others in subordinate roles. "Churchman Conquers Mt. McKinley," said the *Valdez Daily Prospector,* while a full-width all-caps headline announced STUCK REACHES TOP OF CONTINENT on the front page of *The Alaska Daily Empire.*

An early edition of the *New York Times* on June 21, in a small article without a headline, had quoted Stuck as saying, "The chief credit for our success is due to Karstens' good judgement, resourcefulness, and caution. We did not have a single mishap." But later editions of the *Times* that day dropped the quote. DR. STUCK SCALES MT. M'KINLEY, the later *Times* article was headed, as it described how the party "led by" Stuck, "and his assistants" Tatum, Karstens, and Harper (in that order) accomplished the feat.[6] Nor was there mention in the *Times* of Harper's reaching the top first.

Stuck left Tanana on the *Pelican* on July 5. Three days later, Tatum returned to Tanana after a brief time away. According to his journal, "Well we arrived at 10 A.M. found every body well & happy Karstens had left but an hour before and when he was here he said all sorts of things slandering the Arch deacon. Much to my surprise as he vowed he would say nothing to the out siders about our little differences."

Two days later, on July 10, the *Fairbanks Daily Times* announced, CONQUERER OF MT. M'KINLEY IS HOME AGAIN. The headline referred to Karstens, who "desired the *Times* to rectify an impression prevailing concerning the leadership of the expedition." Though the expedition was "always referred to as the Stuck McKinley party, he asks that it be referred to as the Stuck-Karstens party, as Archdeacon Stuck and he, as partners, were equally interested in it, one to assume one phase of preparation for the expedition, and the other another phase."

The article mentioned the upcoming *Scribner's Magazine* article, pointedly stating that "Mr. Karstens gets one-half of the proceeds of the story." Karstens also told the *Daily Times* that the sight of the Sourdough's pole on the North Summit "was a good one" for him personally.

Sometime that July or August, Karstens penned an extraordinary thirty-four-page letter to Charles Sheldon. Responding to Sheldon's letter of July 10, and urged on by his fiercely protective and ambitious fiancee, Frieda Louise Gaerisch, Karstens detailed every resentment he had toward Stuck.

> Sheldon "O" Sheldon why didn't you come in and make that trip as you suggested doing I have worked slept and raised the duce in general on the mountains thinking of it why souldent I have a man with me one worthy of the accent and not & absolute parasite liar . . .

(Now for the story) You remember while I was in New York I told you about the deacon trying for years to get me to go on this trip, and how fine he was to me now I understand to my sorrow. When I came in over the trail from the states I met the deacon on his way to Tanana crossing he approached me again about making the trip the following spring like a fool I consented he promised to do the cooking and get as many Indians as we needed to do the freighting then he would talk of his hardships and long trips to show what a good man he was. I took it for granted he was he surely has traveled enough (I woke up after the first day) I was to wait in Fairbanks until his return when we would make full preparations we were to be equal partners he was to Finance the Expedition it was not to cost me a cent. I was to furnish the experience. He was to do the cooking keep the records and read the instruments and help around general I told him it would be a case of every one get in and drill—which he agreed to.

He told me of all his experience in the Alps and in the Canadian rockies climbing different mountains but he knew absolutely nothing about mountain work and I had to learn as I went along.

We had everything at Eureka March 30th and so far the deacon would do nothing but make the boys cook him savory foods after their hard days work. He would sit around and make them wait on him he tried me one time and never again I was sick of him by this time . . .

in leaving Fairbanks he gave the paper the story and put me in as his acquired guide and he had climbed goodness knows how many Mts.

[At the next to last camp on Denali] I knew the deacon could not make it from there so I was prepared to make camps to the top as I told him if he would keep still and obey orders . . . In the morning before making the last climb I noticed Stuck's name carved on the Thermometer and Cross I asked him what position I was holding in the party he said I was full partner I told him It dident look like it Stuck carved all over everything, where did I come in his excuse was he dident have time it was to hard a job yet he carved the best part of a prayer on the cross and had nothing else to do that is the man I trusted to look out for my interests while I managed the accent and got him there.

You can easily see what I am getting out of it as a partner I have called him in the papers here and to square himself you will read in inclosed paper he has lied to me on money maters before we left Fairbanks I would have turned back several different times but how could I, I had promised to go through and I would have been a quitter. Never again will I write a letter against a man like this but I can't help it all I asked of him was justice. I have done everything I said I would do and more even when I knew I was getting the worst of it.

Before I promised to go I had a nice little sum of money now I am broke and in debt working my head off to get even so I can go on the new stampede at the head of the Tanana. I trusted him with the Photographs and records of the trip now I have nothing for I cant believe in the man he has made to many promises and broken them, as the boys say here that is what you get for befriending a preacher you get it coming and I think they are right.

"With love to all and plenty of it to the kiddies I remain Yours, HPK"

∽

Meanwhile, unaware of his partner's resentments, Stuck had seen the Fairbanks story with Karstens's comments. He wrote a letter from the steamer *St. Michael* on July 28 which the *Fairbanks Sunday Times* published on August 3.

"In your issue of 10th July is a communication from Mr. Harry Karstens, in which he takes a very natural exception to the continual reference to our expedition as the 'Stuck' expedition. I desire to join my protest to his." He stressed that "before leaving on that enterprise I explained to your reporter that Mr. Karstens and I were partners in the affair." The only statement made by Stuck had been the telegrams sent on June 20, "and I am not in any way responsible for the headings given that communication."

Stuck continued, "Mr. Karstens and I discussed the proposed ascent as long ago as six or seven years, and I should never have attempted it without his co-operation . . . I feel perfectly free to say that without Mr. Karstens we should never have reached the top of that mountain."

He found it "exceedingly painful to me to think that anyone should regard me as desirous of taking any credit that belongs to another," and he hoped to make it clear that in the planning of the expedition, "Karstens and I were colleagues and partners," and that on the mountain, "in the overcoming of the difficulties and successful confronting of the unexpected conditions" of the ascent, "Karstens was always the real leader; which I thought I had indicated as fully as a brief telegram would allow."

Stuck had declined a lecture tour on Denali, "for I am a missionary first and a mountain climber afterwards, and my visit Outside is primarily in the interests of missionary work in Alaska." But whatever income is raised from the climb will, "as you are good enough to inform the public, be divided between Karstens and myself."

∽

Stuck's first published account of the climb appeared in the November 1913 issue of *Scribner's Magazine*. In the first paragraph, Stuck, writing in the third person, says of the expedition, "It was only last year that he found himself in a position to plan the enterprise satisfactorily, and was able to secure the co-operation of Mr. H. P. Karstens, without whom it would not have been entered upon at all. *The expedition was thus a joint one, and this explanation is written because Mr. Karstens has been spoken of in the newspapers as a hired guide"* [emphasis added].[7]

In the first of a stream of letters from the archdeacon to his erstwhile partner, dated September 29 from New York and addressed to "My dear Harry," Stuck updated Karstens on the tie pins he had had Tiffany fashion with the granite taken from Denali's Northeast Ridge. By December he had forwarded $500 to Karstens; "I hope, please God, to make it $1000 before I am done." In February 1914, still in New York, Stuck sent "dear Harry" another $250, raised from "mountain lectures." Two months later, this time from Cranston's Kenilworth Hotel in London, Stuck sent $250, for a total of $1000—"I was anxious that you should get at least that amount." Back in Fairbanks in September 1914, Stuck sent Karstens another $25, from Denali lectures he had given in Colorado Springs and Seattle on his way home. And in November Stuck was pleased to send Harry $72.91, the first royalties from Scribner's for *Ascent of Denali*.

But Stuck's letter to Karstens dated February 8th, 1915, "written at the Ohio Roadhouse," had an altogether different tone. "My dear Mr. Karstens," it began:

> I had hoped to see you when I was in Fairbanks, but I heard such extraordinary statements concerning your feelings to me that I did not care to call at your house, lest I be rebuffed at the door . . .

I am altogether at a loss to understand why you should cherish any but the kindest feeling to me. I have given you, in everything that I have written, from the first telegram sent upon our return, to the completed narrative in the book, the fullest credit for your great part in our joint enterprise. Every newspaper or magazine that has reviewed my book, or commented in any way upon the climb, has made a point of noticing that I gave the credit for our success to you and my other companions, and to you first of all.

I saw you hailed in the local paper the other day as "the world-famous explorer." I have no quarrel with the description whatever, but I would point out that if you are "world famous" it is I who have made you so. In my magazine article, in my book, from every platform on which I have lectured, I have sung your praises and told of your exploits. Who ever heard of you before? Sheldon has written nothing of you. You must remember that in this matter of fame it is not enough to be able to do things, it is also necessary to be able to tell about them.

My conscience is absolutely clear as regards you. I have treated you with entire fairness and justice . . . I have none but the kindliest feelings towards you . . . And you helped me to realize a long and keenly-cherished ambition. It would be pleasant to me if you . . . are able to return my kind feelings.

After suggesting an intermediary—"I can convince him, or any reasonable man, that you have no grievance against me"—Stuck signed the letter "With kind regard, Believe me, Always faithfully yours."

As late as September 1917, Stuck was sending Karstens royalties from his book ("I take pleasure in sending you herewith my cheque for $115.00") and congratulating him on the birth of his son. There is no evidence that Karstens ever replied to any of these letters, or ever saw Stuck again.

✑

Hudson Stuck wrote in *Ascent of Denali* that Karstens, "strong, competent, and resourceful," was "the real leader of the expedition." The book made no mention of friction among the members of the climbing party, but not because Stuck was unaware of it. Perhaps an explanation for his reticence can be found later in the book, where he described Robert Dunn's account of the 1903 Cook circumnavigation of Denali as "a vivid but unpleasant production, for which every squabble and jealousy of the party furnishes literary material . . . One is thankful . . . that it is unique in the literature of travel."[8] Stuck would have had no inclination to produce such a book himself. He existed, and hoped to exist, in the more genteel world of noble polar and Arctic explorers such as Shackleton and Johanssen. Or Sir Martin Conway, "one of the world's greatest travellers and climbers," in the words of Stuck's dedication of *Ascent*, "whose fascinating narratives have kindled in many breasts a love of the great heights and a desire to attain unto them." Conway, son of an Anglican rector, Cambridge-educated scholar, president of the Alpine Club, was unlikely to have ever written an "unpleasant production." Stuck owned Conway's *Climbing and Exploration in the Karakoram-Himalayas*, published in 1894; Conway's colorful, sympathetic descriptions of the East would have appealed to the Archdeacon's love of adventure and wild places.

Stuck's stature as an expatriate Englishman, an Episcopal archdeacon, and a member of the National Geographic Society all conspired to keep him in the headlines in that more class-conscious era. Even after Stuck had given Karstens the agreed half of royalties earned on his writings about the climb, and done all he could to appease his expedition partner, the Sourdough never forgave the Archdeacon, rebuffing all attempts by Stuck to repair the friendship. He called Stuck "a liar and a sneak" and claimed to Charles Sheldon that if he ran into Stuck again, "I sure would have mussed him up." In this he was doubtless goaded on by the very white settlers in Alaska who had felt the full effect of the Archdeacon's condescending scorn ("that is what you get for befriending a preacher"). Stuck's campaigns against drunkenness and mistreatment of Native women by white Alaska were being held against him, and perhaps used to fuel Karstens's injured pride.

Stuck asserted that it was the missionaries "who have fought the flagrant, brutal immorality of low-down whites, . . . who have cheerfully incurred all sorts of personal odium in the struggle to protect the natives from those who for lust or gain would debauch and destroy them." The more effective a missionary was, Stuck suggested, the more vilified he was likely to be; visitors to Alaska "should remember that the measure of the unpopularity of a missionary to the Indians amongst a certain class on the steamboats and in the drinking-shops and on the water-fronts of towns, may very possible be the measure of his usefulness."[9]

∞

After Denali, Karstens returned to freighting over the winter ice and guiding hunting trips, while back on the East Coast, Charles Sheldon continued his efforts to create a national park containing the mountain he and Karstens had so often contemplated. As chairman of the Game Committee of the Boone and Crockett Club, Sheldon leveraged his connections and clout, though he admitted to Karstens, "I have no influence with [President Woodrow] Wilson because I have not believed in him." One connection that bore fruit was with Belmore Browne, who also believed the mountain should be part of a national park.[10] In 1917, Judge Wickersham, now Alaska's Congressional delegate, introduced legislation which Wilson signed, officially establishing Mount McKinley National Park. However, no appropriation was made to fund the park, leaving it with no rangers—and no superintendent. Not until 1920 would Harry Karstens finally become the first Superintendent of the park, its 1.6 million acres second in size only to Yellowstone. He built infrastructure, including cabins for the rangers, and established procedures which set the tone for wilderness preservation in Alaska's great parks. But almost four decades after Denali, Karstens would write, "I have always wished that [Sheldon] had made the climb for I sure would have got much more pleasure out of the trip than I did later on."

When Stuck's *Ascent of Denali* was published in January 1914, the *New York Times* said that the book's pages "make one wish that all mountain climbers might be Archdeacons, if their accounts might thus gain, in the interest of happenings by the way, emotional vision and intellectual outlook." The *Times* noted that Stuck "makes an eloquent protest against allowing the native names of this mountain and its companion, 'Denali's Wife,' to be permanently superseded by the names they now bear."[11]

Stuck included chapters on the previous summit attempts (laying out in detail the case against Cook), the names suggested for various features of the mountain, and, meticulous as always where scientific measurements were concerned, "The Height of Denali, with a Discussion of the Readings on the Summit and During the Ascent." Stuck's aneroid altimeter, invented for use by the British army, used the expansions and contractions of a small air chamber to measure twenty-five-foot increments of altitude. As a modern science journalist, Richard Lovett has written, "Stuck found it useful at low altitudes, but halfway up the mountain it became clear that the scale was wrong. At the summit, the 'mendacious little instrument' was 'confidently' reading 23,300 feet, a number Stuck knew to be wildly out."

Triangulation, measuring from various points using known elevations, also presented problems, as it was unknown how much light would bend in the thin air of high elevations. That meant that, in Lovett's words, "In the era before GPS, the best altitude measurements came from measuring air pressure with a mercury barometer." Because barometric pressure varies in any location due to weather, Stuck asked a friend to take daily readings at Fort Gibbon on the Yukon river, which he would compare with his readings on Denali.

When Stuck found himself unable to work out the calculations required, he found C. E. Giffin, a topographer with the US Geological Survey, who, Lovett wrote, "obligingly crunched the numbers for him, determining that Denali was 20,674 feet above Fort Gibbon, or 21,008 feet above sea level." Giffin then repeated the calculation using barometric pressure in the coastal town of Valdez for comparison. That gave him an elevation of 20,384 feet, "remarkably close to today's value of 20,320 feet (6,194 metres)," as Lovett wrote. "Giffin suggested that the people at Fort Gibbon may have muffed their readings, but Stuck saw no reason to fault his friends. He must have had private misgivings though, because he split the difference and suggested an altitude of 20,700 feet."[12]

∽

In the first sentence of his foreword to *The Ascent of Denali*, Stuck issued what was "forefront in the author's heart and desire . . . a plea for the restoration to the greatest mountain in North America of its immemorial native name."[13] He closed by urging that "the native names of these great mountains remain" in honor of "simple, hardy race who braved successfully the rigors of its climate and the inhospitality of their climate and flourished . . . So this book shall end as it began."

15

"THE LIGHT OF
A BRIGHT EXAMPLE"

After Denali, Walter Harper ventured beyond the borders of his homeland for the first time, accompanying Hudson Stuck outside in August 1913. Following Stuck's plan for his education, Harper was to enter Mount Hermon School in Massachusetts, famous in its day for preparing Native American youth to be leaders in their communities. He planned to later attend medical school and become a medical missionary.

On August 11, Stuck and Harper boarded a new ocean liner, the *Princess Sophia*. The ship was designed to serve the Inside Passage from Skagway to Vancouver. They took the *Imperial Limited* train from Vancouver to Montreal, then another train to New York City. After a few days of sightseeing, Stuck and Harper went to Mount Hermon in Northfield, Massachusetts. Arthur Wright, Stuck's first protegé, who had just finished his third year there, met the two.[1]

> The school was founded by Protestant evangelist Dwight Lyman Moody as the Northfield Seminary for Young Ladies in 1879 (later called the Northfield School for Girls) and the Mount Hermon School for Boys in 1881. Moody built the girls' school in Northfield, Massachusetts, the town of his birth, and the boys' school a few miles away in the town of Gill. Moody's goal was to provide the best possible education for young people without privilege, and he enrolled students whose parents were slaves as well as Native Americans and people from other countries, which was unprecedented among elite private schools at that time. Moody sent out students who founded schools and churches of their own. Moody viewed Christian religious education as an essential objective of his schools. By 1913, the schools were operated under the single moniker 'The Northfield Schools.'[2]

According to his biographer Mary Ehrlander, Harper "enjoyed minor celebrity status at Mount Hermon," because of the Denali climb. During his first semester "a stranger sent him William Ogilvie's book *Early Days on the Yukon*, which featured Arthur Harper prominently as the discoverer of the gold potential in the Alaska-Yukon region." Although Walter's father was "somewhat a mystery" to him, he took pride in Arthur Harper's accomplishments and reputation.

In late October 1913 Charles Sheldon, who had heard about Walter from Stuck as well as Karstens, invited him to his home in Woodstock, Vermont. Amid the fall colors of New England, Sheldon encouraged Walter to educate himself in order to return to Alaska and be of use to his people.[3]

The following summer, Stuck visited Harper and took him to New York. They went to Coney Island on May 31, and according to the *Times*, "ballyhoo men . . . ticket takers, and sight-seers were talking about that visit all day." Harper's first exploit was to hit the strength-testing machine, using a twenty-pound hammer, with such force that two hours were required to repair it. Then he "wandered over to the shooting gallery," where with three shots he dispatched three silver balls floating in water. Finally, at a dunking booth, he dunked a "negro" three times with three pitches. When Harper went to the beach, he began piling sand, until Stuck suddenly said, "Look, he's reproduced Denali." Harper had made a three-dimensional model of the mountain, on which he proceeded to trace with a stick the route he, Stuck, and the others had taken to the summit.[4]

Harper did well in some ways at Mount Hermon and enjoyed himself but struggled academically. His intensive tutoring by Stuck didn't prepare him for studying on his own, or for the academic demands of Mount Hermon. Harper wrote Stuck, "I think the chief trouble with me is that I do not know how to apply my mind properly."[5] In 1916, Stuck decided Harper's best opportunity lay in coming back to Alaska and being tutored by Stuck again, the object being medical school.

After three years at Mount Hermon, Harper returned home and resumed his familiar role as Stuck's assistant on mission trips, as well as resuming his studies under his long-time tutor and mentor. In the winter of 1917–1918, the two embarked on an epic two-thousand-mile trip by dogsled across the northern arc of Alaska, described in Stuck's book *A Winter Circuit of Our Arctic Coast*. From Fort Yukon the two, with the addition of Native guides at various intervals, traveled in a clockwise oval, first west to the coast at Point Hope, then north and east along the Arctic shore to Point Barrow and Herschel Island, before turning south and tracing the Porcupine River back to Fort Yukon, arriving on April 24, 1918. Swapping the trees and rivers of the interior for the barren ice of the Farthest North, Stuck and Harper built shelters from their sleds and snow blocks, shouting at each over the howling winds as they shivered through the night.

Immediately before the Arctic trip, Harper had been seriously ill with typhoid, being cleared to travel only one week before his and Stuck's departure. At Fort Yukon, he had been cared for by Frances Wells, a member of a prominent Philadelphia family working as a mission nurse. Harper, following his heart instead of Stuck's plan for his life, fell in love with Wells and decided to marry her that summer. Stuck was against the marriage at first, as he believed it would interfere with Walter's education and advancement in the world. However, in September, 1918, it was Stuck who presided over their marriage. Seven weeks later, the two left Alaska for Philadelphia and a new life. Frances hoped to work for the Red Cross; Walter aimed for medical school before returning to serve the Natives of the Yukon. On October 23, 1918, the newlyweds boarded the *Princess Sophia*—the same ship Harper and Stuck had taken outside in 1913—bound for Seattle and the East.

Shortly after 2:00 A.M., in a blinding snowstorm and heavy seas, the *Princess Sophia* hit Vanderbilt Reef northwest of Juneau and sank. All 268 passengers and 75 crew were lost. The only survivor, an English setter that may have belonged to the *Sophia*'s captain, was found two days later in Auke Bay outside Juneau, half starved and covered in oil.[6]

Stuck's grief at the loss of protegé, friend, and standard-bearer for Alaskan native hopes was almost unbearable. On All Saints Day, November 1, 1918, at the memorial service held at St. Stephen's Church, Fort Yukon, Stuck said,

> I have not dwelt so long the character of Walter Harper because he was so dear to me, because I loved as a son, nor because I though him faultless or entitled to any sort of saintship in the common use of the term . . . I have dwelt so much upon Walters character because I think there is a lesson in it, because I think it shows that the finest flower of character may spring out of any soil, out of any environment, because I

thing that as he lived here before your eyes he set a most valuable example of conduct.[7]

Later, he would say of Walter Harper, "He has left behind him a sweet memory and the light of a bright example."

∽

Walter Harper's legacy, thanks in part to the 2013 centennial celebrations of the Denali ascent, is strong in Alaska today. A 2018 review of Harper's biography described Harper as "an inspiring example of resilience, character, faith, service, and loving-kindness," and his legacy as "a testament to the native peoples of Alaska, the indomitable human spirit, and the self-lessness of those who work as missionaries in the Church in the harshest and remotest of places."[8]

Harper—and Hudson Stuck—would have been highly gratified to read this passage by Jan Raines-Harper, Walter's great-niece, writing in 2020:

> Walter's fame made otherwise humbled people proud. *One of our own made it.* His legacy to his Harper descendants is more personal: a constella-tion of dreams and stories. My mother—Walter's niece—overcame tuberculosis twice while in college, but became the first Alaska Native woman to grad-uate from the University of Alaska in Fairbanks in 1935, where a building was named after her in 1992. My cousin Michael Harper worked as Governor Jay

Hammond's assistant in the 1970s and later became president of a large Native corporation. Another cousin, Phyllis Fast, obtained a PhD in Anthropology from Harvard University and went on to head the Department of Alaska Native Studies at the University of Alaska in Fairbanks.[9]

Walter Harper would have learned about these descendants of his with strong familial pride, as well as pride for his people. And for Hudson Stuck, these stories, these achievements by Native Alaskans, would have been the living embodiment of what he called "the nobler ideal."

16

THE LONG TRAIL

The fall of 1913 was momentous for Hudson Stuck. The Denali ascent led directly to new acclaim for the archdeacon as a writer, lecturer, and expert on the Far North. In addition to his bitter falling-out with Harry Karstens, the missionary had to deal with new demands on his time, and with the newfound attention on him concurrent with his fame. He also would be separated from his protege Walter Harper for the first time in five years, after he took Walter to the East Coast that August.

Over the next six years he also would make more and longer trips to the US mainland, speaking and writing on behalf of the work in Alaska. His outspoken, informed eloquence earned him headlines across the country.

A *New York Times* article dated July 17, 1913, took an interesting approach to the question of the mountain's name. HE'D RENAME MT. MCKINLEY, stated the headline on the small front-page story. The subhead added, "Archdeacon Stuck will suggest Denali, an Indian word"—as though the idea of calling the mountain Denali was a new one, thought up by Stuck, and not one that had been thousands of years in use. The unsigned report, datelined Seattle, reported that Stuck planned to travel to New York that October to urge the National Geographic Society, "of which he is a member," to support the proposal. Stuck also was to attend the General Convention of the Episcopal Church.[1]

The opinionated, cantankerous Stuck was on full display on June 3, 1916, according to the *New York Times* account of his baccalaureate sermon delivered the day before at Columbia University. In ARCHDEACON FLAYS LIFE'S SHAMS, the *Times* referred to his "direct and forceful language of the Yukon" and "startling words" which sank "deep into the minds of the 2,500 students, guests, and faculty present." His main target was professional philanthropy; he contrasted the attitude of the amateur with that of the professional, the former "keeping always uppermost the human, personal touch," while the latter regarded people as "a thing detached, to be classified and indexed away in the laboratory, plotted in curves and regarded in algebraic formulae."

"I have always had a sort of dread," he told the audience,

> of trained sociologists, of anthropologists with a turn
> for practical benevolence, of political economists, of
> psychological pedagogues, and graduates in similar
> subjects . . . they are always in danger of evacuating
> the human personal element out of their work.

> When philanthropy becomes professionalized, Stuck
> added, "it no longer evokes gratitude, it provokes
> antagonism." Though the relief itself may be just as
> real and necessary, "the whole attitude is changed;
> any sort of warm human sympathy seems destroyed,
> and the obligation presses intolerably upon the sensi-
> tive recipient."[2]

The reaction to this speech was substantial. The *Times* printed a letter in response under the headline THE FIGURES OF MISERY, with the subhead "There May Be Much Love Behind 'the Plotting of a Curve.'" The letter took Stuck to task: "One cannot but regret Archdeacon Stuck's baccalaureate address," as it seemed that "the large compassion which Dr. Stuck feels for the Alaskan poor has been withheld from the American philanthropic worker." Dr. Stuck may have merely been flippant in his remarks, the author wrote; "Nevertheless, clergymen should have that 'large compassion' which Dr. Stuck recommends for social workers."

The letter concluded, "Life is, indeed, too full of beauty and mystery to be wantonly hacked and chopped into statistics . . .

[but] There can be much love in 'the plotting of a curve'; statistics are sometimes consecrated by reverent prayer; a trained mind is not incompatible with a loving heart." It was signed "E. and A. Atherton, Wilkes-Barre, Penn. June 15, 1916"

Stuck felt compelled to respond. The *Times* printed his letter on June 30, under the headline CONFESSIONS OF ARCHDEACON STUCK. He had ignored, he said, "the many public and private criticisms which my baccalaureate sermon at Columbia has provoked, and, having shot my bolt, had not thought to open my mouth again." However, "the fine letter signed "E. and S. Atherton I cannot bring myself to ignore." Admitting that he felt "almost ready to admit that I am rebuked," Stuck said, "I took occasion to insist that before mankind can be helped, mankind must be understood, and that before mankind can be understood mankind must be loved." Everything else, he said, was "the mere garnishment of illustration" or "the joyful airing of personal prejudice."[3]

A story dating from this time tells of a visit by Stuck to Texas. Colonel W. S. Simkins, father of Stuck's former student Ormond Simkins, was a colorful Texas lawyer whose exploits were still being recounted almost twenty years after his death. When the Colonel's "very good friend" Stuck came to Austin for a visit, the Colonel took him for a ride in the country. After fifteen minutes of bouncing over the boulders in the hills north of the city, Stuck asked the Colonel to stop the car. "When the wheels skidded to a stop, the Dean got out of the car and started back toward Austin. 'Where are you going?' asked his host. 'Colonel Simkins,' said he, 'I've braved the terrors of the Alaskan winters, and I've conquered Mount McKinley's twenty thousand feet of snow and ice, but I can't stand your driving—I simply can't take it. I am walking back to Austin.'" The Colonel finally persuaded Stuck back into the car for a more sedate drive back to town.[4]

༨

In addition to publishing Stuck's account of the Denali climb in its magazine, Charles Scribner's Sons had offered him a contract for what would become his first book, *The Ascent of Denali*. Although it received positive reviews, the book's niche subject matter kept sales from being very great. The book Stuck had finished in the tent during the expedition, however, could expect, Stuck felt, to find a wider audience. *Ten Thousand Miles With a Dog Sled*, which Scribner's published in May 1914, was to Stuck "a true book and carefully written," and "if the public won't buy it, the public is an ass and a fool."[5] Stuck was right; the book's portrayal of early-pioneer Alaska has kept it in print, and today it routinely appears on lists of best books about early Alaska.

In *The Ascent of Denali*, Stuck had made a plea to keep the mountain's aboriginal name; he now used the preface of *Ten Thousand Miles with a Dog Sled* to inveigh against liquor and its white purveyors. "A measure of real protection must be given the native communities against the low-down whites who seek to intrude into them . . . and some adequate machinery set up for suppressing the contemptible traffic in adulterated spirits they subsist largely upon."[6]

Stuck added to his account of winter travel throughout the interior with chapters on "Photography," "The Alaska Natives,"

"Dogs of Alaska," and "The Northern Lights." In his imitable style, Stuck disrupted the narrative with his keen perceptions of people, places, and institutions of Alaska. He combined firm, almost dogmatic opinions on almost all topics with a refreshing and sometimes breathtaking openmindedness—of a sort that is unusual in the present day, much less in the early 1900s.

Stuck dedicated the book to Grafton Burke, M.D., the St. Matthew's schoolboy who now served as a medical missionary in Alaska, and Edgar Loomis, M.D., who also had served a stint as a medical missionary at Tanana: "pupils, comrades, colleagues, companions on some of these journeys, always dear friends" and to "the mother of the three of us, Sewanee, the college on the mountain-top where the old ideals are still unflinchingly maintained."

As he would later in his writings about Denali, Stuck downplayed his achievements dogsledding around the Alaskan interior. "There are many men in Alaska who have done more. A mail-carrier on one of the longer dog routes will cover four thousand miles in a winter, while the writer's average is less than two thousand."[7]

∽

Even as he wrote *Ten Thousand Miles* Stuck may have had the idea for what he called a "supplement and complement" to that book. The other main means of Alaskan travel, by boat in warm weather, offered an obvious bookend to tales of winter dogsledding. And so *Voyages on the Yukon and Its Tributaries* appeared in November 1917. The book was dedicated to Walter

Harper, Arthur Wright, and John Fredson, his Native Alaskan
protegés, who "during the past ten years have been engineers
and pilots of the launch 'Pelican' as well as dog-drivers and
trail attendants on many thousand miles of the author's winter
journeys," in "affectionate acknowledgement of faithful and
kindly service."

Voyages was one of two Stuck books to be edited by Maxwell
Perkins. Then twenty-nine, Perkins had joined Scribner & Sons
four years earlier; in 1919 Perkins would sign F. Scott Fitzgerald
to Scribner's, and in 1926 would publish Ernest Hemingway's
first novel, *The Sun Also Rises.* Stuck, who had proclaimed that
he would publish for a major house or not at all, would have
been pleased to know that he had worked with a literary star
who was at the onset of his career. Perkins, for his part, seemed
to enjoy working with Stuck, whom he considered a "very rare
individual," on *Voyages on the Yukon and Its Tributaries,* as well as
its successor. Stuck wrote prolifically to Perkins and Scribner's,
asking that books be shipped to Fort Yukon and demanding to
know why royalty payments had not been forthcoming. In one
letter to Perkins, Stuck wrote, "Don't worry about my petulan-
cies or I shall be afraid to write frankly to you and then I might
as well not write at all."[8]

❧

Stuck had thought *Voyages on the Yukon* would be his last book.
After describing winter travel via dogsled and summer travel via
the rivers of Alaska, and then the ascent of Denali, he wrote,
"there would seem little need to chronicle further wanderings."

But the 1917–18 trip with Walter Harper to the Alaskan regions above the Arctic Circle, "a distinct region of great interest," had been for Stuck "sufficiently full of new impressions and experiences" to justify this, his "fourth, and . . . I am sure . . . my last, book of Alaskan travel," *A Winter Circuit of Our Arctic Coast.*[9] On September 5, 1919—the day after Fitzgerald sent his first novel, *This Side of Paradise*, to Perkins—Stuck wrote his editor that he was headed outside and would be in New York by October 1 to check the proofs. It would be May 1920 before *Winter Circuit* reached booksellers.[10]

Although he admitted "no discoveries of explorations to record," Stuck did claim the first circuit of the coast having for its purpose "a general inquiry into Eskimo conditions," even though "the winter is the time when the normal activities of the villages, with their schools and missions, are in operation." By contrast, when such visits had been made previously, in summer, "the natives are scattered and their activities intermitted." As Stuck stated, "Winter life is the normal life."[11]

A contemporary review in the journal of the Royal Geographic Society noted that Stuck "gives some interesting information on reindeer . . . on seals and whale-fishing . . . and on furs and the fur trade." The review described Stuck's remarks "on other subjects also, not geographical or zoological" as "characterized by shrewdness and common sense, which lend variety to an interesting narrative."[12] And Mary Ehrlander, Walter Harper's biographer, described *Winter Circuit* as "in many ways Stuck's masterpiece, an historical, literary, biographical, and ethnographic treasure."[13] To Ehrlander, the book "illustrates Stuck's maturity as a thinker and stylist, exhibiting greater introspection and lyricism than his earlier publications."[14] Readers of the book, Ehrlander wrote, "learn to know this extraordinary intellect and outdoorsman whose service to Alaskan peoples in the face of widespread indifference Outside and hostility within Alaska, leaves no doubt that the Archdeacon lived up to his motto—'I persevere.'"[15]

⚬⁓⚬

A Winter Circuit, as it turned out, wasn't Stuck's last book, either. In 1920, the Episcopal Church published *The Alaskan Missions of the Episcopal Church*, with a preface by Bishop Rowe. The man under whom Stuck had worked since arriving in Alaska described Stuck as "interested in [Alaska's] welfare, sympathetic in the needs of its people, a keen observer and investigator, and an enthusiastic builder in the growing Kingdom of God." He was sure that the public, which had "already become charmed with the author's literary ability" in Stuck's previous books, would be similarly interested in this "interesting, lucid and vigorous" volume.

As of 1920, Stuck could state that "there are today, speaking broadly, no upbaptized natives left in Alaska."[16] In their "material condition of life," Stuck claimed that there had been "slow if gradual advance." And as to their future, Stuck saw it as "reasonably bright," except for "one present menace," the threat to native salmon fisheries. He pushed back forcibly against the idea that Alaska Natives were only valuable as contributors to the economic value of the United States, as summed up in the question a US Senator asked Stuck: "What do your Yukon Indians contribute to the welfare of the world?" Stuck wrote:

The contemptuous dismission of all the little peoples of the world as beneath the regard of the great races, or even a supercilious rating of them by the white man's own standards, does not seem to reflect the feeling of thoughtful men today as much, perhaps, as it did some decades ago.[17]

In contrast to that view, Stuck describes the Alaska Natives of the Yukon as "gentle, simple, kindly people" who have occupied the land "for untold generations" in a "rigourous environment" into which they have "ground themselves . . . to perfect adjustment." Absent as always with Stuck is any sense that the proper thing for Alaska Natives to do is to throw over their old ways, and subscribe fully to twentieth-century Western ideas of progress or desired ways of life.[18]

↜

In the summer of 1914, Johnny Fredson took the place of Walter Harper, who was outside at Mount Hermon, on board the *Pelican* with Stuck. Beginning that winter, Fredson would also assume Harper's other chief role, accompanying the archdeacon on his winter travels by dogsled. In another parallel with Harper, Fredson had school lessons with Stuck every night after docking or setting winter camp; he would become the first Athabascan Alaska Native to complete high school. In August 1916 Fredson followed in Harper's footsteps yet again, enrolling at Mount Hermon. He returned home in August 1921 after graduation, surprised to find himself on the same steamer as Robert Tatum.

The newly-ordained Tatum was headed inside to fill in for Stuck's successor as archdeacon, F. B. Drane.

The next year Fredson began his studies at the University of the South. Although ten years older than his classmates, he made friends and fit in well in Sewanee. During the summer of 1923, while working at a summer camp in upstate New York, he was interviewed extensively by linguistics scholar Edward Sapir, who was conducting a study of the Gwich'in languages. Sapir, a student of the famous ethnographer Franz Boas, "had invented a classification scheme for Native American languages that would become the standard among American linguists." He also urged his fellow anthropologists to "pay attention to the spoken word as an archival record of a distinct way of life."[19]

Fredson's people were the Netsi Gwich'in of the Chandalar region, who had "hunted the muskeg and scrubby forests of the Yukon Flats northward toward the snowcapped Brooks Range, and traveled northeastward toward Yukon Territory for trade with coastal Eskimos for more than a thousand years,"[20] in the words of Fredson's biographer Clara Childs Mackenzie. Sapir recorded Fredson as he recounted "stories from [his] early life, his father's experiences, and special memories, like the speech Chief Jonas had made at . . . Archdeacon Stuck's grave."[21]

After returning to Alaska for three years, Fredson in 1930 went back to Sewanee and earned a B.S. Degree from the University of the South, becoming the first Alaska Native to graduate from college. Back again in Alaska, he worked at the hospital in Fort Yukon and taught school in the village of Venetie. Eventually Fredson became a tribal leader, responsible for the creation of the Venetie Indian Reserve, one of the largest

Native reserves in Alaska, in 1941. After his death in 1945 from pneumonia, Fredson was remembered for his personal abilities as well as his contributions to Alaska Native culture:

> As a folk and classical musician, orator, narrator, trapper, wood carver, river pilot, mechanic, carpenter, surveyor, teacher, and scholar, Fredson was truly one of the most gifted of twentieth-century Alaskan Indians. Not only was he resourceful and diligent in virtually everything he attempted, but from an anthropological perspective, he was one of the key informants who shaped our scientific understanding and appreciation of northern Athabascan languages and cultures.[22]

Perhaps even more than Walter Harper, John Fredson personified Hudson Stuck's hopes for Alaska Natives. Stuck wanted Fredson, and all Alaska Natives, to have the tools to navigate the uncertainties and hazards of the early twentieth century, retaining the links to his heritage while finding success in the new era which was dawning in Fredson's ancestral land.

To Evon Peter of the University of Alaska, Stuck assisted in making that a reality. "Certainly, the outcome of Hudson Stuck's support of Harper and John Fredson was that there was real advancement for the human and civil rights of Gwich'in people," according to Peter. "A portion of [Fredson's leadership] I think can be attributed to the support Hudson Stuck provided him."

As a participant in the 2013 centennial of the first ascent put it, "[Johnny Fredson and Esaias George] weren't there just to help. Stuck had the opinion that if Alaska Natives were to withstand the inevitable changes to their lives brought by the gold rush, then the brightest and best of indigenous people needed to be given the best formal education possible. Then they could go back and help their people."[23]

⚬

Hudson Stuck had always been an outspoken and controversial advocate for indigenous rights as against what he saw as the rapaciousness of some white commercial interests. His last significant battle was fought against the large-scale salmon fisheries, which he saw as serious threats to the very existence of the natives. As he pointed out in his book *The Alaskan Missions of the Episcopal Church*, "Not only is dried salmon a very large part of the native food but it is almost the whole food of the indispensable dog," without which "the whole present Indian economy would be destroyed." Supported by natives as well as the majority of whites in the interior, Stuck wrote letters to officials, gave interviews to the Fairbanks press, and even testified before Congress, telling the House Merchant Marine and Fisheries Committee, "These people . . . resent the destruction of their natural food supplies by the canners, who have adopted a get-rich-quick policy with no regard to the conservation of the fish supply." Just as in Dallas, he drew the ire of powerful business interests, but showed no sign of being intimidated.

While in New York in January 1920, Stuck had printed a small pamphlet, *The Salmon Cannery at the Mouth of the Yukon*, in which he laid out his argument in favor of banning the cannery. He reprinted a lengthy letter from the man who would succeed him, Rev. Frederick B. Drane, head of the Tanana Valley Mission, concluding, "If you will consider the opinion of us who depend on the catch of salmon for our charges, for both man and dog feed, you will say the cannery ought to go." Drane was tempted to "launch forth into a tirade against this cannery, but I have kept back the indignation we of the Interior feel." Instead, he would "merely let this go as a statement of fact, or observations made by one who feels that it is his duty to speak a word for the Indians and the whites who depend from year to year on the catch of salmon."[24]

Stuck and the famous Arctic explorer Vilhjalmur Stefansson traded correspondence about the salmon situation, and Stuck sent Stefansson published statements by Bishop Rowe as well as Stuck, urging the prohibition of canning operations on the Yukon River. In a letter from the Church Mission House in New York, he told Stefansson, "I am greatly obliged to you . . . for your efforts in Washington to effect the removal of the cannery that has caused such distress." Stuck also told him that he didn't think "any Indians will starve in the interior this winter because we shall not let them." But, he added, "there is great distress," as Natives were killing their dogs to keep them from starving, "and without their dogs I know not what the Indians will do." He described the "touchy and rather pompous" Fish Commissioner "(I have never met him but I judge from his irascible correspondence)," then added, "Personally, I am not interested in attacking the Fish Commission but . . . in securing for the natives their continued right to the supply of food which the Yukon has immemorially afforded."[25] Stuck planned to visit

Washington, D.C., that month to press for a bill "prohibiting, once for all, any canneries upon the Yukon River," which seemed to him "the simple and only satisfactory way to deal with the situation."

Eventually, due to many factors not the least of which was Stuck's advocacy, Congress passed legislation in 1924, four years after Stuck's death, regulating the salmon fishery industry in Alaska.

∽

In July 1918 Stuck was nominated for the Explorers Club by Vilhjalmur Stefansson, and seconded by Frederick Dellenbaugh, the club's cofounder, himself an explorer and member of John Wesley Powell's second trip down the Colorado River. Dellenbaugh noted of Stuck on the application, "He's travelled extensively in Alaska and in other regions. Climbed Mt. McKinley." Stuck was elected that October.[26]

The following year Stuck was finally made a Fellow of the Royal Geographic Society. In March of that year he learned that he had received the Society's Back Grant "for your travels in Alaska and ascent of McKinley." The writer noted that the grant, recognizing "applied or scientific geographical studies which make an outstanding contribution to the development of national or international public policy" honored George Back, a noted Arctic explorer, adding, "it seems particularly appropriate that it should go to a traveller who has made his name in the same part of the world."

Stuck then began an exchange of letters with Arthur R. Hinks, the Secretary of the Society, who had been awarded the

Gold Medal of the Royal Astronomical Society for his work in determining the distance between the Sun and the Earth before joining the RGS in 1912. Stuck suggested that the Society undertake the publication of a world atlas, Hinks demurring because of the expense and time involved; Stuck asked for details about Arctic geography ("In the northern part of Hudson's Bay lies . . . a strait named 'Roe's Welcome.' Can you tell me the origin of that name?") and offered to speak to the Society on his visits to England.

Stuck's response to the Back Grant was to pen a letter to Hinks that began, "I am very much concerned about the name of the mountain with which the Council of the Royal Geographical Society has associated my name in the award with which they have recently honoured me." A paragraph followed detailing the names and backgrounds of Denali and "Denali Bo-awt (ought as in bought) or Denali's wife." After pointing out that the RGS had a policy elsewhere of retaining native names, he ended, "Much as I feel gratified and honoured at the award which the Society has conferred upon me, I would cheerfully forego it for the greater satisfaction which the restoration of these native names would bring."[27]

"My dear Archdeacon," came the reply, dated July 21, "We entirely sympathise with you in your views about the undesirability of European names for mountains which have native names." The Society, however, was powerless to do anything, as "the responsible authority . . . is the United States Board on Geographic names. We have to accept their decisions."[28]

∽

After the Denali expedition and his time outside in 1913–14, Stuck had returned to his work in Alaska, tirelessly promoting the work of the Episcopal mission work there. He had also continued his practice of taking on Native boys as assistants for his trips by dogsled and on the *Pelican*. Although he was growing older, Stuck still showed plenty of youthful energy. One of the last of his Native protegés, Moses Cruikshank, later remembered that Stuck "was good with his fists, I remember. Boxing, you know. Wrestling, too, yeah."[29] His unceasing efforts on behalf of Alaska and his missions, however, would take their toll on his health by the end of the decade.

Since relocating to Fort Yukon in 1908, Stuck and the Burkes, Hap and Clara, had been extremely close, the closest thing to family that the Archdeacon had had since leaving England. The Burkes' first child, born in 1911, was named Hudson Stuck Burke. When the namesake and godfather heard the news while on the Yukon, the *Pelican* flew all her flags and sounded her siren to salute the new infant as the boat came into Fort Yukon.[30] Stuck presented the child with a Tiffany sterling silver cup engraved with the design of a dog team and a facsimile of the mission house, bearing the legend: "From Hudson to Hudson," and spoke of wanting Hudson Burke to be enrolled at the University of the South.[31]

Stuck was living in the attic of the mission hospital in 1919 when the Burkes invited Stuck to share their house in Fort Yukon. Four days before the sinking of the *Princess Sophia*, in October 1919, the archdeacon moved into his last home.

When Stuck left Alaska that same fall, the Burkes weren't at all certain that he would ever return. Despondent over Walter

Harper's death, fearing that he had fought a losing battle to preserve the salmon for Alaska Natives on the Yukon, Stuck had been considering offers of professorships in English by Harvard and Sewanee, as well as the rectorship of a small English church. In an August 1919 telegram to John Wood declining the Sewanee offer, he had added, "If appointment open next June will consult and consider. With present inclination accept."[32] In addition, a nagging, debilitating shoulder injury and years of overwork in brutal weather had left him in such poor health that a doctor in Dallas urged him not to return to Alaska. However, when Bishop Rowe, himself sick and possibly going blind, asked Stuck to preside over the diocese until Rowe recovered, Stuck returned to Fort Yukon by the last boat of the year.[33]

By the fall of 1920, Stuck's chronic cold turned into bronchitis, and the shoulder pain which had eased returned at excruciating levels. Burke wrote Wood, "His nervous system seemed to go all to pieces." Bronchitis became bronchial pneumonia. One evening in early October, Clara Burke wrote, "I heard the crash of glass from the Archdeacon's room . . . I . . . found him lying on the floor. He had suffered a stroke and fallen against the glass door of the bookcase." She got him into bed and sent a runner for her husband, who found Stuck in a semicoma, blinded by a cerebral hemorrhage.[34] He became semi-comatose, but when Hap Burke told Stuck that he loved him, Stuck replied, "I am glad, Hap, you love me—I am poor on love."[35]

Hudson Stuck died on October 11, 1920, a month before his fifty-eighth birthday. Clara Burke wrote,

To Fort Yukon and all the Alaskan missions, Hudson Stuck's death was like the crashing of a great tree which had given them moral and spiritual fruit. For sixteen years he had traveled over river and trail to teach and comfort his congregations. Irritable and impatient with white transgressors, his gentleness toward the native people . . . had made them love him and welcome him wherever he went.[36]

The telegram from Fort Yukon announcing Hudson Stuck's death to the outside world said, "He is on the long trail now." Notices and obituaries were published across the country. *The Times* of London said, "America has lost one of her most notable missionaries and explorers by the recent death of Archdeacon Stuck, of Alaska."[37] A typical note on his passing, printed in the Philadelphia *Evening Public Ledger* three days later, related that "Archdeacon Stuck was said by his friends to have been of a highly nervous temperament." His energy, though, "carried him far, it is said, when more stolid men would have been balked by the obstacles encountered." As for Alaska Natives, "The Indians idolized him."

William Alexander Percy would remember Stuck in the Sewanee chapter of *Lanterns on the Levee: Recollections of a Planter's Son*:

[He] . . . appeared on the front pages of newspapers because he had climbed with amazing pluck and calculated foolhardiness a hitherto unconquered mountain peak, an Indian boy his only companion

[sic]. But what we who loved him like best to recall about that exploit is an inch cube of a book he carried along with him and read through—for the hundredth time, likely—before the climb was completed. It was *Hamlet*.[38]

The Gwich'in Chief Jonas spoke of Stuck to his community, referring to Stuck by his Gwich'in name *Ginkhii Choo*, meaning "Big Preacher." He said in part:

> My relatives; with weeping and great sorrow I speak to you again of the Great Preacher . . . what great work he did so that our future might be good! . . . What a good man he was! Indeed, he worked only so that the future would be good . . . My relatives, a man who loved us greatly has labored among us; so let us truly seek to live as he did.[39]

At Walter Harper's memorial service in Fort Yukon, Stuck had pondered life after death. "In one's youth I think one is certain that the world to come is a world of action and high endeavor as well as this one," he said. "But as one grows older one feels with Browning that perhaps: 'The uses of labor are past and done—there remaineth a rest for the people of God. And I have had troubles enough for one.'"[40]

∞

In 1942, a US Army expedition to Denali named the small eminence just northwest of the South Summit Archdeacon's Tower. The fourth-highest peak in Alaska, it stands at 19,700 feet.

In Dallas, programs he set in motion, including the night school for mill workers and the children's home and school, functioned in modern versions into the 1990s.

In All Saints Chapel at the University of the South, a statue of Hudson Stuck in sledding gear, a dog jumping on Stuck's legs, graces the wall behind the altar. And on the Episcopal Church's Calendar of Lesser Feasts and Fasts, April 22—Earth Day—is the feast day of John Muir, the father of the national parks, and of Hudson Stuck.[41]

EPILOGUE

2013: THE CENTENNIAL

The centennial of the ascent in 2013 brought renewed focus on Walter Harper—as Stuck would have wished. Descendants of the 1913 party, including Stuck's great-great-nephew Dan Hopkins; two great-grandsons of Harry Karstens, Ken Karstens and Ray Schuenemann; and Dana Wright, great-grandnephew of Walter Harper, launched a successful attempt to summit Denali in commemoration. The Stuck-Karstens controversy resurfaced as new cultural sensitivities, about both the Native-born Harper's achievement and the feats of Karstens on Denali, led modern-day commentators to paint Stuck in a less flattering light. However, the people of Alaska and the mountaineering world celebrated the undoubtedly heroic effort of the 1913 expedition, which claimed the highest summit in North America and left its mark in history.

The following July, the National Park Service dedicated the Walter Harper Talkeetna Ranger Station in Denali National Park and Preserve. "The ranger station is the base of operations for Denali National Park's mountaineering operations, and climbers from all over the world pass through its doors prior to beginning their attempt on the peak."

In 2012, Mark MacDonald, then National Indigenous Bishop and now Archbishop of the Anglican Church of Canada, wrote, "Archdeacon Stuck made the excursion in 1913 to show the tremendous capacity of native technology and skill. He was confident that the presence of the living word of God in creation gave to the peoples of the land a wisdom that had much to teach others." For Stuck, MacDonald wrote, "The gospel made the conditions for a creative exchange. To say that the gospel implied the end of native wisdom was, he insisted, a monstrous conceit."

The Bishop of Alaska, Mark Lattime, had planned to be part of the summit party, hoping to carry the communion kit that Hudson Stuck took to Denali and use it to celebrate the Christian Eucharist at the summit. However, in a May letter to the diocese, Bishop Lattime took himself off the team, while celebrating the addition of a descendant of Robert Tatum to the expedition. The team summitted on June 28, accompanied by four Alaska Mountaineering School guides.

John Fredson's granddaughter met the returning climbers at the trailhead, "to recreate my grandfather's role of 100 years ago." As to which climber was the first on top, "It was always Dana," Ken Karstens said. "It was always going to be him. It was never going to be any other way."

In his letter, Bishop Lattime pointed out that in 2009, the General Convention of the Episcopal Church passed Resolution D035, "Repudiation of the Doctrine of Discovery." The resolution, the first of its kind among Christian denominations, pronounced the doctrine "fundamentally opposed to the Gospel of Jesus Christ and our understanding of the inherent rights that individuals and peoples have received from God." The Church of Alaska's website cited "the claiming and naming of Mt. McKinley without regard for the fact that the mountain had been called Denali for thousands of years" as an example of the principles of this doctrine, which legalized white, Western claims to lands and minerals in the New World.

On August 28, 2015, Sally Jewell, Interior Secretary in the Obama administration, officially restored the name "Denali" to the peak. In her secretarial order, Jewell noted that "This name change recognizes the sacred status of Denali to many Alaska Natives." The act was a delayed but fitting answer to Hudson Stuck's plea almost a century before, in the preface to his book, for that which was "forefront in the author's heart and desire . . . the restoration to the greatest mountain in North America of its immemorial native name."

BIBLIOGRAPHY

"About Us." Mazmas. Accessed January 22, 2020. https://mazamas.org/about/.

Ackroyd, Peter. *London: The Biography*. London: Chatto & Windus, 2000.

Adams, Mark. *Tip of the Iceberg: My 3,000 Mile Journey Around Wild Alaska, the Last Great American Frontier*. New York: Dutton, 2018.

Armentrout, Donald Smith. *The Quest for the Informed Priest: A History of the School of Theology*. Sewanee, TN: School of Theology, University of the South, 1979.

——— & Robert B. Slocum, eds. *An Episcopal Dictionary of the Church: A User-Friendly Reference for Episcopalians*. New York: Church Publishing, 2000.

Arnold-Baker, Charles. *The Companion to British History, Routledge*. 2nd ed. London: Routledge, 2001.

Baird, Julia. *Victoria the Queen: An Intimate Biography of the Women Who Ruled an Empire*. New York: Random House, 2016.

Baker, Lily, Charlotte Gailor, Rose Duncan Lovell, and Sarah Hodgson Torian, eds. *Sewanee*. "Published for the benefit of the University Library collection of Sewaneeana," Sewanee, TN, 1932.

Barkman, James. "What It's Like to Climb Denali, North America's Highest Peak." *Field Mag*. June 11, 2018. https://www.fieldmag.com/articles/james-barkman-what-it-like-climb-denali.

Berton, Pierre. *Klondike: The Last Great Gold Rush, 1896-1899*. Toronto: McClelland and Stewart, 1972.

Bowman, David. *Sewanee in Stone: Architecture & History*. Sewanee, TN: Proctor's Hall Press, 2003.

Browne, Belmore. *The Conquest of Mount McKinley*. Cambridge: The Riverside Press, 1956.

Burke, Clara Heintz, as told to Adele Comandini. *Doctor Hap*. New York: Coward-McCann, 1961.

Campbell, Randolph B. *Gone to Texas: A History of the Lone Star State*. New York: Oxford University Press, 2003.

Campbell, Robert. *In Darkest Alaska: Travel and Empire Along the Inside Passage*. Philadelphia: University of Pennsylvania Press, 2007.

Childs, Craig. *Atlas of a Lost World: Travels in Ice Age America*. Chapter 3. New York: Pantheon, 2018. Kindle.

Chitty, Arthur Ben. *Hudson Stuck of Alaska.* Pioneer Builders for Christ series, vol. 4. New York: The National Council of the Episcopal Church, 1962.

———, ed. *Purple Sewanee.* Quoted in Martin Knoll and Jason Price, *Climber's Guide to Sewanee.* Sewanee, TN: By the author, 2001.

———. *Reconstruction in Sewanee: The founding of the University of the South and its first administration, 1857-1872.* Sewanee, TN: University Press, 1954.

Conefrey, Mick, and Tim Jordan. *Mountain Men: A History of the Remarkable Climbers and Determined Eccentrics Who First Scaled the World's Most Famous Peaks.* Cambridge, MA: Da Capo Press, 2002.

Cook, Frederick, Belmore Browne, and Hudson Stuck. *Denali: Deception, Defeat, & Triumph.* Edited by Art Davidson. Seattle: The Mountaineers Books, 2001.

Cooke, James J. *Billy Mitchell.* Boulder: Lynne Rienner Publishers, 2002.

Crouch, Gregory. *The Bonanza King: John Mackay and the Battle Over the Greatest Riches in the American West.* New York: Scribner, 2018. Kindle.

Dean, David M. *Breaking Trail: Hudson Stuck of Texas and Alaska.* Athens, OH: Ohio University Press, 1988.

———. "Stuck, Hudson." *Handbook of Texas Online.* https://www.tshaonline.org /handbook/entries/stuck-hudson.

Demuth, Bathsheba. *Floating Coast: An Environmental History of the Bering Strait.* New York: W. W. Norton, 2019.

Das, Nandini, and Tim Youngs, eds. *The Cambridge History of Travel Writing.* Cambridge: Cambridge University Press, 2019.

Drury, Bob. *The Rescue Season: The Heroic Story of Parajumpers on the Edge of the World.* New York: Simon & Schuster, 2001.

Duke, Escal F. "San Angelo, TX." *The Handbook of Texas Online.* Texas State Historical Association. June 15, 2010. Retrieved January 15, 2020. https:// www.tshaonline.org/handbook/entries/san-angelo-tx.

Ehrlander, Mary F. *Walter Harper: Native Alaska Son.* Lincoln, NE: University of Nebraska Press, 2017.

Elrington, C. R., ed. *A History of the County of Middlesex: Volume 9, Hampstead, Paddington.* London, 1989. *British History Online.* http://www.british -history.ac.uk/vch/middx/vol9/pp198-204.

Enstam, Elizabeth York. *Women and the Creation of Urban Life: Dallas, Texas, 1843-1920.* College Station, TX: Texas A&M University Press, 1998.

Fehrenbach, T. R. *Lone Star: A History of Texas and the Texans.* Boulder, CO: Da Capo Press, 2000.

"First Airplane Flight in Alaska – A Special Fourth of July Celebration." *The Alaska Life.* July 4, 2017. https://www.thealaskalife.com/journals-stories /first-airplane-flight/.

Fredson, John, and Edward Sapir. *John Fredson Edward Sapir Haa Googwandak: Stories Told by John Fredson to Edward Sapir.* Fairbanks: Alaska Native Language Center, University of Alaska, 1982.

Friesen, T. M. and Owen K. Mason. *The Oxford Handbook of the Prehistoric Arctic*. New York: Oxford University Press, 2016.

Gailor, Thomas Frank. *Some Memories*. Kingsport, TN: Southern Publishers, 1937.

"GTT." *Handbook of Texas Online*. Accessed November 21, 2019. http://www .tshaonline.org/handbook/online/articles/pfg01.

Haley, James L. *Wolf: The Lives of Jack London*. New York: Basic Books, 2010. Kindle Edition.

Hall, Donald E., ed. *Muscular Christianity: Embodying the Victorian Age*. Cambridge Studies in Nineteenth-Century Literature and Culture. New York: Cambridge University Press, 1994.

Handwerk, Brian. "Ice Age Child Found in Prehistoric Alaskan Home." *National Geographic*. February 25, 2011. https://www.nationalgeographic.com /news/2011/2/110224-ice-age-child-cremation-human-remains-alaska -science.html.

Hankinson, Alan. *A Century on the Crags: The Story of Rock Climbing in the Lake District*. London: Dent, 1988.

Harper-Haines, Jan. *Cold Water Spirits: The Legacy of an Athabascan-Irish Family from Alaska's Yukon River*. Anchorage: Epicenter Press, 2000.

Hill, Patricia Everidge. *Dallas: The Making of a Modern City*. Austin: University of Texas Press, 1996.

"History of child labor in the United States—part 1: little children working." *Monthly Labor Review*. Bureau of Labor Statistics. January 2017. https:// www.bls.gov/opub/mlr/2017/article/history-of-child-labor-in-the -united-states-part-1.htm.

"The History of the FA." *The Football Association*. Accessed November 21, 2019. http://www.thefa.com/about-football-association/what-we-do/history.

"The History of the Hash House Harriers." *Runner's World*. June 13, 2019. https://www.runnersworld.com/training/a20785273/why-are-runners -often-called-harriers/.

Kari, James and James A. Fall. *Shem Pete's Alaska: The Territory of the Upper Cook Inlet Dena'ina*. Fairbanks: University of Alaska Press, 2016.

King, Charles. *Gods of the Upper Air: How a Circle of Renegade Anthropologists Reinvented Race, Sex, and Gender in the Twentieth Century*. New York: Doubleday, 2019.

Krakauer, Jon. *Eiger Dreams: Ventures Among Men and Mountains*. New York: Lyons & Burford, 1980.

Jenkins, Mark Collins. "The Story of National Geographic Society's Youngest Founder." *National Geographic* (blog). January 10, 2018. https://blog .nationalgeographic.org/2018/01/10/the-story-of-the-national-geographic -societys-youngest-founder/.

Jenkins, Thomas. *The Man of Alaska: Peter Trimble Rowe*. New York: Morehouse-Gorham, 1943.

Labor, Earle. *Jack London: An American Life*. New York: Farrar, Straus and
     Giroux, 2013.

Lattka, Ann. "The Princess Sophia." National Park Service. Accessed February 9,
     2020. https://www.nps.gov/articles/khns-princess-sophia.htm.

"The Lectionary Page." Episcopal Church of the USA. Accessed January 26, 2020.
     http://www.lectionarypage.net/CalndrsIndexes/TxtIndexLFF.htmlApril.

London, Jack. *Burning Daylight*. New York: Macmillan Company, 1910. Project
     Gutenberg ebook.

Lovett, Richard. "Nearer my god to thee." *New Scientist* 185, no. 2492 (2005): 52+,
     https://link.gale.com/apps/doc/A131163236/ITOF?u=tel_s_tsla&sid
     =ITOF&xid=318ac50b.

Luker, Ralph. *A Southern Tradition in Theology and Social Criticism, 1830-1930:
     The Religious Liberalism and Social Conservatism of James Warley Miles,
     William Porcher DuBose and Edgar Gardner Murphy*. Studies in American
     Religion Volume 11. New York: The Edwin Mellen Press, 1984.

MacDonald, Mark. "Peter John's last trip." *Anglican Journal* 138, no. 7 (2012): 2.
     Accessed May 28, 2020. https://link.gale.com/apps/doc/A325175608
     /ITOF?u=tel_s_tsla&sid=ITOF&xid=d9a310b3.

Macfarlane, Robert. *Mountains of the Mind: How Desolate and Forbidding Heights
     Were Transformed into Experiences of Indomitable Spirit*. New York: Pan-
     theon, 2003.

Mackenzie, Clara Childs. *Wolf Smeller (Zhoh Gwatsan): A Biography of John
     Fredson, Native Alaskan*. Anchorage: Alaska Pacific University Press, 1985.

McArthur, Judith N., and Harold L. Smith. *Texas Through Women's Eyes: The
     Twentieth-Century Experience*. Austin: University of Texas Press, 2010.

McDermott, James. *Martin Frobisher: Elizabethan Privateer*. New Haven, CT:
     Yale University Press, 2001.

McDonald, William L. *Dallas Rediscovered: A Photographic Chronicle of Urban
     Expansion 1870-1925*. Dallas: The Dallas Historical Society, 1978.

Modzelewski, Michael. *Inside Passage: Living with Killer Whales, Bald Eagles, and
     Kwakiutl Indians*. New York: Harper Collins, 1991.

Moore, Terris. *Mt. McKinley: The Pioneer Climbs*. College, Alaska: University of
     Alaska Press, 1967.

Morris, Edmund. *The Rise of Theodore Roosevelt*. New York: Ballantine, 1979.

"Mountaineering." University of Alaska Museum of the North. Accessed
     February 28, 2020. https://www.uaf.edu/museum/education/educators
     /teaching-through-collecti/mountaineering/.

"Muldrow Glacier." *Mt. McKinley Climber's Guide*. Accessed July 15, 2019.
     http://cliffhanger76.tripod.com/mckinley/muldrow_glacier/index.html.

Muccigrosso, Robert. *American Gothic: The Mind and Art of Ralph Adams Cram*.
     Washington, DC: University Press of American, 1974.

National Park Service. "The Alaska Range and Denali: Geology and Orogeny."
     Updated January 7, 2020. https://www.nps.gov/articles/denali.htm.

"Origin of the Name Dallas." Dallas City Hall. Accessed April 16, 2020. https://dallascityhall.com/government/citysecretary/archives/Pages/Archives_DallasNameOrigin.aspx.

"Our Founder." TMI Episcopal School. Accessed December 18, 2019. https://www.tmi-sa.org/About/History/Our-Founder.

Patterson, Brown. *The Liberal Arts at Sewanee: A History of Teaching and Learning at the University of the South.* Sewanee, TN: University of the South, 2009.

Percy, William Alexander. *Lanterns on the Levee: Recollections of a Planter's Son.* New York: Alfred A. Knopf, 1941.

Phillips, Carol A., ed. *A Century of Faith.* Fairbanks, AK: Centennial Press, 1995.

Potter, Ben A., Joel D. Irish, Joshua D. Reuther, and Holly J. McKinney. "New insights into Eastern Beringian mortuary behavior: A terminal Pleistocene double infant burial at Upward Sun River." *Proceedings of the National Academy of Sciences* 111, no 48 (2014): 17060–17065; first published November 10, 2014. https://doi.org/10.1073/pnas.1413131111.

Potter, Ben, and Robert Sattler. "Upward Sun River Site Frequently Asked Questions." Tanana Chiefs Conference. November 14, 2014. https://www.tananachiefs.org/upward-sun-river-site-faq/.

Purple Sewanee. Sewanee, TN: Association for the Preservation of Tennessee Antiquities, Sewanee Chapter, 1961.

Raines-Harper, Jan. *Cold River Spirits: The Legacy of an Athabascan-Irish Family from Alaska's Yukon River.* Kenmore, WA: Epicenter Press, 2000.

———. "Denali, A Universe." *Alpinist.* October 23, 2019. http://www.alpinist.com/doc/web19f/wfeature-a67-wired-denali-universe.

Roberts, David, ed. *Points Unknown: A Great Century of Exploration.* New York: Outside Books/W. W. Norton, 2000.

Robinson, Michael F. *The Coldest Crucible: Arctic Exploration and American Culture.* Chicago: University of Chicago, 2006. Kindle Edition.

Rosenberg, Matt. "Largest Cities Throughout History." *Thoughtco.* Updated November 4, 2019. https://www.thoughtco.com/largest-cities-throughout-history-4068071.

Seatree, George. "In Memoriam: John W. Robinson." *The Journal of the Fell & Rock Climbing Club of the English Lake District* 1, no. 1 (1907). https://www.frcc.co.uk/wp-content/uploads/2016/01/Vol1-1.pdf.

"Scafell & Wasdale." *Fell & Rock Climbing Club.* Accessed November 7, 2019. https://www.frcc.co.uk/rock-climbing/scafell-wasdale/.

Scherer, Logan. "Bedfellows Forever." *Oxford American,* Issue 106, Fall 2019. https://www.oxfordamerican.org/magazine/item/1819-bedfellows-forever.

Scott, Doug. *Big Wall Climbing: Development, Techniques, and Aids.* Oxford: Oxford University Press, 1974.

Scull, E. Marshall. *Hunting in the Arctic and Alaska.* Philadelphia: John C. Winston, Co., 1915.

Secor, R. J. *Aconcagua: A Climbing Guide.* Seattle: Mountaineers, 1999.

Sheldon, Charles. *The Wilderness of Denali: Explorations of a Hunter-naturalist in Northern Alaska.* Lanham, NY: Derrydale Press, 1958. Kindle Edition.

Smith, Gerald L. *Hudson Stuck and Sewanee.* Pre-Orientation Talk, University of the South, August 1994. http://smith2.sewanee.edu/texts/Sewanee/Hudson.html.

Sponagle, Jane. "Forgotten Voyage." CBC News. October 27, 2018. https://news interactives.cbc.ca/longform/forgotten-voyage.

Stark, Peter. *Astoria: John Jacob Astor and Thomas Jefferson's Lost Pacific Empire: A Story of Wealth, Ambition, and Survival.* New York: Ecco, 2014.

Stefansson, Vilhjalmur. *Discovery: The Autobiography of Vilhjalmur Stefansson.* New York: McGraw-Hill, 1964.

Stoler, Ann Laura, ed. *Haunted by Empire: Geographies of Intimacy on North American History.* Durham, NC: Duke University Press, 2006.

Stuck, Hudson. *The Alaskan Missions of the Episcopal Church.* New York: Domestic and Foreign Missionary Society, 1920.

———. *The Ascent of Denali (Mount McKinley).* New York: Charles Scribner's Sons, 1914.

———. *The Salmon Cannery at the Mouth of the Yukon.* New York, 1920.

———. *Ten Thousand Miles With a Dog Sled: A Narrative of Winter Travel in Interior Alaska.* Lincoln, NE and London: University of Nebraska Press, 1988.

———. *Voyages on the Yukon and its tributaries; a narrative of summer travel in the interior of Alaska.* New York: Charles Scribner's Sons, 1917.

———. *A Winter Circuit of Our Arctic Coast.* New York: Charles Scribner's Sons, 1920.

Townsend, Brad. "A New Religion: Football Caught On Early and Became Texas' Passion." *Dallas Morning News,* December 6, 2010. https://www.dallasnews.com/sports/2010/12/06/a-new-religion-football-caught-on-early-and-became-texas-passion.

Vance, Norman. *The Sinews of the Spirit: The Ideal of Christian Manliness in Victorian Literature and Religious Thought.* Cambridge, UK: Cambridge University Press, 1985.

Walker, Tom. *The Seventymile Kid: The Lost Legacy of Harry Karstens and the First Ascent of Mount McKinley.* Seattle: The Mountaineers Books, 2013. Kindle Edition.

Waterman, Jonathan. *Chasing Denali: The Sourdoughs, Cheechakos, and Frauds Behind the Most Unbelievable Feat in Mountaineering.* Guilford, CT: Lyons Press, 2019.

West, Frederick H. and Constance F. West. *American Beginnings: The Prehistory and Paleoecology of Beringia.* Chicago: University of Chicago Press, 1996.

Wickersham, James. *Old Yukon: Tales, Trails, and Trials.* Edited and abridged by Terrence Cole. Fairbanks: University of Alaska Press, 2009.

Williams, Maria Shaa Tláa, ed. *Alaska Native Reader: History, Culture, Politics.* Durham, NC: Duke University Press, 2009.

Yarrow, Andrew L. "History of U.S. Children's Policy, 1900-Present." Firstfocus .org. April 2009. https://firstfocus.org/wp-content/uploads/2014/06 /Childrens-Policy-History.pdf.

Yong, Ed. "Ancient Infant's DNA Reveals New Clues to How the Americas Were Peopled." *The Atlantic.* January 3, 2018. https://www.theatlantic .com/science/archive/2018/01/upward-sun-river-infants-genome -peopling-americas/549572/.

NOTES

PROLOGUE

1. Hudson Stuck, *The Ascent of Denali (Mount McKinley)* (New York: Charles Scribner's Sons, 1914), p. 94.
2. Ibid., p. 75.
3. Stuck, *Ten Thousand Miles With a Dog Sled: A Narrative of Winter Travel in Interior Alaska* (Lincoln, NE, and London: University of Nebraska Press, 1988), 251-252.
4. Mary F. Ehrlander, *Walter Harper: Native Alaska Son* (Lincoln, NE: University of Nebraska Press, 2017), p. 25.
5. Stuck, *Ascent*, p. 6.
6. Ibid., p. 6.
7. Ibid., p. xii.
8. Ibid., p. 4.
9. Randolph B. Campbell, *Gone to Texas: A History of the Lone Star State* (New York: Oxford University Press, 2003), pp. 303-304.
10. Hudson Stuck, *Voyages on the Yukon and its tributaries; a narrative of summer travel in the interior of Alaska* (New York: Charles Scribner's Sons, 1917), p. 233.
11. Hudson Stuck Diary, July 4, 1904.
12. Stuck, *Ascent*, p. 3.
13. Stuck, *Ten Thousand Miles*, pp. 225–226.

CHAPTER 1

1. "The Alaska Range and Denali: Geology and Orogeny," National Park Service, updated January 7, 2020, https://www.nps.gov/articles/denali.htm.

2. Ben A. Potter et al., "New insights into Eastern Beringian mortuary behavior: A terminal Pleistocene double infant burial at Upward Sun River," *Proceedings of the National Academy of Sciences* 111, no 48 (December 2, 2014): 17060–17065; first published November 10, 2014, https://doi.org/10.1073/pnas.1413131111.

3. Craig Childs, *Atlas of a Lost World: Travels in Ice Age America* (New York: Pantheon, 2018), Chap. 3, Kindle.

4. Paul Colinveaux, "Reconstructing the Environment," in Frederick H. West and Constance F. West, *American Beginnings: The Prehistory and Paleoecology of Beringia* (Chicago: University of Chicago Press, 1996), p. 13.

5. Ed Yong, "Ancient Infant's DNA Reveals New Clues to How the Americas Were Peopled," *The Atlantic*, January 3, 2018, https://www.theatlantic.com/science /archive/2018/01/upward-sun-river-infants-genome-peopling-americas/549572/.

6. T. M. Friesen and Owen K. Mason, "Introduction: Archaeology of the North American Arctic," in *The Oxford Handbook of the Prehistoric Arctic*, eds. T. Max Friesen and Owen K. Mason (New York: Oxford University Press, 2016), p. 13.

7. Yong, "Ancient Infant's DNA Reveals New Clues to How the Americas Were Peopled."

8. Craig Childs, *Atlas of a Lost World: Travels in Ice Age America* (New York: Pantheon, 2018), Chap. 1, Kindle.

9. Claire Alix, "A Critical Resource: Wood Use and Technology in the North American Arctic," in *The Oxford Handbook of the Prehistoric Arctic*, eds. T. Max Friesen and Owen K. Mason (New York: Oxford University Press, 2016), p. 114.

10. Ted Goebel and Ben A. Potter, "First Traces: Human Settlement of the Arctic," in *The Oxford Handbook of the Prehistoric Arctic*, eds. T. Max Friesen and Owen K. Mason (New York: Oxford University Press, 2016), p. 236.

11. Ben Potter and Robert Sattler, "Upward Sun River Site Frequently Asked Questions," *Tanana Chiefs Conference*, https://www.tananachiefs.org/upward -sun-river-site-faq/.

12. Email from Dr. Ben Potter to the author, August 26, 2019.

13. Brian Handwerk, "Ice Age Child Found in Prehistoric Alaskan Home," *National Geographic*, February 25, 2011, https://www.nationalgeographic.com/news /2011/2/110224-ice-age-child-cremation-human-remains-alaska-science.html.

14. Childs, *Atlas of a Lost World*, Chap. 4, Kindle.

15. Book resides in the University of the South Archives, Sewanee, TN.

16. Email from Dr Ben Potter to the author, August 26, 2019.

17. Katerina G. Solovjova and Aleksandra A. Vovnyanko, "The Fur Rush: A Chronicle of Colonial Life," in *The Alaska Native Reader: History, Culture, Politics*, ed. Maria Shaa Tláa Williams (Durham, NC: Duke University Press, 2009), p 29.

18. James Kari et al, "*Lazeni 'linn Nataelde Ghadghaande:* When Russians Were Killed at 'Roasted Salmon Place' (Batzulnetas)," in *The Alaska Native Reader*, ed. Maria Shaa Tláa Williams (Durham, NC: Duke University Press, 2009), pp. 15–27.

19. Solovjova and Vovnyanko, "The Fur Rush: A Chronicle of Colonial Life," p. *30 ff.*

20. Gwenn A. Miller, "'The Perfect Mistress of Russian Economy': Sighting the Intimate on a Colonial Alaskan Terrain, 1784-1821," in *Haunted by Empire: Geographies of Intimacy on North American History*, ed. Ann Laura Stoler (Durham, NC: Duke University Press, 2006), p. 299.

21. Bathsheba Demuth, *Floating Coast: An Environmental History of the Bering Strait* (New York: W. W. Norton, 2019), p. 86.

22. Peter Stark, *Astoria: John Jacob Astor and Thomas Jefferson's Lost Pacific Empire: A Story of Wealth, Ambition, and Survival* (New York: Ecco, 2014), p. 70.

23. Stuck, *Alaskan Missions*, p. 2.

24. Ehrlander, p. 18.

25. Eherlander, p. 19.

26. Maria Shaa Tláa Williams, "The Comity Agreement," in *Alaska Native Reader* (Durham, NC: Duke University Press, 2009), pp. 152–153.

27. Ehrlander, p. 20.

28. Charles King, *Gods of the Upper Air: How a Circle of Renegade Anthropologists Reinvented Race, Sex, and Gender in the Twentieth Century* (New York: Doubleday, 2019), p. 85.

29. Demuth, p. 215.

30. Earle Labor, *Jack London: An American Life* (New York: Farrar, Straus and Giroux, 2013), p. 99.

31. Demuth, p. 212.

CHAPTER 2

1. Julia Baird, *Victoria the Queen: An Intimate Biography of the Women Who Ruled an Empire* (New York: Random House, 2016), p. 325 ff.

2. "Largest Cities Throughout History," *Thoughtco*, updated November 4, 2019, https://www.thoughtco.com/largest-cities-throughout-history-4068071.

3. Charles Arnold-Baker, "Underground," in *The Companion to British History,* 2nd ed. (London: Routledge, 2001).

4. "The History of the FA," *The Football Association,* accessed November 21, 2019, http://www.thefa.com/about-football-association/what-we-do/history.

5. Peter Ackroyd, *London: The Biography* (London: Chatto & Windus, 2000), p. 111.

6. David Dean, *Breaking Trail: Hudson Stuck of Texas and Alaska* (Athens, OH: Ohio University Press, 1988), p. 1.

7. Hudson Stuck, *A Winter Circuit of Our Arctic Coast: A Narrative of a Journey with Dog-Sleds Around the Entire Coast of Alaska* (New York: Charles Scribner's Sons, 1920), pp. 86–87.

8. Clara Heintz Burke, as told to Adele Comandini, *Doctor Hap* (New York: Coward-McCann, 1961), p. 175.

9. Hudson Stuck letter to Joshua Kimber, June 27, 1904. Archives of the Episcopal Church, Austin,

10. T. F. T. Baker, Diane K. Bolton, and Patricia E. C. Croot, "Paddington: Westbourne Green," in *A History of the County of Middlesex: Volume 9, Hampstead, Paddington,* ed. C R Elrington (London, 1989), pp. 198-204, http://www.british-history.ac.uk /vch/middx/vol9/pp198-204.

11. Stuck, *Winter Circuit*, p. 122.

12. Ibid., p. 86.

13. Ibid.

14. Stuck, *Ascent*, p. 4.

15. "From Cowboy to Missionary," *The Courier and Argus* (Dundee, Scotland) June 24, 1913, p. 5.

16. Alan Hankinson, *A Century on the Crags : The Story of Rock Climbing in the Lake District* (London: Dent, 1988), pp. 14–15.

17.   George Seatree, "In Memoriam: John W. Robinson," *The Journal of the Fell & Rock Climbing Club of the English Lake District* 1, no. 1 (1907), https://www.frcc.co.uk /wp-content/uploads/2016/01/Vol1-1.pdf.

18.   Hankinson, *Century*, p. 16.

19.   "Scafell & Wasdale," *Fell & Rock Climbing Club*, accessed November 7, 2019, https://www.frcc.co.uk/rock-climbing/scafell-wasdale/.

20.   Hankinson, *Century*, p. 8.

21.   Doug Scott, *Big Wall Climbing: Development, Techniques, and Aids* (Oxford: Oxford University Press, 1974), quoted in Hankinson, *Century*, p. 26.

22.   Frank A. Juhan, unpublished manuscript dated February 4, 1961; University of the South archives.

23.   "In The Steerage of a Cunard Steamer," in the *Pall Mall Budget: Being a Weekly Collection of Articles Printed in the Pall Mall Gazette from day to day with a Summary of News*, London, Vol. XXII, 16 August 1879, pp. 9–12, https://www.gjenvick.com /Steerage/1879-SteerageAccommodations-Cunard.html.

24.   Grafton Burke, "Hudson Stuck from Texas to Alaska," *Alaska Churchman* p. 39.

25.   "GTT," *Handbook of Texas Online*, accessed November 21, 2019, http://www .tshaonline.org/handbook/online/articles/pfg01.

26.   Randolph B. Campbell, *Gone to Texas: A History of the Lone Star State* (New York: Oxford University Press, 2003), p. 290.

27.   Burke, "Hudson Stuck," p. 40.

28.   Ibid., pp. 41–42.

29.   Campbell, *Gone to Texas*, p. 295.

30.   "The Indians," *Trenton State Gazette* (published as *Daily State Gazette*), June 28, 1878, p. 2.

31.   "Summary of the News," *New York Daily Herald*, July 11, 1883, p. 6.

32.   "Mr. Roosevelt Among the Cowboys," *New York Tribune*, July 28, 1884.

33.   Burke, "Hudson Stuck," pp 42.

34.   Escal F. Duke, "San Angelo, TX," *The Handbook of Texas Online*, Texas State Historical Association, June 15, 2010, https://www.tshaonline.org/handbook /entries/san-angelo-tx.

35.   Burke, "Hudson Stuck," pp. 43-44.

36.   T. R. Fehrenbach, *Lone Star: A History of Texas and the Texans* (Boulder, CO: Da Capo Press, 2000), p. 599.

37.   Burke, "Hudson Stuck," p. 44.

38.   "Archdeacon, Hudson Stuck Dead," *The Junction Eagle* (Junction, Texas), December 10, 1920, https://texashistory.unt.edu/ark:/67531/metapth801011 /m1/2/?q=hudson%20stuck.

39.   "Our Founder," TMI Episcopal, accessed December 18, 2019, https://www.tmi-sa .org/About/History/Our-Founder.

40.   Burke, "Hudson Stuck," p. 10.

CHAPTER 3

1.   William Alexander Percy, *Lanterns on the Levee: Recollections of a Planter's Son* (New York: Alfred A. Knopf, 1941), p. 96.

2.   David Bowman, *Sewanee in Stone: Architecture & History* (Sewanee, TN: Proctor's Hall Press, 2003), p. 22.

3. Professor Gerald Smith, email to the author, September 23, 2020.

4. Ralph Luker, *A Southern Tradition in Theology and Social Criticism, 1830-1930: The Religious Liberalism and Social Conservatism of James Warley Miles, William Porcher DuBose and Edgar Gardner Murphy*, Studies in American Religion Volume 11 (New York: The Edwin Mellen Press, 1984), p. 2.

5. Hudson Stuck to Dr. Benjamin Lawton Wiggins, 9 March, 1893, Typescript, Hudson Stuck Collection, William R. Laurie University Archives and Special Collections, the University of the South.

6. Arthur Ben Chitty, *Reconstruction in Sewanee: The founding of the University of the South and its first administration, 1857–1872* (Sewanee, TN: University Press, 1954), p. 63.

7. Brown Patterson, *The Liberal Arts at Sewanee: A History of Teaching and Learning at the University of the South* (Sewanee, TN: University of the South, 2009), p. 12.

8. Donald Smith Armentrout, *The Quest for the Informed Priest: A History of the School of Theology* (Sewanee, TN: School of Theology, University of the South, 1979), p. 32.

9. Thomas Frank Gailor, *Some Memories* (Kingsport, TN: Southern Publishers, 1937), p. 80.

10. Patterson, *The Liberal Arts at Sewanee*, p. 19.

11. Armentrout, *Quest for the Informed Priest*, p. 131.

12. Patterson, *The Liberal Arts at Sewanee*, p. 20.

13. Archives, University of the South, Sewanee, Tennessee.

14. Armentrout, *Quest for the Informed Priest*, p. 475.

15. Ibid., pp. 129–130.

16. Stuck to Wiggins, March 9, 1893.

17. Armentrout, *Quest for the Informed Priest*, p. 101.

18. "Archdeacon, Hudson Stuck Dead," *The Junction Eagle*, Junction, Texas, December 10, 1920. https://texashistory.unt.edu/ark:/67531/metapth801011/m1/2/?q=hudson%20stuck.

19. Lily Baker et al., eds. *Sewanee* ("Published for the benefit of the University Library collection of Sewaneeana," Sewanee, TN, 1932), p. 77.

20. *Cap & Gown*, University of the South, 1892, https://dspace.sewanee.edu/bitstream/handle/11005/17/CapandGown1892.pdf?sequence=1&isAllowed=y.

21. Stuck to Wiggins, 9 March, 1893.

22. "Archdeacon Stuck Flays Life's Shams," *New York Times*, June 5, 1916, p. 11, ProQuest Historical Newspapers.

23. Armentrout, *Quest for the Informed Priest*, p. 96.

24. "Previous Vice-Chancellors," The Univeristy of the South, https://www.sewanee.edu/about/vc/previous-vice-chancellors/.

25. Stuck to Wiggins, Oct 4 1893. Sewanee archives.

26. Stuck to Wiggins, March 8, 1893.

27. *The Gazette*, Fort Worth, Texas, June 19, 1894.

CHAPTER 4

1. William L. McDonald, *Dallas Rediscovered: A Photographic Chronicle of Urban Expansion 1870-1925* (Dallas: The Dallas Historical Society, 1978), p. 7.

2. "Origin of the Name Dallas," Dallas City Hall, https://dallascityhall.com/government/citysecretary/archives/Pages/Archives_DallasNameOrigin.aspx.

3. Patricia Everidge Hill, *Dallas: The Making of a Modern City* (Austin: University of Texas Press, 1996), p. xx.

4. McDonald, *Dallas Rediscovered*, p. 19.

5. Hill, *Dallas*, p. xxv.

6. Campbell, *Gone to Texas*, p. 309.

7. Hill, *Dallas*, p. 5.

8. Campbell, *Gone to Texas*, p. 306.

9. "Jubliee of Bishop Garrett," *Houston Daily Post*, December 21, 1899, p. 5.

10. Quoted in "Our History," St. Matthews Cathedral, accessed April 14, 2020, http://www.episcopalcathedral.org/our-history/.

11. McDonald, *Dallas Rediscovered*, p. 67, p. 112.

12. Don S. Armentrout and Robert B. Slocum, eds., *An Episcopal Dictionary of the Church: A User-Friendly Reference for Episcopalians* (New York: Church Pubilshing, 2000), p. 68.

13. Donald E. Hall, ed., *Muscular Christianity: Embodying the Victorian Age,* Cambridge Studies in Nineteenth-Century Literature and Culture (New York: Cambridge University Press, 1994), p. 7.

14. Stuck to Wiggins, Nov 5, 1898.

15. Stuck to Wiggins, November 12, 1898.

16. Brad Townsend, "A New Religion: Football Caught On Early and Became Texas' Passion," *Dallas Morning News,* December 6, 2010, https://www.dallasnews.com/sports/2010/12/06/a-new-religion-football-caught-on-early-and-became-texas-passion.

17. "The History of the Hash House Harriers," *Runner's World*, June 13, 2019, https://www.runnersworld.com/training/a20785273/why-are-runners-often-called-harriers/.

18. "St. Matthew's Harriers," *Dallas Morning News*, September 28, 1902.

19. Robert Macfarlane, *Mountains of the Mind: How Desolate and Forbidding Heights Were Transformed into Experiences of Indomitable Spirit* (New York: Pantheon, 2003), 92.

20. Townsend, "A New Religion."

21. "Vanity of the World: The Sermon of Rev. Hudson Stuck," *Dallas Morning News*, July 21, 1902, p. 3.

22. Stuck, *Voyages*, p. 48.

23. Stuck to Wiggins, October 31, 1894.

24. *The Churchman,* November 14, 1896, p. 653.

25. "Some Broad Charities," *Dallas Morning News*, November 19, 1899, p. 24.

26. Hill, *Dallas*, p. 48.

27. "Some Broad Charities," p. 24.

28. Dean, *Breaking Trail*, p. 33.

29. Ibid., p. 32.

30. "Some Broad Charities," p. 24.

31. St. Matthew's Cathedral Newsletter, Second Week in Lent, 1899.

32. Ibid.

33. "The Archdeacon of the Yukon," *The Churchman*, July 23, 1904, p. 151.

34. Dean, *Breaking Trail*, p. 29.

35. Frank A. Juhan, unpublished manuscript dated February 4, 1961; University of the South archives, p. 1.

36. Stuck to Wiggins, November 7, 1890.
37. Logan Scherer, "Bedfellows Forever," *Oxford American*, no. 106 (Fall 2019), https://www.oxfordamerican.org/magazine/item/1819-bedfellows-forever.
38. Juhan, "Stuck," p. 3.
39. Stuck to Wiggins, October 31, 1894.
40. Stuck to Wiggins, March 9, 1893.
41. Stuck to Wiggins, October 20, 1897.
42. Register of Students, Registrar's records, UA17, Box 7. Archives, University of the South.
43. "Illiteracy of a City," *Dallas Morning News*, October 29, 1900.
44. Burke, *Hudson Stuck*, p. 45.
45. James N. Young to Arthur Ben Chitty, April 25, 1953. Sewanee archives.
46. McDonald, *Dallas Rediscovered*, p. 32.
47. Judith N. McArthur and Harold L. Smith, "Maternalist Legislation: Child Labor, Compulsory Education, and Mothers' Pensions Mills," in *Texas through women's eyes: the twentieth-century experience* (Austin: University of Texas Press, 2010), p. 88, EBSCOhost.
48. "History of child labor in the United States—part 1: little children working," *Monthly Labor Review*, Bureau of Labor Statistics, January 2017, https://www.bls.gov/opub/mlr/2017/article/history-of-child-labor-in-the-united-states-part-1.htm.
49. Andrew L. Yarrow, "History of U.S. Children's Policy, 1900-Present," First Focus, April 2009, https://firstfocus.org/wp-content/uploads/2014/06/Childrens-Policy-History.pdf.
50. Hill, *Dallas*, p. xxvii.
51. Hill, *Dallas*, p. 2.
52. "Child Labor Condemned," *Dallas Morning Herald*, January 12, 1902.
53. Judith N. McArthur and Harold L. Smith, "Clubwomen Investigate Child Labor in the Dallas Cotton Mills (1902)," in *Texas Through Women's Eyes: The Twentieth-Century Experience* (Austin: University of Texas Press, 2010), p. 88, EBSCOhost.
54. "Clubdom," *Dallas Morning News*, September 23, 1901.
55. Elizabeth York Enstam, *Women and the Creation of Urban Life: Dallas, Texas, 1843–1920* (College Station, TX: Texas A&M University Press, 1998), p. 240, note 9.
56. "A Broader View of the Child-Labor Question," *Dallas Morning News*, April 15, 1902, p. 6.
57. Hudson Stuck, "Against Child Labor," *Dallas Morning News*, April 17, 1902, p. 12.
58. "The Child in the Mill and Out of the Mill," *Dallas Morning News*, April 20, 1902, p. 18.
59. H. W. Fairbanks, "Reply to Dean Stuck," *Dallas Morning News*, April 20, 1902, p. 4.
60. Hudson Stuck, "Reply to Mr. Fairbanks," *Dallas Morning News*, May 1, 1902, p. 5.
61. Hudson Stuck, "Dean Stuck's Position," *Dallas Morning News*, May 4, 1902, p. 30.
62. Hudson Stuck, "Open Letter to Democrats," *Dallas Morning News*, July 16, 1902, p. 9.
63. "Refused to Adjourn," *Dallas Morning News*, March 3, 1903, p. 2; "Approved by Governor," *Dallas Morning News*, March 7, 1903, p. 8.
64. Dean, *Breaking Trail*, pp. 42-43.
65. Ibid, p. 48.
66. Ibid, p. 50.
67. Stuck to Wiggins, October 20, 1897.
68. Grafton Burke, "Hudson Stuck," p. 11.

69.   "The Archdeacon of Alaska," *Spirit of Missions*, August 1904, pp. 600-601.

70.   Stuck to Wiggins, March 8, 1904. Sewanee Archives.

CHAPTER 5

1.   Hudson Stuck, "On the Way to Central Alaska: Some Notes from a Missionary's Journal," *Spirit of Missions*, December 1904, p. 879-880.

2.   Michael Modzelewski, *Inside Passage: Living with Killer Whales, Bald Eagles, and Kwakiutl Indians* (New York: Harper Collins, 1991), p. xvii.

3.   Stuck, *Voyages*, p. 3.

4.   Ibid., pp. 5-6.

5.   Ibid., p. 6.

6.   "The Archdeacon of the Yukon," and "Archdeacon Stuck's Impressions of the St. Louis Fair," *The Churchman*, July 23, 1904, p. 151.

7.   Stuck, "On the Way to Central Alaska," pp. 879-880.

8.   Hudson Stuck Diary, August 6, 1904.

9.   Stuck, *Alaskan Missions*, p. 17.

10.   Letter of John Bell to George Simpson, August 1, 1845, Hudson Bay Company Archives, D.5/14, fos. 212-215d. Quoted at https://en.wikipedia.org/wiki/Yukon _River.

11.   Stuck, "On the Way to Central Alaska," p. 880.

12.   Dean, *Breaking Trail*, p. 69.

13.   Stuck, "On the Way to Central Alaska," p. 880.

14.   Ibid.

15.   Stuck, *Alaskan Missions*, p. 82-83.

16.   James Wickersham, *Old Yukon: Tales, Trails, and Trials,* edited and abridged by Terrence Cole (Fairbanks: University of Alaska Press, 2009), p. 27.

17.   Wickersham, *Old Yukon*, p. 151.

18.   Ibid., pp.148–155.

19.   Ibid., p. 32.

20.   Stuck, *Alaskan Missions*, p. 48.

21.   Ibid., p. 51.

22.   "The Church in Two Alaska Communities," *Spirit of Missions*, May 1904, p. 317.

23.   Stuck, *Ten Thousand Miles*, p. 251.

24.   Stuck diary, Sept 1, 1904.

25.   Stuck, *Alaskan Missions*, p. 117.

26.   "The Meeting of the Board of Managers," *Spirit of Missions*, August 1904, p. 514.

27.   Stuck, *Alaskan Missions*, p. 117-118.

28.   "How the Church Went to Alaska, and What Has Been Done There," *Spirit of Missions*, March 1905, p. 264.

29.   Hudson Stuck, "The Outlook at Fairbanks," *Spirit of Missions,* August 1905, p. 631.

30.   Rev. Charles E. Betticher, Jr., "A Reading-Room at Work," *Spirit of Missions*, December 1906, p. 993-4.

31.   Hudson Stuck, "A Missionary Gramophone in Central Alaska," *Spirit of Missions*, January 1906, p. 51.

32.   Debbie Carter, "Alaska's longest-running weather station to be honored," *UAF news and information,* July 31, 2018, https://news.uaf.edu/alaskas-longest-running -weather-station-to-be-honored/.

33. Hudson Stuck, "A Visit to the Miners of the Fairbanks District," *Spirit of Missions*, September 1905, p. 705.

34. "Rev. Mr. Stuck Will Preach," *The Daily Alaskan*, August 1, 1908, p. 1.

35. Rowe quoted in Dean, *Breaking Trail*, p. 85.

36. Rev. Mr. Kippenbrock to Arthur Ben Chitty, n.d., ABC file, University of the South Archives.

37. Hudson Stuck, *Voyages*, p. 84.

38. Lorna Coppinger, *The World of Sled Dogs: From Siberia to Sport Racing* (Howell Book House, 1977), quoted in Thom Swan, "'Marche': Sledge Dogs in the North West Fur Trade," *Swanny's Place*, archived from the original on 17 June 2009, https://web .archive.org/web/20090617050554/http://www.tworiversak.com/sleddoghx1.htm.

39. see James McDermott, *Martin Frobisher: Elizabethan Privateer* (New Haven: Yale University Press, 2001), chs. 8, 10, and 12.

40. Email from James McDermott to the author, June 15, 2020.

41. Jennifer A. Leonard, Robert K. Wayne, Jane Wheeler, Raúl Valadez, Sonia Guillén, and Carles Vilà, "Ancient DNA Evidence for Old World Origin of New World Dogs," *Science* 298 (5598), pp. 1613-1616, doi: 10.1126/science.1076980.

42. "A Brief History of Dog Sledding," *Outdoor Dog World*, updated April 30, 2020, https://outdoordogworld.com/dog-sledding-history/.

43. Stuck, *Ten Thousand Miles*, p. 397.

44. Lydia Black, *Russians in Alaska, 1732-1867* (Fairbanks: University of Alaska, 2004), p. 279, https://www.google.com/books/edition/Russians_in_Alaska_1732_1867 /NSRxrDm0JYYC?hl=en&gbpv=1&bsq=dog.

45. "A Brief History of Dog Sledding," *Outdoor Dog World*.

46. Wickersham, *Old Yukon*, p. 191.

47. Hudson Stuck, "With Bishop Rowe on the Arctic Trail," *Spirit of Missions*, March 1905, p. 267.

48. Ibid.

49. Stuck, *Ten Thousand Miles*, pp. 19, 35, and 36.

50. Joanna Cohan Scherer, "Historical Photographs of the Subarctic: A Resource for Future Research," *Arctic Anthropology* 18, no. 2 (1981), p. 5, http://www.jstor.com /stable/40315997.

51. Hudson Stuck, "The Third Cruise of the *Pelican*," *Spirit of Missions*, May 1911, p. 397.

52. Hudson Stuck, "The First Voyage of the Pelican," *The Churchman*, January 1909, p. 22.

53. Ibid., p. 16.

54. Scott Fisher, former rector of Stuck's church, St. Matthew's Fairbanks, pointed out to the author that this is a play on Psalm 60, verse 8.

55. Stuck, *Voyages*, p. 224.

56. "Archdeacon Stuck Visiting Iditarod," *Iditarod Pioneer*, March 18, 1911. *Chronicling America: Historic American Newspapers*, https://chroniclingamerica.loc.gov/lccn /sn95060032/1911-03-18/ed-1/seq-3/.

57. Stuck, *Ten Thousand Miles*, pp. 16, 46, and 41.

58. Stuck, "The Third Cruise of the *Pelican*," pp. 397–398.

59. Mackenzie, *Wolf Smeller*, p. 65.

60. Stuck, *Voyages*, p. 274.

61. Hudson Stuck, "How the Church Went to the Most Northern Gold Fields," *Spirit of Missions*, July 1905, p. 552.

62. Stuck, *Voyages,* pp. 216, 314.
63. Ibid., pp. 87-88.
64. Ibid., p. 191.
65. Hudson Stuck, "The Yukon Indians," *Spirit of Missions,* February 1906, p. 105.
66. Burke, *Doctor Hap,* p. 36.
67. Ibid., p. 37.
68. Ibid., pp. 40–41.

CHAPTER 6
1. Stuck diary, December 15, 1904.
2. Robert Campbell, *In Darkest Africa: Travel and Empire Along the Inside Passage* (Philadelphia: University of Pennsylvania Press, 2007), p. 5.
3. Campbell, *In Darkest Africa,* p. 10.
4. Harold Napoleon, "Yuuyaraq," in Maria Shaa Tláa Williams, ed., *Alaska Native Reader: History, Culture, Politics* (Durham: Duke University Press, 2009), p. 129.
5. Robert J. Wolfe, "Alaska's Great Sickness, 1900: An Epidemic of Measles and Influenza in a Virgin Soil Population," *Proceedings of the American Philosophical Society,* April 8, 1982, p. 91, http://www.jstor.com/stable/986355.
6. Napoleon, "Yuuyaraq," p. 129.
7. Ibid., p. 122.
8. Stuck, *Voyages,* pp. 178–9.
9. "The Torch of the Gospel," *Dallas Morning News,* December 12, 1898.
10. Hudson Stuck, "The Yukon Indians," *Spirit of Missions,* February 1906, p. 113.
11. Hudson Stuck, "By Boat and Sled to the Koyukuk Country," *Spirit of Missions,* January 1909, p. 25.
12. Hudson Stuck, "The Many-Sided Missionary," *Spirit of Missions,* January 1908, p. 45.
13. Ibid., pp. 47–48.
14. *The Churchman,* October 19, 1907, p. 600.
15. *The Churchman,* July 6, 1907, p. 30.
16. *The Churchman,* December 7, 1907, p. 883.
17. *The Churchman,* December 28, 1907, p. 1007.
18. *The Churchman,* February 1, 1908, p. 162.
19. Theodore Roosevelt, *Theodore Roosevelt Papers: Series 9: Desk Diaries, -1909; 1907, Jan. 1–1908, Dec. 31; 1909, Jan. 7–Feb. 18, 1907,* Manuscript/Mixed Material, https://www.loc.gov/item/mss382990726/; Stuck quoted in Dean, *Breaking Trail,* p. 127.
20. Dean, *Breaking Trail,* p. 129.
21. Rev. John W. Chapman, "The Yukon River and Its Value to the Alaskan Mission," *Spirit of Missions,* April 1904, p. 264.
22. Evon Peter, interview with the author.
23. Stuck, "A New Book on Alaska," *The Sewanee Review,* July 1910, https://www.jstor.org/stable/27532395.
24. Wickersham, *Old Yukon,* 40–41.
25. Ehrlander, *Walter Harper,* p. 19.
26. Steven C. Dinero, "'The Lord Will Provide': The History and Role of Episcopalian Christianity in Nets'aii Gwich'in Social Development - Arctic Village, Alaska," *Indigenous Nations Studies Journal* 4, no. 1 (Spring 2003), p. 10.
27. Stuck, *Alaskan Missions,* pp. 24–25.

28.   Stuck, *Voyages*, pp. 184–185.

29.   Ibid.

30.   Stuck, *Ten Thousand Miles,* p. 81.

31.   Ibid., p. 23.

32.   Edith Pritchard, "The Mission Children of Ketchikan," *Spirit of Missions*, March 1904, p. 215.

33.   Hudson Stuck, "Little Brethen of the North," *Spirit of Missions*, February 1907, p. 121.

34.   Cornelius Osgood, *Contributions to the Ethnography of the Kutchin*, Yale University Publications in Anthropology, Number 14 (New Haven: Yale University Press, 1936), p.3.

35.   Ibid., pp. 173–174.

36.   Dinero, "The Lord Will Provide," p. 22.

37.   Stuck, *Ten Thousand Miles,* p. 24.

38.   Ibid.

39.   Clara Carter, "Alaska Notes," *Spirit of Missions*, April 1909, p. 286.

40.   Susie Williams, interview by Wendy Arundale, Jukebox Project, University of Alaska Fairbanks Oral History Program, November 16, 1992, http://jukebox.uaf.edu/site7/interviews/201.

41.   Moses Cruikshank, interview by Bill Schneider, Jukebox Project, University of Alaska Fairbanks Oral History Project, February 21, 1986, http://jukebox.uaf.edu/site7/interviews/2289.

42.   Stuck, *Alaskan Missions, pp. 127–128.*

43.   Jan Harper-Haines, *Cold Water Spirits: The Legacy of an Athabascan-Irish Family from Alaska's Yukon River* (Anchorage: Epicenter Press, 2000), p. 17.

44.   Pierre Berton, *Klondike: The Last Geat Gold Rush, 1896–1899* (Toronto: McClelland and Stewart Limited, 1972), p. 11.

45.   Thomas K. Bundtzen and Charles C. Hawley, "Arthur Harper," Alaska Mining Hall of Fame Foundation, 1998, revised 2009, http://alaskamininghalloffame.org/inductees/harper.php.

46.   Jan Harper-Haines, "Denali: A Universe," *Alpinist,* October 23, 2019, http://www.alpinist.com/doc/web19f/wfeature-a67-wired-denali-universe.

47.   Harper-Haines, "Denali."

48.   Stuck, *Ten Thousand Miles*, p. 315.

49.   Ehrlander, *Walter Harper*, p. xix.

CHAPTER 7

1.   Quoted in C. Hart Merriam, "Introduction," in Charles Sheldon, *The Wilderness of Denali: Explorations of a Hunter-naturalist in Northern Alaska* (Lanham, NY: Derrydale Press, 1930), Kindle Edition.

2.   Tom Walker, *The Seventymile Kid: The Lost Legacy of Harry Karstens and the First Ascent of Mount McKinley* (Seattle: The Mountaineers Books, 2013), Kindle Edition, loc. 1474.

3.   Ibid.

4.   Charles Sheldon, *The Wilderness of Denali: Explorations of a Hunter-naturalist in Northern Alaska* (Lanham, NY: Derrydale Press, 1958), p. 24, Kindle Edition.

5.   Gregory Crouch, *The Bonanza King: John Mackay and the Battle Over the Greatest Riches in the American West* (New York: Scribner, 2018), Chap. 2, Kindle.

6. James L. Haley, *Wolf: The Lives of Jack London* (New York: Basic Books, 2010), Kindle Edition.

7. Campbell, *In Darkest Alaska*, pp. 272–273.

8. Stuck, *Voyages*, p. 14.

9. Stuck, *Alaskan Missions*, p. 74.

10. Walker, *Seventy-Mile Kid*, loc. 304.

11. Jack London, *Burning Daylight* (New York: Macmillan, 1910), kindle locations 112–117.

12. Earle Labor, *Jack London: An American Life* (New York: Farrar, Straus and Giroux, 2013), p. 108.

13. Stuck, *Voyages*, p. 76.

14. Harry Karstens, autobiographical notes quoted in Terris Moore, *Mt. McKinley: The Pioneer Climbs* (Fairbanks: University of Alaska Press, 1967), pp. 184–185.

15. *The Alaska Citizen*, October 02, 1911, p. 5.

16. Stuck, *Ten Thousand Miles*, p. 215.

17. Wickersham, *Old Yukon*, p. 73.

18. In Moore, *Mt. McKinley*, p. 185.

19. Walker, *Seventy-Mile Kid*, loc. 725.

20. James J. Cooke, *Billy Mitchell* (Boulder: Lynne Rienner Publishers, 2002), p. 36.

21. In Moore, *Mt. McKinley*, p. 185.

22. Walker, *Seventy-Mile Kid*, loc. 747.

23. In Moore, *Mt. McKinley*, p. 185.

24. Ibid., pp. 186–7.

25. *The Alaska Prospector* (Valdez), August 18, 1904, Image 4.

26. "Horse racing at Model park," *The Alaska Citizen*, July 09, 1910, p. 3.

27. *Iditarod Pioneer*, December 11, 1910, p.1.

28. E. Marshall Scull, *Hunting in the Arctic and Alaska* (Philadelphia: John C. Winston, Co., 1915), p. 30.

29. Edmund Morris, *The Rise of Theodore Roosevelt* (New York: Ballantine, 1979), pp. 383–384.

30. "History of the Boone & Crockett Club," Boone and Crockett Club, https://www.boone-crockett.org/history-boone-and-crockett-club.

31. "Charles Sheldon: One Man's Quest to Create the Alaskan Park," *worldhistory.us,* July 6, 2017, https://worldhistory.us/american-history/charles-sheldon-one-mans-quest-to-create-the-alaskan-park.php.

32. Dean, *Breaking Trail*, p. 160.

33. Sheldon, *The Wilderness of Denali*, p. 4.

34. Ibid., p. 213.

35. "Charles Sheldon," *worldhistory.us.*

36. "A History of the Denali-Mount McKinley Region, Alaska," National Park Service, 1991, https://irma.nps.gov/DataStore/DownloadFile/462515.

37. Sheldon, *The Wilderness of Denali*, p. 23.

38. Dean, *Breaking Trail*, p. 160.

39. Walker, *The Seventymile Kid*, loc. 1726.

40. Sheldon, *The Wilderness of Denali,* p. 65.

41. Ibid., p. 274.

42. Ibid., p. 213.

43. "New York Society," *New-York Tribune,* March 10, 1909.

44. Walker, *The Seventymile Kid*, loc. 2311.

45. Stuck, *Ascent*, pp. 4–5.

46. Walker, *The Seventymile Kid*, loc. 2410.

47. Stuck diary, June 26, 1912.

48. Stuck diary, July 31, 1912.

49. Dean, *Breaking Trail*, p. 161.

CHAPTER 8

1. "Introduction," in David Roberts, ed., *Points Unknown: A Great Century of Exploration* (New York: Outside Books/Norton, 2000), p. 12.

2. Michael F. Robinson, *The Coldest Crucible: Arctic Exploration and American Culture* (Chicago: University of Chicago, 2006), loc. 70-72, Kindle Edition.

3. Stuck diary, April 27, 1913.

4. Dean, *Breaking Trail*, pp. 156–7.

5. Stuck, *Winter Circuit*, p. 193.

6. Stuck to Wood, March 19, 1904.

7. Stuck diary, July 22, 1904.

8. Stuck diary, July 23, 1904.

9. Stuck diary, July 24, 1904.

10. "Peter Kaufmann (Alpine Guide)," Wikipedia, updated November 5, 2020, https://en .wikipedia.org/wiki/Peter_Kaufmann_(Alpine_guide)#cite_ref-18; "Christian Kaufmann (Alpine Guide)," Wikipedia, updated November 5, 2020, https://en .wikipedia.org/wiki/Christian_Kaufmann_(alpine_guide).

11. Stuck diary, July 25, 1904.

12. "Alpine Huts," *Alpine Club of Canada,* p. 3, https://www.alpineclubofcanada.ca /web/ACCMember/Huts/Abbot_Pass_Hut.aspx.

13. Stuck diary, July 26, 1904.

14. Stuck, *Ten Thousand Miles,* pp. 225–226.

15. Stuck, *Voyages*, p. 272.

16. Ibid., p. 278.

17. Stuck diary, June 20, 1912.

18. Belmore Browne, *The Conquest of Mt. McKinley* (Boston: Houghton Mifflin, 1956), pp. 338–340.

CHAPTER 9

1. The book resides in the Archives of the University of the South, Sewanee, TN.

2. Terrence Cole, "Introduction," in Wickersham, *Old Yukon*, p. xxiv.

3. Ibid, p. 172.

4. Ibid, p. 178.

5. Art Davidson, "Foreword," in *Denali: Deception, Defeat, and Triumph* (Seattle: The Mountaineers Books, 2001), p. 8.

6. Wickersham, *Old Yukon*, p. 184.

7. Ibid, p. 186.

8. Ibid, p. 190.

9. Stuck, *Ascent*, p. 160.

10. Wickersham, *Old Yukon*, p. 242.

11. Terrence Cole in Wickersham, *Old Yukon*, note p. 242.

12. Stuck, *Ascent*, p. 161.

13. Art Davidson, "Foreword," in *Denali*, p. 9.

14. Ibid.

15. Stuck, *Ascent*, p. 166.

16. Carolyn Kremers, "Denali, Thinking Like a Glacier," National Park Service, updated March 29, 2017, https://www.nps.gov/dena/getinvolved/dca_kremers.htm.

17. Browne, *Conquest*, pp. 70–71.

18. Stuck letter to Royal Geographic Society, London, October 20, 1909. RGS Archives.

19. Unsigned RGS letter to Stuck, December 31, 1909. RGS Archives.

20. Jonathan Waterman, *Chasing Denali: The Sourdoughs, Cheechakos, and Frauds Behind the Most Unbelievable Feat in Mountaineering* (Guilford, CT: Lyons Press, 2019), p. iv.

21. Stuck, *Ascent*, pp. 170–171.

22. "About Us," Mazamas, https://mazamas.org/about/.

23. C. E. Rusk, "On the Trail of Dr. Cook," *The Pacific Monthly*, October 1910, p. 430.

24. Bradford Washington, "Introduction," in Browne, *Conquest*, p. xxv.

25. Browne, *Conquest*, p. v.

26. Ibid., p. 74.

27. Ibid., pp. 121–122.

28. Stuck, *Ascent*, p. 175.

29. Ibid., p. 178.

30. Stuck diary, July 29, 1912.

31. Mackenzie, *Wolf Smeller*, p. 36.

CHAPTER 10

1. In Chapters 10-14, all quotations not otherwise cited are from the diaries of the four members of the Denali expedtion.

   Stuck had two journals, one for 1913 and another smaller one for the ascent. Both are in the American Geographical Society Library, University of Wisconsin-Milwaukee Libraries. The smaller one can be accessed via https://collections.lib.uwm .edu/digital/collection/agsny/id/2117/rec/1 and the larger via https://collections .lib.uwm.edu/digital/collection/agsny/id/2247.

   Karstens's diary is in the American Alpine Club library, Boulder, CO. It was transcribed by Bradford Washburn, noted Denali photographer, cartographer, and alpinist. Washburn's transcription can be accessed via http://publications .americanalpineclub.org/articles/12196933900/The-First-Ascent-of-Mount -McKinley-1913.

   Tatum's diary resides in the University of Tennessee, Knoxville, and be accessed via https://digital.lib.utk.edu/collections/islandora/object/tatum%3A1#page/1/mode/2up.

   Harper's diary is transcribed in full in *Denali: Deception, Defeat, & Triumph*, listed in the bibliography.

2. "Will Attempt to Scale Highest Peak," *Alaska Citizen,* Fairbanks, March 17, 1913, p. 7.

3. Walker, *Seventymile Kid*, loc. 2718.

4. Mackenzie, *Wolf Smeller*, p. 34.

5. Stuck, *Ascent*, p. 7.

6. Ehrlander, *Walter Harper,* p. 55.

7. See Amrita Dhar, "Travel and Mountains," in *The Cambridge History of Travel Writing*, Nandini Das and Tim Youngs, Eds. (Cambridge: Cambridge University Press, 2019), pp. 345–60.

8. Davidson, "Hudson Stuck: Triumph," in *Denali*, p. 493.

9. Yvonne Mozee, "Walter Harper," in *Denali*, p. 620.

10. Bradford Washburn, preface to "The First Ascent of Mount McKinley: A Verbatim Copy of the Diary of Harry P. Karstens," *American Alpine Journal*, February 2, 1969, p. 339.

11. Davidson, "Foreword," in *Denali*, p. 7.

12. Eherlander, *Walter Harper*, p. 60.

13. Ibid.

14. Jon Krakauer, "Club Denali," in *Eiger Dreams: Ventures Among Men and Mountains* (New York: Lyons & Burford, 1980), p. 66.

15. Ibid, p. 65.

16. Bob Drury, *The Rescue Season: The Heroic Story of Parajumpers on the Edge of the World* (New York: Simon & Schuster, 2001), p. 36.

17. R. L. Frost, "A Climatological Review of the Alaska-Yukon Plateau," in W. J. Humphreys, ed., *Monthly Weather Review* 62, no. 8 (August 1934).

18. "The Alaska Range and Denali: Geology and Orogeny," National Park Service, updated January 7, 2020, https://www.nps.gov/articles/denali.htm.

19. James Barkman, "What It's Like to Climb Denali, North America's Highest Peak," *Field Mag*, June 11, 2018, https://www.fieldmag.com/articles/james-barkman-what-it-like-climb-denali.

20. Gordy Megroz, "Karl Egloff Just Beat Kilian Jornet's Denali Record," *Outside Online*, June 21, 2019, https://www.outsideonline.com/2298706/community-rocks.

CHAPTER 11

1. "Muldrow Glacier," *Mt. McKinley Climber's Guide*, http://cliffhanger76.tripod.com/mckinley/muldrow_glacier/index.html.

2. Carolyn Kremers, "Denali, Thinking Like a Glacier," National Park Service, updated March 29, 2017, https://www.nps.gov/dena/getinvolved/dca_kremers.html.

3. Mark Collins Jenkins, "The Story of National Geographic Society's Youngest Founder," *National Geographic*, January 10, 2018, https://blog.nationalgeographic.org/2018/01/10/the-story-of-the-national-geographic-societys-youngest-founder/.

4. Stuck, *Ascent*, p. 24.

5. Walker, *Seventymile Kid*, loc. 3072.

6. Stuck, *Ascent*, pp. 33–34.

7. Browne, *Conquest*, pp. 298–299.

CHAPTER 12

1. Stuck, *Ascent*, pp. 40–42.

2. Ibid., p. 38.

3. Joseph S. Dixon, *Fauna of the National Parks of the United States* (National Park Service, 1938), cited in "Denali," Wikipedia, https://en.wikipedia.org/wiki/Denali#cite_note-dixon-97.

CHAPTER 13

1. Stuck, *Ascent*, p. 72.

2.   Ibid., p. 85.

3.   R. J. Secor, *Aconcagua: A Climbing Guide* (United States: Mountaineers, 1999), p. 17.

4.   "Mountaineering," University of Alaska Museum of the North, https://www.uaf .edu/museum/education/educators/teaching-through-collecti/mountaineering/.

5.   Stuck, *Ascent*, p. 121.

6.   Mackenzie, *Wolf Smeller*, p. 42.

CHAPTER 14

1.   Stuck, *Ascent*, p. 131.

2.   Tessa Hulls, "Fannie Quigley, the Alaska Gold Rush's All-in-One Miner, Hunter, Brewer, and Cook," *Atlas Obscura*, August 21, 2017, https://www.atlasobscura.com /articles/fannie-quigley-alaska-gold-rush August 21, 2017.

3.   Stuck, *Ascent*, p. 140.

4.   "First Airplane Flight in Alaska – A Special Fourth of July Celebration," *The Alaska Life* (blog), July 4, 2017, https://www.thealaskalife.com/journals-stories/first -airplane-flight/.

5.   Dirk Tordoff, "Airplanes on Denali," *Alaska History Journal* 9, no. 4 (Fall 1994).

6.   "Dr. Stuck Scales Mount M'Kinley," *New York Times,* June 21, 1913, p. 1, ProQuest Historical Newspapers.

7.   Descendants of Harry Karstens believe that Charles Sheldon prevailed on Stuck to make changes to the *Scribner's* article, including the sentence emphasized here. Although certainly willing to believe this, the author found no direct evidence of it. Sheldon did write a letter to *Scribner's* on behalf of his friend Karstens. In a reply, the magazine reassured Sheldon that Stuck had *already* added a sentence on Karstens's behalf to the article — presumably, the sentence in question.

8.   Stuck, *Ascent*, p. 163.

9.   Stuck, *Voyages*, p. 193.

10. Walker, *Seventymile Kid*, loc. 3796.

11. "Exploration: Adventures in Strange Lands by Many Travelers," *New York Times (1857–1922),* May 31, 1914, ProQuest Historical Newspapers: *The New York Times,* pg. BR251.

12. Richard Lovett, "Nearer my god to thee," *New Scientist* 185, no. 2492 (March 26, 2005), p. 52, https://link.gale.com/apps/doc/A131163236/ITOF?u=tel_s_tsla&sid =ITOF&xid=318ac50b.

13. Stuck, *Ascent*, vii.

CHAPTER 15

1.   Ehrlander, *Harper*, p. 90.

2.   "History," *Northfield Mount Hermon School,* https://www.nmhschool.org/about /history.

3.   Ehrlander, *Harper*, p.90.

4.   "Yukon Indian Opens Coney Island Eyes," *New York Times*, January 1, 1914, p.4.

5.   Ehrlander, Harper, p. 97.

6.   Jane Sponagle, "Forgotten Voyage," CBCNews, October 27, 2018, https://news interactives.cbc.ca/longform/forgotten-voyage.

7.   "Vale of Walter Harper," *Fairbanks Daily News Miner*, December 4, 1918.

8. Jason VanBorssum, review of *Walter Harper: Alaska Native Son,* by Mary F. Ehrlander, *Anglican and Episcopal History* 87, no. 3 (September 2018), pp. 335–336, https://www.jstor.org/stable/10.2307/26532540.

9. Jan Raines-Harper, "Denali, A Universe," *Alpinist,* October 23, 2019, http://www .alpinist.com/doc/web19f/wfeature-a67-wired-denali-universe.

CHAPTER 16

1. "He'd Rename Mt. McKinley," *New York Times,* July 17, 1913, p. 1.

2. "Archdeacon Stuck Flays Life's Shams," *New York Times,* June 5, 1916, p. 11.

3. "Confessions of Archdeacon Stuck," *New York Times,* June 30, 1916, p. 10.

4. Charles S. Potts, "Old Simp and His Jackasses," *Southwest Review* 31, no. 1 (Fall 1945), pp. 23–27, https://www.jstor.org/stable/43463037.

5. Stuck to *Scribner's,* November 4, 1914. Archives of Charles Scribner's Sons, C0101, Manuscripts Division, Department of Special Collections, Princeton University Library.

6. Stuck, *Ten Thousand Mile*s, p. xxii.

7. Ibid., p. xvii.

8. Hudson Stuck to Maxwell Perkins, December 11, 1918, Princeton.

9. Stuck, *Winter Circuit*, p. vii.

10. Hudson Stuck to Maxwell Perkins, September 5, 1919; Perkins to Stuck, April 24, 1920.

11. Stuck, *Winter Circuit*, p. vii.

12. W.A.T., review of *A Winter Circuit of Our Arctic Coast* by Hudson Stuck, *The Geographical Journal* 56, no. 2 (August 1920), p. 139.

13. Mary Ehrlander, "*A Winter Circuit of Our Arctic Coast*: Hudson Stuck's Literary, Ethnographic and Historical Masterpiece," *Alaska History*, Alaska Historical Society, Fall 2014, p. 22.

14. Ibid., p 27.

15. Ibid., p 37.

16. Stuck, *Alaskan Missions*, p. 167.

17. Ibid., pp. 169-170.

18. Ibid., p. 170.

19. King, *Gods of the Upper Air*, p. 137.

20. Mackenzie, *Wolf Smeller*, p. 5.

21. Ibid., p. 122.

22. Craig Mishler, "John Fredson: A Biographical Sketch," in *John Fredson Edward Sapir Haa Googwandak: Stories Told by John Fredson to Edward Sapir* (Fairbanks: Alaska Native Language Center, University of Alaska, 1982), p. 10.

23. Beth Bragg, "Alaska Native teens get official credit for assisting historic Denali ascent," *Anchorage Daily News,* November 21, 2018, https://www.adn.com/sports /2018/11/21/alaska-sports-hall-of-fame-plaque-honoring-historic-denali-ascent -gets-an-edit/.

24. Hudson Stuck, *The Salmon Cannery at the Mouth of the Yukon* (New York, 1920), p. 9.

25. Hudson Stuck to Vilhjalmur Stefansson, January 2, 1920.

26. Archives of the Explorers Club, New York, NY.

27. Stuck to RGS, June 4th, 1919. Copy in author's possession.

28. RGS to Stuck, July 21, 1919. Copy in author's possession.

29. Moses Cruikshank, interview by Bill Schneider, Jukebox Project, University of Alaska Fairbanks Oral History Project, February 21, 1986, http://jukebox.uaf.edu /site7/interviews/2289.

30. Mackenzie, *Wolf Smeller*, p. 23.

31. Burke, *Doctor Hap*, p. 175.

32. Copy in Karstens family collection.

33. Burke, *Doctor Hap*, p. 238.

34. Ibid., p. 239.

35. Quoted in Dean, *Breaking Trail*, p. 299.

36. Burke, *Doctor Hap*, p. 239-240.

37. "Archdeacon Hudson Stuck," *The Times* (London), October 30, 1920, p. 13.

38. Percy, *Lanterns on the Levee*, pp. 100-101.

39. Mackenzie, *Wolf Smeller*, p. 108.

40. "Vale of Walter Harper," *Fairbanks Daily News Miner*, December 4, 1918.

41. "The Lectionary Page," *Episcopal Church of the USA*, http://www.lectionarypage .net/CalndrsIndexes/TxtIndexLFF.html#April.

ACKNOWLEDGEMENTS

E arly in my research I came upon a statement in *The Alaska Native Reader:* "The history of Alaska is often told from the perspective of outsiders and those who view the resources of Alaska as amazing treasures to exploit." It gave me pause. This outsider has been determined not to exploit the people and events of Alaska, past and present, but rather to tell a story that I hope Alaskans, as well as those outside, will consider to be accurate, fair, and respectful.

This goal was complicated by the coronavirus outbreak of 2020. Planned trips to Alaska, as well as to the Episcopal Archives in Austin and to the plains of west Texas where Stuck first lived in the US, were canceled. This book, therefore, is in large debt to many, many people who know more about Alaska and its people than I, and who helped me with my research from afar. Evon Peter gave me background on the Episcopal

Church in Alaska, and Stuck's legacy as reflected in the lives of Walter Harper and John Fredson. Helen Hegener helped me with the history of dogsledding and the Gold Rush. And Dr. Ben Potter checked my work concerning Alaskan prehistory and the Upward Sun archaeological find.

Scott Fisher, retired rector of St. Matthew's, Fairbanks— Stuck's church—became a friend, advisor, and proofreader. He also connected me with Allan Haymon, descendant of John Fredson, who corrected my Gwich'in spelling and furthered my Alaskan education. Invaluable to this book were Ken and Gene Karstens, great-grandson and grandson of Harry, who shared documents, photographs, and their family's views of Stuck and the Denali ascent. So did Tom Walker, author of *Seventymile Kid*, the Karstens biography which was foundational for my own book.

The other work upon which this book was built is *Breaking Trail: Hudson Stuck of Texas and Alaska*, by Dr. David Dean (a wonderful coincidence—but no relation), the only previous biography of Stuck. Dr. Dean and his son corresponded with me and offered me help in the early stages of my work. I am truly grateful to him and Tom Walker for going before me and breaking this particular trail.

Rachel Cohen and Fawn Carter at the Alaska and Polar Regions Collections & Archives, Elmer E. Rasmuson Library, University of Alaska Fairbanks were so helpful with documents, photographs, and artifacts, as was Angela Linn at the University of Alaska Museum of the North. Kimberly Arthur, museum curator at Denali National Park, and the rangers there responded promptly to my requests for information and photo permissions.

For insight into the world of 19th-century British mountaineering, I am grateful to Chris Sherwin of the Fell and Rock Climbing Club of the English Lake District, Lancashire, UK.

For a first book, one wants to go way back, to thank early influences and mentors. I was fortunate to work at Lemuria Bookstore in Jackson, Mississippi, in my 20s, where John, Tom, and Valerie showed me what the literary life could be. During that time, obsessed with Africa and Alaska, I snatched up a paperback copy of *Ten Thousand Miles with a Dog Sled*, by Hudson Stuck; I used that very copy for this book. John Evans continues to lead Lemuria, one of the best independent bookstores in the country. I'm glad to make a small contribution to support Lemuria, and local bookstores everywhere.

I am fortunate to have lived for two decades on the Mountain that nurtured Stuck's intellect and that is home to the University of the South. A number of Sewanee professors came to my aid: Woody Register gave me photocopies of Stuck's diaries from an earlier project; Ben King checked my chapter on London, and discussed Muscular Christianity with me; Brown Patterson, Gerald Smith, and Chris McDonough gave me advice and information about early Sewanee history.

The staff at Sewanee's Jessie L. DuPont Library and William R. Laurie University Archives and Special Collections were rockstars, guiding me through online research, bringing me interlibrary loans from faraway places, and basically holding my hand through the process. My thanks to Courtnay Zeitler, Cari Reynolds, Heidi Syler, Linnea Minich, Matt Reynolds, and Mandi Johnson. Mandi, the archives' director, deserves special mention, photocopying for me entire sections of books and archival materials which were otherwise inaccessible due to the pandemic.

Nearly a decade ago, as I began to think of Stuck's life as a possible book with myself as its writer, Henry Hamman assured me that I had a story to tell. The Rivendell Writers' Colony, David Coe, Laura Willis, April Alvarez, Megan Roberts, Virginia Craighill, Adam Latham, and Brooks Egerton, were crucial to this book's creation. Their insights and encouragement enabled its formulation and eventual liftoff. Thanks also to Carmen Toussaint, guiding force behind Rivendell Writers' Colony, for giving the group a home, and fostering a literary community on the Mountain, however sadly short-lived.

Cycling buddy and consummate writing professional Kim Cross gave me valuable critiques and pro tips, and made the fateful suggestion that I apply to the Archer City Story Center's book proposal workshop. In summer 2017's Texas heat, Glenn Stout led me through the process of making Stuck's story saleable. His support then and since has been integral. Thanks also to my fellow Archer City workshoppers, Kathy Floyd, Coretta Perkins, and David Tannenwald, for their engagement and advice. Eva Holland offered to read my proposal; when life intervened, she asked Andrea Pitzer to fill in, and Andrea did so wonderfully, making valuable suggestions.

April Alvarez gets a second round of my gratitude; she slotted me into Sewanee's School of Letters program, where I was fortunate enough to be in nonfiction workshops led by Neil Shea and Meera Subramanian. I learned, and continue to learn, so much from them both, about how to write and how to be a writer.

Farley Chase of Chase Literary Agency took a chance on a first-time author, worked with me on the proposal, and found it and me a publishing home. Jessica Case of Pegasus Books has answered all my annoying newbie questions and made me feel well cared-for while getting this manuscript honed, packaged, and ready to release to the world. Thank you both for a gratifying, enjoyable, and exciting publishing process.

When I lost both parents in my 13th year, my older brother Michael ("Dino") and his wife Janice ("Honey") took me on to raise, as we say in Mississippi. In their house, full of art and literature, was born in me a love of ideas and the written word of which this book is a direct result. My greatest regret is that my brother is not here to hold this book in his hands. But he and Honey have left a wonderful legacy: their children and grandchildren, my nephews, nieces, and "greats," who are some of the best people I know, and whom I love dearly.

Finally, my wife Susan has encouraged me in this dream, as she's supported me throughout our time together. She won't want me to go on here, so I'll just say that the words "without whom . . ." were never truer. Thank you, Susan, for everything.

Archdeacon Stuck used the prefaces and afterwords of his books to argue for justice and equal treatment for Alaska Natives, whether in the proper naming of their mountain, Denali, or the enforcement of laws concerning alcohol in the territory. I have asked my new Alaska friends what Stuck might focus on if he were alive today. Most often mentioned was the fight to preserve the Arctic National Wildlife Refuge, a center of Gwich'in life and culture on the land. Anyone interested in perpetuating Hudson Stuck's legacy can lend their support in this struggle through organizations such as Defend the Sacred Alaska (defendthesacredalaska.org) and the Gwich'in Steering Committee (gwichinsteeringcommittee.org).

Monteagle, Tennessee